Any Place, Any Time, Any Where

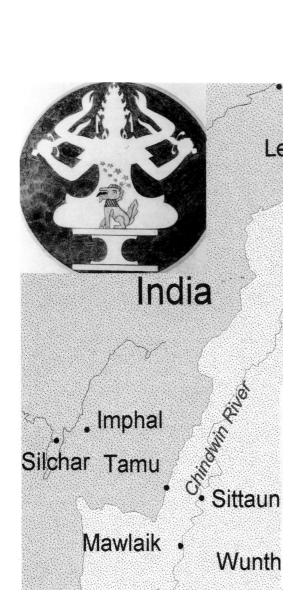

Dinjan

Ledo

India

Mogaung

Myitkyina

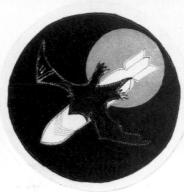

China

Imphal

Silchar Tamu

Sittaun

amo

Wanting

Mawlaik

Wunth

Lashio

Kalewa

Tiddim

Yeu

Shwebo

Irrawaddy

Gangaw

Monywa

Maymyo

Mandalay

kku

Meiktila

n

Taunggyi

Thazi

Magwe

Salwee

Any Place, Any Time, Any Where

The 1st Air Commandos in WWII

R. D. Van Wagner

R. D. Van Wagner

Schiffer Military/Aviation History
Atglen, PA

Cover artwork by Steve Ferguson, Colorado Springs, CO:

YANKEE AIR PIRATES ON BROADWAY- The cover art depicts a pair of 1st Air Commando P-51 Mustangs flown by Fighter Section Leader Lieutenant Colonel Grant Mahony and his Operations Executive Major Bob Petit (in "Mrs. Virginia") crossing over C-47 transports descending upon their home airstrip codenamed BROADWAY. Supplied exclusively by air at this remote airdrome far behind enemy lines, the Commandos employed their service weary fighter-bombers, and B-25 Mitchell cannon-armed medium bombers to exact a horrendous toll of targets at the farthermost reaches of the theater. Whether establishing air supremacy or interdicting enemy supply lines, the self professed "Yankee Air Pirates of Burma" accomplished their mission with distinction and established a new precedent in total battlefield airborne support.

In Memory of My Father

"So that Broadway will never again become worthless ground."

Book Design by Ian Robertson.

We are interested in hearing from authors with book ideas on related topics.

Published by Schiffer Publishing Ltd.
4880 Lower Valley Road
Atglen, PA 19310
Phone: (610) 593-1777
FAX: (610) 593-2002
E-mail: Schifferbk@aol.com
Please write for a free catalog.
This book may be purchased from the publisher.
Please include $3.95 postage.
Try your bookstore first.

Contents

Preface

This work examines the 1st Air Commando Group of World War II—an experiment looking toward future air warfare. Employed in the China-Burma-India Theater, the organization made military history by conducting the first Allied all-aerial invasion—Operation THURSDAY. Because of more glamorous campaigns in Europe and the Pacific, Operation THURSDAY and the 1st Air Commandos have been generally overlooked by military historians. This study calls attention to that lost piece of air power history; however, it is not a definitive work. That undertaking would be enormous considering the group never published a unit history, instead adopting the theme: "To hell with the paper work, go out and fight." Therefore, this account focuses on the circumstances which brought about the requirement for and the employment of the 1st Air Commando Group in Burma. Intended as a 6-month excursion, the unit proved so valuable it was extended in the field until the end of the war. By using unorthodox procedures, the group serves as a model organization for use in both conventional and unconventional conflicts today.

The primary impetus for this study of the 1st Air Commando Group is my father, Fred H. Van Wagner. He joined the air commandos after their deployment to India but before Operation THURSDAY. He remained in Burma through much of the 1944-45 Dry Season Campaign. Greatly influenced by the events and camaraderie experienced in India, he passed on his acquired values and philosophy concerning duty and love of country to me. This study has been well worth the time spent; it has helped me to know my father better. Therefore, with warmth and love, I dedicate my research to him.

This study would not have been possible without the help of many former members of the 1st Air Commando Group. I am grateful to Major General John R. Alison, co-commander of the unit, for his contribution and participation. I hold a great respect for him and the accomplishments of his organization. I also was aided by the men of the 1st Air Commando Association. Particularly I wish to express my appreciation to the association secretaries, Robert Moist and William W. Johnson, Jr., for their time and information. Additionally, interviews with William S. Burghardt; Arthur Burrell; Maximo A. Cheng; William T. Cherry, Jr., Frank Clifford; Joseph Cochran; Andrew L. Cox; Lemuel Davis; John Derdak; Thomas Doherty; Patrick Driscoll; Dr. Cortez Enloe; Paul Forcey; Duane K. Fudge; Allen Hall, Jr.; Neville Hogan; John Hyland; Felix Lockman, Jr.; Roland R. Lynn; Joseph Lysowski; Rodney E. Petty, Jr.; Stamford Robertson; Raymond Ruksas; Lloyd Samp; Howard Smith; Tom Taketa; Vincent Ulery; F. H. Van Wagner; and Carl E. Zeigler, Jr. provided invaluable insights. Their responses to my questions and enthusiastic support of this endeavor were an inspiration. As I attempted to turn this collection of anecdotes into a serious work of history, Jim Lansdale provided encouragement and direction. I would not have finished without his guidance.

I am indebted to the personnel of the USAF Historical Research Center, Herb Huie of the Graphics Arts organization at Maxwell AFB, Alabama, Chuck Noland, and to Mark Hanley, my photographer. I would like to formally thank my advisor, Lieutenant Colonel Robert Gregory, for his encouragement, technical assistance, and advice. Finally, I would be remiss if I did not thank the members of my family for their patience and understanding during this task. Many kind people have helped and encouraged me in writing this account; I thank them all.

Opposite Page: Map 1—South-East Asia, Circa 1942

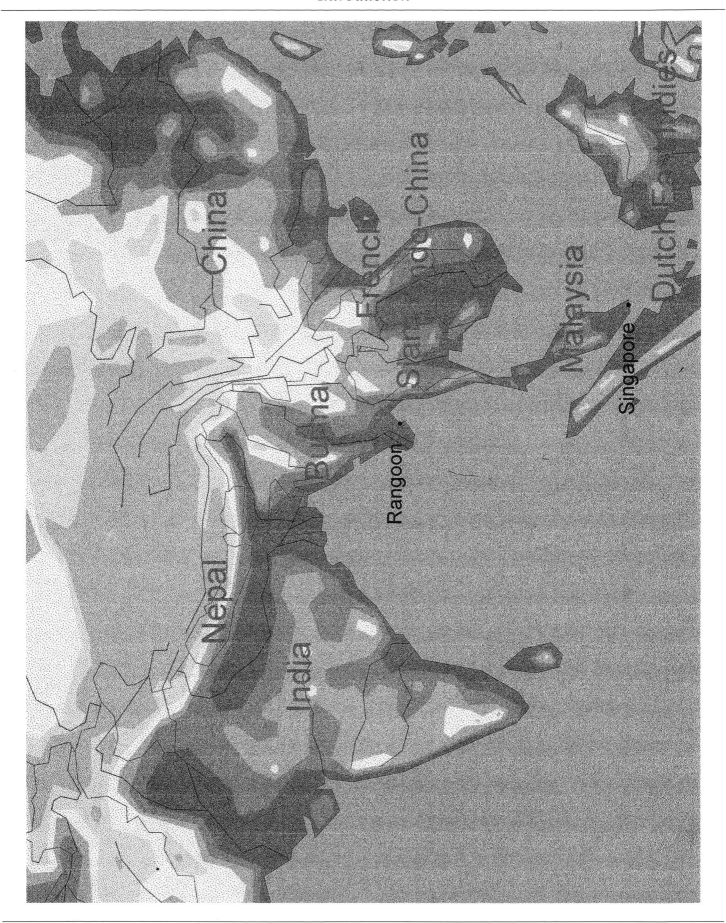

1

Burma

Bolstered by recent successful attacks on Pearl Harbor and the Philippines, Japan's Prime Minister and War Minister Hideki Tojo announced his intention to invade the small country of Burma on 23 December 1941. On that date, the Japanese launched an air raid on the key Burmese port of Rangoon. The damage inflicted by the raid was questionable; the intent of the Japanese action, however, was well defined and of tremendous strategic impact. From the secure, sophisticated shores of the United States, the Emperor's attack was not well publicized and consequently, scarcely understood. Why would the Nipponese Empire be interested in the obscure land of Burma? For those aware of that sleepy nation in Southeast Asia, the question posed was about the Burmese defensive capability. What resistance would Emperor Hirohito's soldiers face as they tried to take such a rugged and foreboding land? And finally, would this British colony hold out against the might of Japan's finest troops? How these questions were answered during the invasion of Burma would affect future campaign strategy.

The question of *why?* was answered by the Japanese desire to use Burma as a wedge, a springboard, and a shield. By appealing to all these desires, Burma promised to be a vitally strategic trophy. Falling under Japan's *Greater East Asia Co-Prosperity Sphere* Program, Burma was a natural extension of Prime Minister Tojo's expansionism started a decade earlier in China. In harmony with the 1927 Tanaka Memorial, the Land of the Rising Sun annexed Manchuria in 1931, and in 1937, had begun a systematic march on China's major cities of Peking, Tientsin, Shanghai, Nanking, and Hankow. After almost 10 years of fighting, the Japanese managed to make the Chinese Nationalist government move its capital to Chungking and effectively cut off China from the outer world. By 1941, the Japanese fundamentally closed the door on China, but resistance soon was being met with the help of a supply line, the Burma Road. Winding through the Himalayas, this inadequate road extended from Burma to Kunming, a small mountain town in China's Yunnan province.

As they looked at Burma, Prime Minister Tojo's strategists saw a wedge—a way to stop China's flow of munitions, equipment, and

The Burma Road
Before the Japanese slammed the door, virtually all supplies to China traveled the Burma Road. Its hairpin course began at the railhead of Lashio, Burma, and snaked through the mountains to the stronghold at Kunming, China. *Courtesy of Historical Research Center, Maxwell AFB AL*

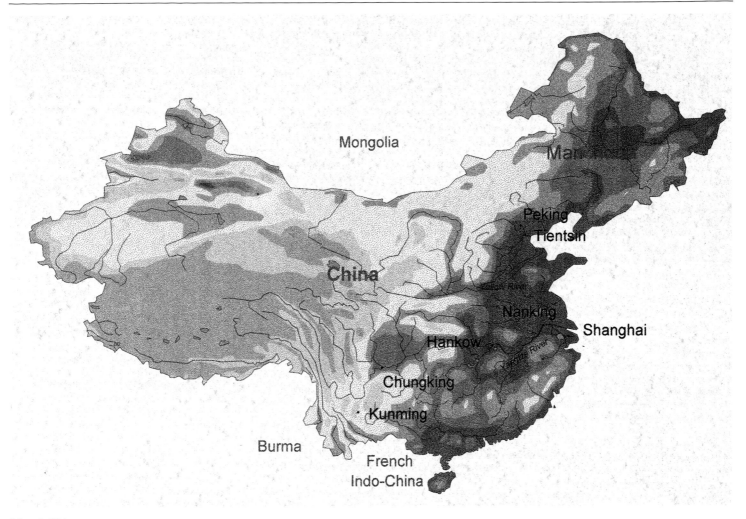

Map 2-China

provisions. If the Japanese could seize Central Burma and control interior transportation lines, the deep horseshoe mountains along the border of India and China provided a natural barrier to conclusively seal off China and starve her into submission. With Burma occupied, the Japanese could stabilize China and release Nippon's continental forces for other potential conquests.

The Chinese element may have been the impetus for the invasion, but Japan saw other strategic prizes in Burma. As well as establishing a roadblock for Chinese supplies, Burma also could become the springboard for an offensive into the riches of India. The Japanese sensed an opportunity to take advantage of civil unrest, stirred by India's Mohandas K. Gandhi, to absorb the greatest British colony in Asia. If Japan invaded, they anticipated the support of Indian nationals to dislodge the British.

India was certainly a prize worth having, as great, if not more so, than China itself. World War I had given a stimulus to commercialization in India. In 1941 she offered an economy with burgeoning industrial capability. Production of coal and cotton had begun in India before 1920, but since that time, the iron and steel, arms and munitions, and chemical industries had emerged with gusto.

Most important though was the Japanese grand strategy to overrun India and link with a planned Axis push in Persia under the command of German General Erwin Rommel. Burma was the way to people, industry, and a possible strategic union. Indeed, the very idea of Burma brought a gleam of covetousness to the eyes of the Japanese generals.

As a pivot point, Burma offered China and India, but Burma, by itself, also beckoned to the Japanese. Three reasons are given— rice, natural resources, and natural defense. In 1940, the mainstay of Burma's internal and external economy was rice; almost 12,000,000 acres were under cultivation. To Japan, Burma represented a rice bowl capable of producing nearly 8,000,000 tons of this staple crop. Prime Minister Tojo believed Burma's rice export of 3,000,000 tons could be re-channeled to his already overextended Imperial Army. Additionally, Burma offered an abundance of natural resources, primarily oil and manganese. Finally, a Japanese-occupied Burma would act as a barrier or shield for the entire Far East territory. Japanese occupation of Burma would put distance between the Allies and Emperor Hirohito's new possessions of the Philippine Islands, French Indochina, Siam, Singapore, and the Dutch East Indies.

For the question of *why?* there was plenty of rationale. With so many reasons to invade—China, India, and Burma's food and natural resources—the question of the unknown Burmese defense plans waited to be answered. The only way to find out was to try, and that Japan decided to do in earnest when the new year, 1942, rolled around.

There were three factors that comprised the British defensive scheme for Burma. Collectively the Japanese had to overcome them all. Separately, they posed no appreciable problem, but together, each contributed to a viable British plan for the defense of Burma against the Japanese invasion. They were as follows:

(1) The impact of Burma's rugged geography,
(2) The effect of the Burmese climatic conditions, and
(3) The preparedness of Burma's defense.

Geography and God's handiwork divided Burma into several zones. The 8,000-foot crests of the Chin Hills separated India from Burma and protected "Burma Proper," the original settlement area. The region was defined by the surrounding mountains and dominated by river valleys. Here was the agricultural heart of the country. Because of distinctively different climates and historical developments, within this central belt dramatic differences existed between Upper and Lower Burma. Farther west between the Chin Hills and the graceful coastline along the Bay of Bengal were the isolated islands and sandy beaches of the Arakan. To the north along the Sino-Burman border stood peaks and crouching subtropical gorges in the Kachin Hills anchored by Hkakabo Razi, highest peak in Southeast Asia. Known as the foothills of the Himalayas, the Kachin Hills towered majestically to heights of more than 10,000 feet. Along the Siam and French-Indochina border, European-type climates and undulating contours characterized the Shan Plateau. Working southward, the plateau funneled into the Tenasserim coastal range still providing a natural barrier between Burma and Siam.

Physically, Burma resembled a waterfall. All the natural elements that composed the country paralleled each other, running from north to south—her mountains, rivers, roads, central plain, valleys, and even her railway system. As a result, travel in Burma from east to west was an enterprise contrary to the rules of nature. Along the Indo-Burman border, the country's sudden and irregular mountains isolated one ravine from another. The roads connecting these valleys snaked across the mountains and progress was always slow. Additionally, the mountainsides were covered with jungles thick enough to form a natural canopy. Hiding beneath this umbrella were leeches, malaria-carrying mosquitoes, and diseases by the score.

Therefore, it was obvious for the British to assume that an invader would be confined to the meager road system, limited railroads, or the great rivers. If given a choice, travelers generally used the waterways because Burma possessed three major and two smaller river systems. During the colonial period, British settlers depended on the largest, the Irrawaddy River, to such an extent it was called the "Road to Mandalay." Fed from the Himalayan Mountains to the north, the Irrawaddy flowed swiftly down the center of the country and was joined from the northwest by the next largest in size, the Chindwin River. Together these two mammoth rivers and their tributaries provided over 15,000 miles of navigable waters to the near geographic center of Burma. After it was joined by the Chindwin, the Irrawaddy emerged from Burma's central valley and emptied itself into the Bay of Bengal through a 9-arm delta area just west of Rangoon. Farther east, the swift Salween River churned southward from its headwaters in China determining the border between Burma and Siam. Extending down the southeast finger of Burma, the unpredictable Salween tumbled from the interior of Burma near the town of Moulmein later to be unleashed into the Andaman Sea.

Because of the north/south topography of Burma, choke points—the confluence of rivers, roads, and railroads—were commonplace. Under the circumstances, the British felt sure the Japanese could be held at bay by a relatively small force taking advantage of the natural contours and formation of the land. Herein was the defensive strength of Burma.

The British also felt time was on their side in Burma because of the recurring monsoons. Rain! Probably the most dominant feature of Burma was the monsoons. Lasting from mid-May until late October, the monsoons limited all military operations to the dry season. Annual rainfalls varied from about 200 inches in the area of Rangoon, 100 inches in the Irrawaddy Delta, 80 inches in the hills, and up to 45 inches in the dry zone of North Central Burma. Effects of the rain created pools of ankle-deep mud and mire. The monotony of the incessant downpour also had a psychological impact— sapping the strength of fighting men. The British hoped topography would slow the Japanese enough so the monsoons could deliver the knockout punch. Key to British success was their ability to hold out until mid-May; this key was in the hands of General Archibald Wavell, Commander-in-Chief of British Forces, India.

When the military responsibility for Burma transferred from Singapore to India on 12 December 1941, General Wavell was greatly concerned by the extent of unpreparedness in Burma's defense. He did concede, however, it was understandable because Burma was protected from sea invasion by Singapore and from land attack by three friendly neighbors. As long as Singapore, Siam, Indochina, and India remained strong, there was no need for a buildup in Burma.

This dependence on regional stability was reinforced by the fact that the Burmese Army had only been activated since April 1937. By late 1941, Burma had two British infantry battalions, two India infantry brigades, eight battalions of Burma Rifles, four mountain artillery batteries, and the equivalent of six battalions of the Burma Frontier Force. The latter mostly worked under the control of the Civil Power and had little fighting value. The forces avail-

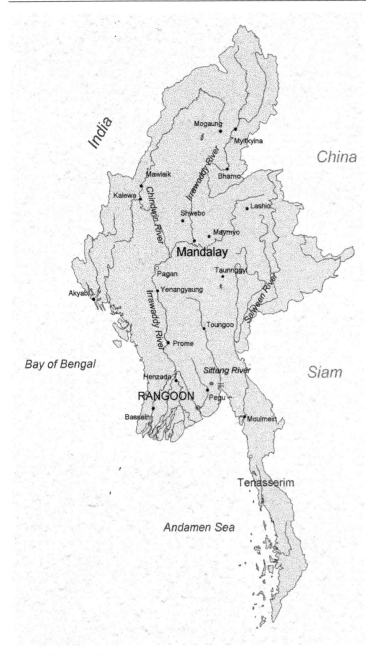

Map 3-Political Map of Burma

able for the defense of Burma were only partially trained and almost without artillery, signal equipment, and antiaircraft weapons. The air force was practically nonexistent. It consisted of one fighter squadron equipped with outmoded Brewster Buffaloes.

To assist in the defense of Burma, Generalissimo Chiang Kai-shek's offer of the Chinese 5th and 6th Armies, complicated by demands for separate lines of communication, finally was accepted by General Wavell in February 1942. It must be stated, however, General Wavell questioned Chinese willingness to fight in Burma if their homeland became threatened. Many attributed the problem to the internal struggle between General Chiang's loyalist, the Kuomintang, and Mao Tse-tung's Communist followers. In part,

when General Wavell accepted Chinese help, his decision included the realization that the American Volunteer Group, Colonel Clair L. Chennault's famous *Flying Tigers*, was part of the package.

Lacking equipment, aircraft, manpower, and training, the military was clearly the weak link in the Burma defense plan. General Wavell counted on India for possible reinforcements and was beginning to mobilize for the fortification of Burma when Japan dropped its first bombs on Rangoon. India Command hoped the combination of two aspects, terrain and national defense, was sufficient to impede any offensive until the arrival of the monsoons. General Wavell believed when the operation resumed in late October, he would have a sufficiently strong army in place to resist the Japanese. In matter of fact, General Wavell's hope proved to be groundless. His forces could not even hold out until mid-May.

In systematic fashion, Japan's air force attacked first the weakest link in the military infrastructure of Burma. Airplanes of the Rising Sun quickly established air superiority, and began to harass British attempts to reinforce with soldiers from Malaysia and Singapore. Only Chennault's American Volunteer Group provided noticeable resistance to Japanese air attacks. The Nippon air raids on Rangoon helped spread panic among the Burmese citizens; movement came to a standstill when the roads and port facilities swelled with refugees seeking safety. This confusion proved advantageous to the Japanese and allowed their ground troops to begin a race against the monsoons to overtake the British and Chinese Armies.

Yet even before they dropped a bomb or set foot on Burma soil, Nippon's plans for the Southeast Asia region foreshadowed the demise of the British in Burma. The Army of the Rising Sun accomplished the first step in their plan, occupation of Siam, after only eight hours of fighting. By December 1941, Japan's war machine converged on the Malay Peninsula and Britain's fortress of Singapore. Emperor Hirohito's master plan called for the fall of the citadel in 100 days. Unfortunately for the British, on 15 February 1942, Japan took Singapore—70 days after initiating action.

With the defeat of Singapore, Burma lost its protection from a sea invasion; the swiftness of the Japanese occupation of the vital links of Siam and Singapore left Burma naked. General Wavell could not react quickly enough to overcome the Japanese momentum. Additional troops from the 16th Indian Brigade were still landing at Rangoon when Lieutenant General Shojira Iida's 15th Army began its move on Burma in strength.

The British readied for a westward advance from Siam, but instead the Japanese turned south and moved into the tail of Burma. After initially securing airfields along the Tenasserim coast, General Iida mounted his attack on the port of Rangoon itself. Lieutenant General T. J. Hutton was placed in command of the Burma land forces and he was joined by Major General J. G. Smyth in January 1942. General Smyth moved forward to cut off the Japanese before they reached the supply sites of Central Burma. Establishing a defensive position with the Bilin and Sittang Rivers behind him, General Smyth's troops dug in to oppose the expected Japanese advance.

Unfortunately, the Japanese 17th Division soon turned the advantages around and General Smyth became concerned about his troop's only means of escape—the Sittang Bridge. Orders were issued to begin a withdrawal at 0800 on 22 February. Relayed in the clear, the Japanese intercepted the orders and began an all-out assault to capture the trestle. During the fighting, General Smyth faced the possibility General Iida would overrun his troops and the bridge would become a Japanese thoroughfare. He regretfully ordered Lieutenant Bashir Ahmed Khan to destroy the span before all British troops could cross. Of the 8,500 men who were isolated on the Japanese side, only 3,500 managed to rejoin their units on the east bank. Additionally, General Smyth lost almost all his transportation and artillery. With just a remnant of an army, many without boots or rifles, the dispirited British were unable to withstand the Nippon assaults on Rangoon.

Shortly after the Sittang Bridge tragedy, General Hutton was replaced by General the Right Honourable Sir Harold Alexander. His arrival in Burma coincided with a lull in the fighting and General Alexander held out hope the British Army could secure the area. But the respite was short lived; the Japanese Army, having fought for a month without re-supply, had regrouped and restarted its offensive. On 8 March, General Alexander faced the agonizing truth and was forced to abandon Rangoon. The loss of Burma's principal port gave little hope of re-supply or reinforcement to the troops fleeing into the jungle-clad interior of Burma or to the resistance fighters in the mountains of China. With this action, General Alexander set in motion the longest and most inglorious retreat in British military history. During this *strategic withdrawal* two personalities emerged: British Major General William J. Slim and American Lieutenant General Joseph W. Stilwell. From a tactical perspective their viewpoint of the rout showed the chaos and terror of the tumultuous flight back to India.

General Slim, son of a hardware store owner, had spent most of his career in the Indian Army; during the 1942 campaign he commanded Burma Corps. Included under his control were the 17th Indian Division and the 1st Burma Division. During the retreat, Chinese troops joined General Slim around Toungoo. For a time, the Chinese fought well and stubbornly, but their operations were uncoordinated. When General Iida invaded, the British were unprepared for the speed of the Japanese advance. While the British troops were roadbound and expected the Japanese to be also, the truth was the opposite. The Nippon Army used the jungle to their advantage. They often divided into small units and bypassed enemy troop movements. Well behind the British lines, they would establish roadblocks by felling trees and emplacing machine guns. Although highly regarded as fighting men, General Slim's command was particularly vulnerable to this type of attack as they had been trained for mechanized desert warfare.

Using this hooking method, the Japanese continued to harass General Slim by pushing the Burma Corps northward along the Irrawaddy Valley toward the oil fields of Yenangyaung. Forced to live on bully beef and biscuits, Slim's troops were strafed by Japanese planes, suffered from lack of water, and became enveloped by enemy troops. Under these conditions, on 15 April General Slim gave the order to blow up the oil fields and oil storage facilities before they fell into the hands of the advancing horde. Almost waiting too long, he just managed to cut a path through the jungle and escape. In doing so, the Commoner General lost most of his vehicles and heavy equipment.

With no more reasons to stay and fight in Burma, Slim began a general retreat. At the Chindwin River near the towns of Shwegyin and Kalewa, General Slim ordered his men to cross at the only available point, the Basin—a natural site for ambush. He placed

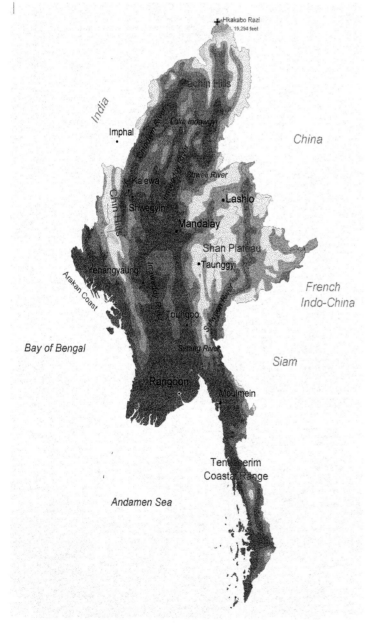

Map 4-Topographical Map of Burma

Gurkhas, fierce soldiers from Nepal, in position to guard the rear of his columns. When he began the crossing, Slim learned the Gurkhas' radio had failed and the Japanese forces were overrunning the bridgehead. The fighting intensified, but General Slim continued to direct the decaying situation until all his men boarded the last ferry and made it to safety on the other side.

Fortunately, the Japanese decided not to press the attack and General Slim finally marched into India on 16 May. With him were over 12,000 troops; more important, he left almost 13,000 men behind. The Commoner General relinquished his hollow command to Lieutenant General N. M. S. Irwin of IV Corps. The long flight across swollen rivers and up the steep banks of the Chin Hills had virtually finished Burma Corps as a fighting force. Slim noted the following as his battered, exhausted men shuffled into India:

> On the last day of that 900-mile retreat I stood on a bank beside the road and watched the rearguard march into India. All of them, British, Indian and Gurkha, were gaunt and ragged as scarecrows. Yet, as they trudged behind their surviving officers in groups pitifully small, they still carried their arms and kept their ranks, they were still recognizable as fighting units. They might look like scarecrows, but they looked like soldiers too. (44:87)

For General Stilwell, the results were the same and the performance of the Chinese gave new currency to previous concerns. Stilwell was originally slated to supervise the distribution of American military aid, act as the Commander of all the Chinese Forces in Burma, and serve as Chief of Staff to Generalissimo Chiang Kai-shek. Upon arrival in Chungking two days before the fall of Rangoon, Stilwell immediately assumed the job of holding the Sittang Valley and the railroad between Rangoon and Mandalay. General Alexander planned to establish a defensive line about 150 miles north of Rangoon to protect Northern Burma. Seeing the disadvantages of this strategy, General Stilwell proposed a counteroffensive using the Chinese 5th Army's 22nd and 96th Divisions. However, Generalissimo Chiang Kai-shek delayed approval; then Major General Tu Yu-ming found excuses and finally refused to fight. He feared the 96th Division might lose the only field artillery in the Chinese Army.

Other instances were noted of the Chinese lack of resolve, and some had an apocryphal flavor. General Stilwell said that when attacked by a Japanese regiment, China's 55th Division completely vanished when they fled from an inferior Japanese force. Stilwell added that he accomplished his one bright spot, the retaking of Taunggyi, only after offering the Chinese troops monetary rewards. That too came to naught as the Japanese detoured around the town and drove on to Lashio and the Burma Road.

Originally planning to retreat by rail, General Stilwell had to start north in a convoy because of a train wreck. Finding travel by road virtually impossible and the Japanese slowly encompassing his position, Stilwell abandoned his vehicles and set out for India on foot. With the monsoons soon due to begin, he managed to get his men, now only numbering few more than a hundred, to the Chindwin River. Here he made a perilous crossing and drove on across the steep, forested mountains, finally arriving in Imphal, India, during a pouring rain on 19 May 1942. The monsoons had abated just long enough. The Infantry General summed up his feelings while offering an outspoken challenge in this manner: "...we got a hell of a beating. We got run out of Burma and it is humiliating as hell. I think we ought to find out what caused it, go back and retake it." (52:293-300)

As the monsoon season started in 1942, the Japanese juggernaut had run the King's Own from the rice paddies and teakwood forests of Burma. Japan had cut the overland road to China and had fortified her land conquests to the east of Burma. India lay temptingly to the west. The Japanese had overcome all the defensive obstacles of Burma within the time of the impending monsoons. Britain had failed to realize the advantages of the bush; to the contrary, Emperor Hirohito's Army had employed them to perfection. Now the Japanese used the natural barriers of Burma to establish their defense. The Land of the Rising Sun thus was firmly entrenched in Burma; her troops were fanned out in a border defense that effectively barricaded the door to Southeast Asia.

For the defeated British troops, there was despair. Not only was this because of the humiliating trek back to India, but also for the memory of encounters in the primeval rain forests of Burma. One soldier's account relates the dispirited emotion of the British at that time:

> Unlike the campaigns in Italy and Normandy...the very nature of the country in Burma dictated that brutal hand-to-hand clashes decided the outcome of countless encounters. Gloomily we sensed that, inevitably, our future lay in the jungles of Burma and our nightmares contained grinning Japanese, ready to open fire at us from cunningly concealed ambush positions. It was to take a considerable time before we ceased to think of the Japanese soldier as a superman, ten feet tall... (45:10, 12)

But even as the last stragglers of the British Army returned to India, a former artillery officer was already studying the contours, rivers, jungles, and situation in Burma to answer the challenge of General Stilwell. To mount an offensive, he would have to overcome the terrain, fear, and organizational malaise shown during the Japanese conquest of Burma. Recognizing these facts, this lone figure's unorthodox mind began to scheme and conceive of a bold and unprecedented operation. His plan would ultimately plant the seed for the formulation of a totally new concept in military history. To take back the wedge, springboard, and shield, he would have to beat the Japanese at their own game.

2

Wingate's Plan

British Colonel Orde C. Wingate arrived in India on 19 March 1942 and promptly plunged into an intense evaluation of the situation. He visited the Burmese front, began studying the training and tactics of the Japanese, religion and customs of Burma and Japan, climate and topography, and every available report on Japanese fighting in Burma. He agreed with India Command's assessment: the invincible Chin Hills and Japanese troop emplacements prevented a standard frontal attack. From India there were a number of possible routes into Burma, but all were too fragile to sustain large-scale military operations. Contrary to commonly held beliefs, though, Wingate felt strongly British soldiers could equal Nippon soldiers in the rain forests because they were more flexible and had more imagination.

To overcome the enemy's stranglehold on Burma, Colonel Wingate theorized the Japanese should never know British intentions or strength. Additionally, he felt the British army should present the Japanese with unconventional situations whenever possible. Slowly he constructed the concept of Long-Range Penetration (LRP) in his mind. At first just a collection of ideas, later Wingate talked incessantly about organizing a force to employ hit-and-run tactics well behind Japanese lines in Burma. Although there were many disbelievers on India Command's staff, Colonel Wingate's ideas caught the imagination of General Alexander. He liked the boldness of the idea and directed Wingate to transform his theories into a completed plan. However, because it was innovative and unconventional, Wingate's LRP theory actually evolved in stages.

During his 1942 study of Burma, Wingate concluded the combination of Burma's wilderness and Japanese perimeter defense could not be assaulted head on, yet they still were exploitable. Noting Imperial troops were strung out with only a thin supply line connecting them to the interior, Colonel Wingate proposed an offensive to weaken Japan's grip on Burma. Employing an indirect approach to operations in Burma, Colonel Wingate constructed his LRP theory around three principles:

(1) The light concentration of Japanese troops in the core of Burma,

(2) Use of surprise and mobility, and

(3) Employment of aerial firepower and re-supply.

Simply stated, Wingate's theory of LRP was to place highly mobile forces in the enemy's rear to harass Japanese lines of communication and destroy supplies. Reminiscent of Confederate Lieutenant General Nathan Bedford Forrest's raids during the American War Between the States, Colonel Wingate proposed an offensive based on the indirect approach. By intercepting munitions, food, and medical supplies, LRP sought to cut off the tail of the dragon so the main body became too weak to fight.

The Japanese defensive posture after the 1942 offensive pointed to the soft underbelly of the dragon. Wingate stated the enemy was most vulnerable far behind the front where Japanese troops were of inferior quality. Here, he reasoned, a small force could wreak havoc out of all proportion to its number. The size and composition of each group would vary with conditions, the governing principle being strength enough to cause damage but small enough to slip through the enemy's net. LRP-trained soldiers would conduct operations and movements during the day; if required to disperse, rendezvous would always be made after dark.

The consequence of successful LRP would be widespread confusion and uncertainty behind the enemy's forward areas. Cutting off supplies would lead to a progressive weakening and misdirection of General Renya Mutaguchi's main forces. Colonel Wingate insisted LRP units were not to fight on the front lines and must be used only in conjunction with a major campaign. If an offensive did not occur, LRP would focus, not redirect, the Japanese forces and the small LRP bands would be annihilated by the full force of the Nippon troops.

Wingate's LRP units were not strong enough to withstand the main force; their greatest strength emerged from their ability to maneuver. Each LRP group would strike, disappear, and turn up somewhere else without the enemy being able to follow their move-

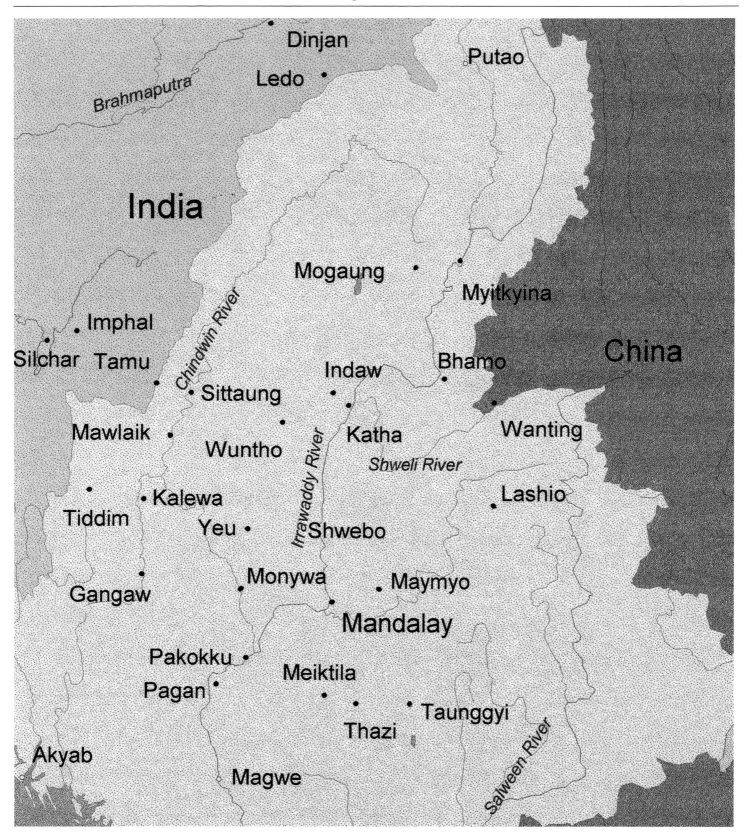

Map 5-Northern Burma, 1943

ments through the jungle. The commander of the LRP group would dictate the choice of engagement. Whenever possible, the objective of LRP was to hit the confluence of supply and communication lines. If LRP units struck a railroad bridge at dawn and a supply dump in the afternoon, the Japanese would be unable to guess the true strength of the columns and probably overestimate their numbers. Furthermore, if two LRP units worked in unison, they could utterly confuse the enemy. Wingate wrote, "Long-Range Penetration affords greater opportunity of mystifying and misleading the enemy than any other form of warfare." (79:1) At the root of Colonel Wingate's theory of penetration was the value of one fighting man deep in the heart of enemy territory.

Colonel Wingate further theorized the only limit to the number of fighting men and length of their operations was the availability of supplies. He called this the air support factor and he proposed using cargo and consumable airdrops as his flexible supply line. Incorporated into his theory of warfare, Colonel Wingate intended to capitalize on air re-supply capability developed during the British withdrawal from Burma. Additionally, because LRP units required too much mobility to manipulate artillery pieces behind the lines, Wingate had another use for air power. He anticipated using high precision bombing and strafing in the place of artillery and tanks.

This departure from recognized methods of warfare called for the use of portable communications to maintain contact with base camps and detached columns. Wingate could not rely on normal supply lines, so as he colorfully stated, "Have no Lines of Communication on the jungle floor. Bring in the goods like Father Christmas, down the chimney." (22:164) The dropping of supplies was nothing new, nevertheless, the degree of accuracy required did present problems. For this reason, he requested Royal Air Force (RAF) flying officers be assigned to each ground unit to direct aircraft to drop zones and to mark targets in forward areas. This notion was complicated and time consuming because RAF procedures did not allow direct outside communication with British pilots. Further limiting the effectiveness was the lack of British air superiority over Burma. Even with this drawback and the complex communication scheme, Colonel Wingate submitted an outline to General Alexander who approved the plan and forwarded it to India Command.

Despite the audacity of the strategy, General Wavell supported the plan totally. He included it as a part of a coordinated offensive called ANAKIM. The fulcrum of the plan called for the capture of the airfield at Akyab Island. From Akyab, the British could increase the security of the Bay of Bengal, thereby relieving the pressure on Burma and China from the Nippon Navy and Air Force. If such protection could be realized, General Wavell contended the re-conquest of all of Burma was possible. The details of the ANAKIM plan involved coordination among a variety of military units, British and Chinese. Colonel Wingate's role in the plan would help secure Northern Burma from the Japanese. As the British advanced,

a new road from Ledo would be built to connect with the Burma Road, thus reopening the supply line to China. The ANAKIM operational plan was as follows:

(1) In mid-October 1942, XV Corps would mount an offensive into the Arakan region to recapture the port of Akyab;

(2) Amphibious strikes at strategic points along the Arakan coast would supplement the XV Corps offensive;

(3) Ultimately joining forces, the amphibious units and XV Corps would continue their attack to Rangoon;

(4) In late January 1943, IV Corps, commanded by Lieutenant General A. F. P. Christison, would launch an assault on the Burmese towns of Sittaung and Kalewa;

(5) The Chinese Ramgarh Force under General Stilwell would move south across the Pangsau Pass to engage Japanese forces at Myitkyina, Bhamo, and Lashio; and

(6) The LRP group would infiltrate the central portion of Burma to confuse and disrupt Japanese lines of communication.

Orde C. Wingate
He conceived, planned and commanded Operation LONGCLOTH—the infiltration of Central Burma. *Courtesy of 1ˢᵗ Air Commando Association*

To seal his endorsement of Wingate's plan, in June General Wavell established the 77th Indian Infantry Brigade expressly for LRP and promoted Colonel Wingate to Brigadier General. In July, General Wingate assembled his troops in the jungle region around Saugor and began preparing for the mission. His command, certainly not hand-picked men, consisted of the following units:

(1)   13th Kings Liverpool Regiment
(2)   3/2nd Gurkha Rifles
(3)   142nd Commando Company
(4)   2nd Burma Rifles
(5)   Mule Transport Company
(6)   RAF liaison officers
(7)   Officers from the Bush Warfare School at Maymyo, Burma

Little did General Wingate know when he assembled his troops that he would be forced to compromise his original LRP tenets. Because of the continuing disunity within General Wavell's command, General Wingate would execute his portion of the ANAKIM plan without the primary requirement of LRP—the presence of a major offensive.

As Wingate prepared to turn a defeated army into jungle fighters, he devised training methods that were physical, exacting, and thorough. The program required all soldiers to move everywhere on the double. General Wingate set the example by sprinting from one viewpoint to another. The regimen was described by one of the officers as follows: "Every movement, from stand to stand, was done on the double. ...When he [Wingate] wished to move to another viewpoint, he ran there, and jolly fast too." (49:376)

At first, the strain of the intensive training program took its toll. Before, during, and after the monsoons, General Wingate's men were swimming rivers, marching long miles, navigating through the jungle, climbing trees, and scaling hills. Within two months, up to 70 percent of the troops had been in the hospital with real and imaginary cases of malaria, dysentery, and jungle sores. Wingate's reaction was severe but logical. He instituted strict punishments for imaginary ailments. Further, he eliminated hospital excuses by having all officers instructed on the treatment of illnesses. For those who collapsed from the heat, Wingate offered little more comfort than a shady tree and a hand-held fan. He reasoned in the jungle, there would be no hospitals and very few medics. The cure slowly showed results as the men hardened under the discipline.

In addition to physical preparedness, General Wingate also trained his men in LRP principles. He did this by extensively using a technique called Tactical Exercises Without Troops. Normally this involved sand tables modeled into miniature terrain maps. Wingate, insisting on extreme detail, had huge 400-square yard pits dug so that all enemy troop strengths, as well as pertinent hills, rivers, roads, and gun emplacements could be depicted to scale. For hours, the officers practiced a spectrum of scenarios envisioned by General Wingate: ambush, attack in position, attack while moving a column, use of light artillery, air re-supply methods, and dispersion/rendezvous procedures. At his Field Headquarters he had a small scale map of enemy-held territory placed on the floor. With his commanders standing on Burma, everyone padded about in socks as he instructed strategy and tactics to the finest detail.

Most important, he taught his soldiers the security and shelter of the jungle. He demonstrated with maps and aerial photographs that closeness to the enemy did not automatically mean contact. Rather than an enemy, Wingate proposed the jungle, at the least, was neutral. Among those who learned the LRP lessons well were two column commanders with totally dissimilar backgrounds. Brigadier Michael Calvert of the Burma Bush Warfare School and Brigadier Bernard Fergusson, previously of General Headquarters India, would later play an important role in Wingate's future plans.

Just prior to the scheduled offensive in January 1943, General Wingate broke camp at Saugar and moved his men forward on foot. After hiking 133 miles to the railway station at Jhansi, the men would travel by train to the railhead in Dimapur. Self-control and strict adherence to procedures were the order of the day. Column actions were directed by four prearranged silent signals:

(1)	*Prepare to March*	All men, equipment, and animals were to be formed up within 30 minutes of notice.
(2)	*Officer's Report*	Every officer received marching orders from column commanders.
(3)	*March*	Columns moved out with precision toward their objective.
(4)	*Halt*	Order given after 90 minutes of march to afford men and animals a 10-minute rest.

During the march, Wingate disciplined his men for deprivations expected in the jungles of Burma. Each man was allowed only 2.5 pints of water a day—1 pint before the march, 1 pint at midday, and .5 pint at the conclusion of the day's march. The men fully soaked canteen covers to produce cool water. To provide columns with food, Wingate administered the last operational test. Departing without rations, he arranged for supplies to be dropped to his columns at prearranged sites after dark. After an 8-day march, he bivouacked outside the town of Imphal, still requiring the brigade to attend long and concentrated lectures. These classroom exercises proved necessary as General Wingate's mission was markedly changing even at this late date.

Little by little, the fabric of ANAKIM unraveled, leaving only the 77th Indian Brigade as a participant. First, in late October 1942, General Wavell recommended moving ANAKIM back to November 1943 and a more modest plan be submitted. The new plan, called RAVENOUS, did not include an amphibious operation and it only sought to retake Northern Burma. Next, IV Corps canceled its operation in the Ledo area because of transportation and road-making materiel shortages. Then Generalissimo Chiang Kai-shek joined the parade by refusing to participate and withdrew the commitment of his Chinese forces to the operation. To make matters worse, in late January 1943, XV Corps encountered stiff Japanese opposition in the Arakan and stalled. They were never able to advance further and subsequently were driven back. In view of the facts, Field Marshall Wavell decided to disband Wingate's LRP forces and thus terminate the last vestiges of the operation.

To Field Marshall Wavell's surprise, General Wingate resisted. Although the primary prerequisite of a coordinated major offensive was lacking, Wingate argued for an opportunity to test his plan. After prolonged discussions, Field Marshall Wavell finally agreed to a new expedition named Operation LONGCLOTH. In allowing General Wingate's excursion, Field Marshall Wavell let stand the specific task of the RAVENOUS plan. The goals given Wingate and his men were as follows:

(1)   To cut the main railway line between Mandalay and Myitkyina,
(2)   To harass the Shwebo area, and
(3)   If possible, cross the Irrawaddy River and sever the railway between Mandalay and Lashio.

After two days of intense planning, General Wingate was ready to test LRP principles in actual combat against the Japanese. Between 8 and 10 February 1943, 2,800 men crossed the Chindwin River into Burma. Organizationally broken into columns, each was commanded by a major. For transportation, the columns included 15 horses and 100 mules or oxen to carry the column's jungle fighting equipment. To avoid detection, General Wingate had ordered each animal's vocal cords be severed. Unable to cover much distance in the dense undergrowth of the jungle, the columns moved slowly toward the railroad lines near Shwebo. Based on RAF liaison officer inputs, clearings were selected along the way for air drops. Between 24 and 26 February, the first series of drops were accomplished. The results were satisfactory although response time was predictably long.

Shortly after the first airdrops, the brigade's reliance on wireless communication was shown when two of General Wingate's columns were ambushed and lost their radios. Without means of communication, the column commanders had no other choice than to return to India. Even with these losses, by 6 March the 77ᵗʰ Indian Brigade had blown up more than 75 sections of the Mandalay-Myitkyina railroad between the Burmese towns of Shwebo and Wuntho. Field Marshall Wavell's first two tasks were accomplished according to plan and with very little loss of personnel. The Irrawaddy River was now between Wingate and the successful completion of Operation LONGCLOTH.

When General Wingate crossed the Irrawaddy, he obliquely proved many LRP premises. In doing so, he almost lost his brigade. With the activity around Shwebo, Major Iwaichi Fujiwara and the rest of General Hisaichi Terauchi's staff were now fully aware of the 77ᵗʰ Indian Brigade's position. The Japanese turned their full attention on the LRP columns. Slowly establishing a pincer movement, Burma Area Army drove Wingate toward an area where the Shweli River formed a loop. Herded into the apex of a triangle with the river on two sides, the force was weakened by the RAF's inability to keep up air re-supply.

India Command responded by recommending General Wingate terminate the operation and return to India. He concurred without hesitation. His men had reached the point of exhaustion, were no longer receiving supplies, and had begun eating pack mules, snakes, and rats. Casualties had also become a major problem. Unfit to keep up with the rapidly moving columns, injured men were often left at Burmese villages or under the shade of a tree with nothing more than a canteen of water, a rifle, and, sometimes, the Bible. Sergeant Tony Aubrey, No. 8 Column, recorded the tragedy:

> That night one man, whose feet were in a very bad state, made up his mind he could go no further. He lay down. His mates, worn out as they were, tried to carry him. But he wouldn't allow them to. All he wanted was to be left alone with as many hand grenades as we could spare. So we gave him the grenades and left him. There wasn't anything else to do. (1:142)

To withdraw the rest of his troops, General Wingate had no other options; on the night of 27 March, he met with his column commanders and decided to re-cross the Irrawaddy River. Over Brigadier Fergusson's objection, Wingate also decided to leave most of the pack-animals on the east bank of the river. Along with the mules and oxen, Wingate left nearly six tons of equipment behind. Unable to shake his Japanese pursuers, General Wingate finally issued the order for the force to form dispersion groups and work their way back to India or China. A massive airdrop was arranged before striking out for India; food, maps, compasses, and boots were included. Major Fergusson's column had difficulty getting to the rendezvous, arrived late, and never got supplied. Even despite these hardships and constant harassment from the Emperor's crack troops, the escape worked as diagrammed.

One group, led by Major Walter P. Scott, greeted C-47 pilots bringing airdrop supplies with an urgent message laid out on the ground. The strips of parachute cloth read *Plane land here*. Without enough of a clearing to do so, the pilot circled over the area before attaching a note to the last parcel. The pilot instructed Major Scott and his men to mark out a flat piece of ground 1200 yards— the Dakota would be back to try the next day. Even though only 800 yards were available the following morning, the pilot decided to risk a landing. The gamble succeeded. In less than 12 minutes, 17 wounded soldiers were loaded aboard the Dakota and the C-47 was again airborne above the jungle, carrying its soldiers back to safety.

Not all the others were so lucky. Operation LONGCLOTH lasted from 8 February until early June. Of the 2,800 who entered

Burma, only 2,182 returned to India but most were unfit for future combat. Notwithstanding these heavy losses and despite suffering from exhaustion, when the 77th Indian Brigade finally reached safety in India, their spirits were high.

General Wingate's troops had reason to feel good about Operation LONGCLOTH. The mission had dealt a blow to the Japanese and proved several elements of LRP theory. LRP was actually able to exploit Japanese weaknesses in the interior of Burma; the successful raids on the railroads amply proved this fact. Secondly, LRP's mobility and surprise had confused the Japanese for nearly 2 months. It was only when air re-supply was unable to respond quickly enough to Wingate's needs that the mission broke down. Because of similarly slow responses, the brigades never exploited the firepower aspect of the theory.

General Wingate's operation brought to light the strengths and weaknesses of LRP operations. Wingate had overcome Burma's terrain and the residual fear from the Japanese invasion, but he did not get the organizational support necessary for complete victory. LRP was never intended to be the primary, let alone the sole, operation; its value was to divide the attention of the enemy. Operation LONGCLOTH simply violated its own principles and the Japanese finally were able to corral the operation and pick it apart. What General Wingate did not foresee was the most devastating flaw; his inability to evacuate the wounded had a grave affect on morale. The later events of the operation did not detract from the mission's overall value, though. For the first time, British troops had fought a jungle war against the Japanese and had delivered punishment. In Wingate's words, "a weapon has been found which may well prove a counter to the obstinate but unimaginative courage of the Japanese soldier." (86:24)

On 21 May, the *London Daily Times* released the invasion story for worldwide distribution. During this report, the name Chindit was given to the 77th Indian Brigade. Incorrectly identifying the Burmese *Chinthe*, General Wingate explained the term described a mythological beast, half-lion and half-griffin. Portrayed as statues that guard Burmese pagodas, the lion-griffin symbolized to Wingate the unique cooperation required between ground and air forces. The description captured the imagination of Englishmen around the globe. The British press was extremely favorable in its treatment of the Chindits; their success contrasted sharply with the failure of XV Corps' Arakan operation. Because of the publicity, General Wingate became the British champion of Burma.

Additionally, the exploits of the Chindits fired the hope and praise of the Allies. Without question, General Wingate's mission influenced future Burma operations. Before the Chindit mission, U.S. and British planners had been at loggerheads about Burma. Since the Japanese had closed all overland supply routes to China in early 1942, American air power, flying over the Himalayas, kept provisions of fuel and materiel flowing to Chiang Kai-shek. However, increased Japanese actions required more stores than feasible using the *Hump* re-supply method. Strategic planners in Washing-

ton realized that if China was unable to hold out against the 20-odd Japanese divisions on their mainland, these experienced units could be released to fight elsewhere in the Pacific. Considering China a cornerstone in the war against Japan, U.S. President Roosevelt wanted the Burma Road reopened.

Britain's Prime Minister Churchill, on the other hand, was more concerned with maintaining the British Empire. Because China had territorial claims on Northern Burma, Churchill wanted a weak China to emerge from the war. Based on these two interconnected priorities, the Prime Minister was not interested in relieving China's supply problems. Britain consistently recommended an amphibious assault in Sumatra with a push toward the recapture of Singapore.

President Roosevelt's trump card was to tie U.S. demands for a Burma offensive to Britain's greatest need, war machinery. The inability of Britain to demonstrate a successful strategy to re-secure the Burma Road had been a source of embarrassment to Churchill and his planning staff. To pump some life into India Command, the Prime Minister's staff proposed the establishment of South-east Asia Command (SEAC) to coordinate the complex interlocking and overlapping areas of command, geography, and operation. A new organization, however, was not a strategy. When he witnessed the press reaction to the Chindits, Churchill realized he had a new means of surmounting the topographic defenses of Burma and a new champion in General Wingate.

In July, Churchill called Wingate back to London to discuss the Chindit LRP operations. After speaking to General Wingate, the Prime Minister invited him to attend the upcoming Quadrant Conference in Quebec, Canada. The purpose of Quadrant was to establish overarching Allied strategy, and although it primarily dealt with the European Theater, operations in Burma were to be discussed. Specifically, Churchill wanted Wingate "to explain his recent operation with a long-range penetration group and to set out his views on their future employment." (80:1) During the conference, General Wingate proposed to expand the number of units, in steps, to eight brigade groups for the forthcoming 1943-44 dry season offensive. Four of the units would lead the operation while four would be held in reserve. Wingate felt LRP units should only be subjected to combat for 90-day periods before being relieved for a rest. In addition to LRP units, a major offensive would be mounted. The objectives were to occupy Bhamo and Lashio; take over the Katha-Indaw airfield and drive toward Pinlebu and Kalewa; and initiate an assault from Ledo toward Myitkyina. General Wingate's fortified LRP groups would act in coordination with British and Chinese forces whose objective was limited to the conquest of Burma north of the 23rd Parallel.

General Wingate's Quadrant plan also included requirements for aircraft support. He asked for approximately 16 DC-3 aircraft for airdrop and an allotment of one bomber squadron per unit for close air support. Additionally, at the insistence of one of his RAF liaison officers, Squadron Leader Robert "Tommy" Thompson, General Wingate sought to overcome previous morale problems by requesting a "Light Plane Force" to help in the evacuation of wounded LRP personnel. The U.S. reaction to a plan to reopen the Burma Road was viewed favorably.

While offering Wingate's LRP plan to secure Northern Burma, the British were forced to request American assistance. With the constant demands on war materiel in Europe, the British supply capability was over-committed. The result was the China-Burma-India (CBI) Theater had the lowest priority in the war. Weapons, vehicles, planes, and other equipment were always in short supply. Critical items regularly included food and medicine. Britain simply could not meet all the demands of General Wingate's Quadrant plan.

Prime Minister Churchill felt that England had the necessary bombers, but he was unable to provide two LRP brigades, the DC-3 Dakotas, and the evacuation aircraft. At the Quadrant Conference, the Prime Minister asked General Wingate to brief President Roosevelt. Then when he had the President's agreement on the mission, Churchill followed up the briefing with a request for American men and materiel.

The President endorsed Wingate's bold strategy and forwarded Churchill's petition for help through channels. The request for aircraft was routed to U.S. General of the Army Henry H. (Hap) Arnold for action. Because of Arnold's experience with air power, his fertile mind saw more in the plan than simple light airplanes. Like Churchill, Arnold wanted to put new life in the CBI Theater because he felt the previous campaigns had sapped the will of the British ground troops. In his mind, Arnold saw an opportunity to exploit and expand air power. He became determined to form a new air organization totally dedicated to supporting Wingate's troops on the ground in Burma. The successful realization of that strategy rested in Arnold's choice of a commander to breathe life into his vision.

Chinthe
Twin chinthes guard the pagoda at Swebo. Major General Orde C. Wingate's mispronunciation of the term led to his forces popularly being called Chindits. To Wingate, the Chinthe, half-lion and half-griffin, symbolized the unique cooperation required between ground and air forces.
Courtesy of 1ˢᵗ Air Commando Association

3

Project 9

On 26 August 1943, newly named Supreme Allied Commander of SEAC, British Admiral Lord Louis Mountbatten met with General Arnold to discuss plans for the CBI Theater. During this discussion, Admiral Lord Mountbatten reportedly brought up the idea of enlarging on General Wingate's mission. General Arnold restated his support of LRP and committed his plan to develop an autonomous organization for this purpose. General Arnold's concept of this new force was as a highly mobile fighting unit complete with

Supreme Allied Commander, South-East Asia
Lord Louis Mountbatten was the son of Prince Louis Alexander of Battenberg and Princess Victoria, a grand-daughter of Queen Victoria.
Courtesy of 1st Air Commando Association

its own transportation and services. It would be an experiment looking toward future air warfare. As the unit evolved, it would change names five times. The evolution included the names Project 9, Project CA 281, 5318th Provisional Unit (Air), No. 1 Air Commando Force, and 1st Air Commando Group.

Arnold's first priority was to find men who would infuse the U.S. *can-do* spirit into the CBI Theater. Having formed other "specials" and monitored their operations, General Arnold had concerns. Too often he had seen theater organizations absorb these unique forces, causing them to fail in their purpose. Therefore, the selection of a commander was critical as he would ultimately decide the composition, morale, and employment of the unit. General Arnold requested members of his staff nominate candidates for command of this experimental organization; five nominations were submitted. In a short time, the search narrowed to two individuals.

The first, Lieutenant Colonel Philip G. Cochran, fit General Arnold's desired qualities: he was confident, aggressive, imaginative, and had a highly distinguished war record as a fighter pilot in Africa. In November 1942, then-Major Cochran had led a group of 35 replacement pilots and planes to North Africa. Informed that casualties were lighter than expected, Cochran ascertained his men were not needed. Without headquarters sanction, he took the pilots to Rabat, Morocco, named them the Joker Squadron and began training for combat. When the Joker Squadron was discovered, higher headquarters ordered it back to Casablanca. However, Cochran and seven of his fellow aviators were sent to Tunisia to reinforce the remnants of two P-40 squadrons. Upon reporting to the airfield near the Kasserine Pass, Major Cochran noted he was the ranking officer and took over the 58th Squadron. Forced to live in caves because of their proximity to the front, 58th Squadron personnel concentrated on attacking Axis truck and train routes to relieve pressure on French and American forces. Because of the success of Cochran's raids, the Germans were forced to begin moving supplies by night and to hiding trucks under haystacks during the day. However, this tactic did not slow Major Cochran's men; they began attacking haystacks with outstanding results. Among his mis-

Project 9 Selection
Lieutenant Colonel Philip G. Cochran poses in full uniform. Milton Caniff's characters from *Terry and the Pirates* **are in the background.** *Courtesy of Historian Office of Hurlburt Field, Florida*

was charged with reassembling the crated planes upon delivery at the Arctic port of Arkhangelsk.

As the planes began to arrive, Captain Hubert "Hub" Zemke, later of the famous *Wolfpack* Squadron, joined the program as Chief of Operations; he and Alison then began teaching Russian pilots to operate the American warplanes. Without technical orders, they put together P-40 Tomahawks and tested every one before delivery. When the numbing Russian winter shut down operations, the State Department allowed Zemke to leave, but Captain Alison stayed on as the Assistant Military Attaché for Air. Finally in January 1942, Alison secured a verbal release from General George C. Marshall's special emissary to the Soviet Union, Lieutenant Colonel Townsen Griffiths.

Captain Alison left Russia and traveled to Basra, Iraq, believing Griffiths would forward written orders upon returning to Washington. The orders never came. Tragically, in April, Alison learned Griffiths' plane had been shot down over the English Channel. Officially, Alison had been absent without leave for over three months. Meanwhile he had attached himself to a small engineering unit that was assisting the British as they received lend-lease A-20s. Although he had not flown the aircraft, Alison took charge of the operation

Flip Corkin
Lieutenant Colonel Philip G. Cochran was the model for Milton Caniff's Flip Corkin of *Terry and the Pirates.* **Advertisement from the Pittsburgh Post-Gazette.** *Courtesy of 1ˢᵗ Air Commando Association*

sions was one in which Cochran loaded a P-40 with two 500-pound bombs and blew up the heavily defended German headquarters at Kairouan, Tunisia.

After 6 months of combat, Cochran had downed two German fighters and won the Distinguished Flying Cross with two clusters, a Silver Star, the Soldier's Medal, the Air Medal with three clusters, and the Croix de Guerre with Star and Palm. Unknown to General Arnold, Lieutenant Colonel Cochran was also the model for the character of Flip Corkin in Milton Caniff's ***Terry and the Pirates*** comic strip.

Although General Arnold did not know Cochran, he recognized the name of the second candidate, Lieutenant Colonel John R. Alison. Like Cochran, Alison represented traits desired by General Arnold, although the qualities were not the same. Alison was tactful, well organized, experienced in Far East flight operations, and a consummate pilot with a superb flying record. A 1936 Engineering School graduate from the University of Florida, Alison drew on his technical training during one of his first assignments: administering the sensitive U.S.-Russian lend-lease program of P-40 aircraft. Dispatched to Russia during the summer of 1941 by Harry Hopkins, trusted advisor of President Roosevelt, then-Captain Alison

Co-commander
General Henry H. "Hap" Arnold selected Colonel John R. Alison to share command of Project 9. *Courtesy of Stan Zajac and the R. T. Smith Family, 1ˢᵗ Air Commando Association*

details of the project separately to Cochran and Alison. After the operation was outlined, each man stated his opposition, thinking of it only as a light plane evacuation organization. Playing *Alphonse and Gaston*, each tried to persuade General Arnold to give the job to the other.

General Arnold solved the problem by naming them co-commanders, adding that there was more to the project than met the eye. General Arnold said, "I not only want you to [take out the wounded] ... but I want the USAAF to spearhead General Wingate's operation." (80:3) General Arnold then terminated the session by saying, "To hell with the paper work, go out and fight." (57:130) Perhaps not intending them to take him literally, Cochran and Alison did just that after setting up offices in the Pentagon and the Hay-Adams House, a Washington hotel.

Trying to better understand LRP and the mission of the new unit, Lieutenant Colonel Cochran immediately flew to England to talk to Admiral Lord Mountbatten and General Wingate. During discussions about the previous campaign and long-range penetration theory, Cochran began to mentally formulate the organization of General Arnold's vision, known as Project 9.

After talking with Wingate, Cochran enlarged his notion of the Project 9 mission. Based on the 1943 Chindit campaign and focusing on the LRP principle of air support, Cochran and Alison decided to take on the responsibility for all of Wingate's air requirements. They began "building a whole small region of warfare where

and cabled the War Department to inform them of his new duties. Duplicating the previous program in Russia, Alison periodically forwarded pencil-written progress reports directly to General Arnold, always with a postscript requesting combat duty when relieved.

In June 1942, he finally was sent to the China Theater as a pilot for U.S. Major General Claire L. Chennault's 23ʳᵈ Fighter Group, known previously as the American Volunteer Group (AVG) *Flying Tigers*. During this tour, Alison organized the first successful night interception of Japanese airplanes. After shooting down two Mitsubishi Type 97 bombers, Alison's plane was hit and he had to make a forced landing in the Siang Kiang River, a tributary of the Yangtze. Later, he became an ace by downing six enemy aircraft and was one of a select few U.S. pilots who flew a captured Japanese Zero. Lieutenant Colonel Alison returned home in May 1943 and was training the 367ᵗʰ Fighter Group on the West Coast when General Arnold summoned him for an interview.

During the meetings, General Arnold hoped to find a man to lead his unique organization who was aggressive, imaginative, and highly organized. Together, Cochran and Alison possessed these qualities. Cochran was cavalier, outspoken, a positive leader, and possessed an innovative mind. By contrast, Alison was disciplined, articulate, a quiet leader, and had displayed a diplomatic demeanor. Unable to make a clear selection, General Arnold explained the

Project 9 Operations Officer
Former AVG pilot, Lieutenant Colonel Arvid E. Olson *Courtesy of A. R. Van de Weghe, 1ˢᵗ Air Commando Association*

Fighter Section Commander
Lieutenant Colonel Grattan "Grant" Mahony. Mahony's name was often misspelled Mahoney in various records. *Courtesy of 1st Air Commando Association*

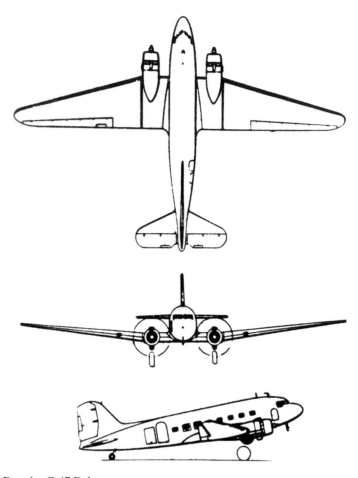

Douglas C-47 Dakota
Also known as the Skytrain and Gooney Bird, the C-47 was the workhorse of Allied air transportation during World War II. *Courtesy of the Graphics Art Department, Maxwell AFB AL*

we had ground troops, artillery, infantry, air-ground support, fighter support, and bombardment support." (107:157-158)

There was no table of organization for a unit of this kind, so Cochran and Alison used their imagination to describe the structure and personnel requirements. They got what they wanted because "General Arnold had given them practically carte blanche orders to gather men and materiel under the highest priority." (113:1) Among the first personnel assignments to Project 9 were Major Samson Smith as Executive Officer; Major Arvid E. Olson, a former AVG pilot, as Operations Officer; and Captain Charles L. Engelhardt as Administrative Assistant. The Project 9 group immediately launched into manning the unit. Heading the various functions of the organization were Captain Robert E. Moist, Adjutant; Major Edwin B. White, Supply Section; Captain John H. Jennette, Engineering Section; Major Richard W. Boebel and Captain Temple C. Moore, Intelligence Section; and Major Earnest O. Bonham, Communication Section. Due to the classification of the project, inter-

Waco CG-4A Hadrian
The glider could carry troopers, jeeps, and howitzers. Its maximum payload was 3,750 pounds. *Courtesy of the Graphics Art Department, Maxwell AFB AL*

Aeronca TG-5 Glider
The Aeronca TG-5 glider was intended for small party infiltration and ex-filtration operations. The glider's size and light weight allowed it to be towed by a UC-64 Norseman. *Courtesy of 1ˢᵗ Air Commando Association*

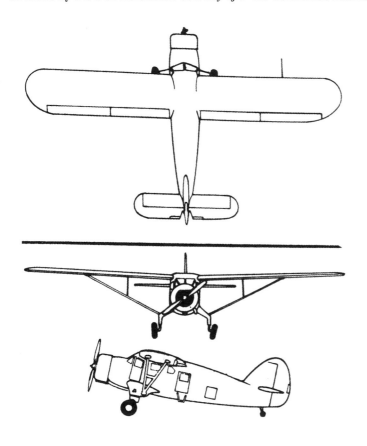

Noorduyn UC-64 Norseman
Norseman pilots joked that the Canadian-built light transport rotated, climbed, cruised, descended, and landed at 160 miles per hour. *Courtesy of the Graphics Art Department, Maxwell AFB AL*

ested personnel were told only a minimum amount of information. Not advised of the destination, applicants were assured the mission included combat, the duration involved would be no more than 6 months, all who joined would be volunteers, and personnel should expect no promotions. At the Quadrant Conference, the RAF had agreed to supply the bomber requirement; therefore, the co-commanders were seeking volunteers for three major types of aircraft—fighters, transports, and light planes.

To provide air support to LRP units, Cochran and Alison proposed an assault force of fighters. The Fighter Section, working directly with the Chindits, would fully test Wingate's theory of airborne artillery. The lure of combat duty and the secret nature of Project 9 made recruiting simple. Lieutenant Colonel Cochran said, "[W]e were allowed to bring in from anywhere—if we knew [a] man's name, we'd send for him. We knew them through our time in the Air Force." (107:161) Cochran and Alison selected Major Grattan "Grant" Mahony to lead the Fighter Section. He had combat experience throughout the Pacific, was an ace (five kills), and had flown with Lieutenant Colonel Alison in China. Major Robert T. "Tadpole" Smith, also an ace (eight kills) and a former AVG pilot, was selected as his deputy. After the composition of the unit was altered in India, Major Robert L. Petit, winner of a Silver Star for air battles at Guadalcanal, replaced Major Smith. As pilots were brought into the unit, they recommended others. Crew chiefs and enlisted men who had previously served under the leaders were asked to join the unit. For aircraft, Project 9 recommended P-38 Lightnings for the close air support requirements. When this request was denied, the co-commanders substituted P-47 Thunderbolts and requested an allocation of 30 aircraft.

For the transport requirements, the Cochran and Alison team defined a need for three separate units. They decided to recruit pilots for transport, glider, and light-cargo airplanes. Each would fill a distinct role in the organization.

The mission of the Transport Section was to provide responsive airland and airdrop support for the Chindits. Major William T. Cherry, Jr., pilot of E. V. "Eddie" Rickenbacker's ill-fated Pacific trip, was selected to command this section. Captain Jacob B. Sartz was chosen to be his deputy. He had the experience and daring wanted by Cochran. Earlier Sartz had bombed the Japanese from a C-87 (a cargo version of the B-24) and flew 72 refugees on one of the last Dakotas out of Rangoon in 1942. To keep the transport aircraft flightworthy, Captain Richard E. Cole, General James H. "Jimmy" Doolittle's copilot on the B-25 Tokyo Raid, was named Engineering Officer. With few exceptions, Major Cherry selected pilots and maintenance men from the 724ᵗʰ Training Group assigned to Baer Field, Ft. Wayne, Indiana, and the 5ᵗʰ Troop Carrier Squadron at Lawson Field, Ft. Benning, Georgia. Interestingly, the men's orders assigned them to Project CA-281. Reportedly this identification signified the Cochran-Alison office temporarily established in room 281 at the Hay-Adams House.

To fully support the Chindits, Cochran proposed using gliders to transport heavy artillery to LRP units. Similarly, Alison saw the potential for gliders to re-supply Wingate by moving men and equipment into small jungle clearings that could not otherwise be accessed. At the recommendation of the Pentagon, Captain William H. Taylor, Jr., and First Lieutenant Vincent Rose were designated Glider Section commander and deputy command respectively. Once assigned, Captain Taylor personally selected all glider pilots and mechanics for the unit from Bowman Field in Louisville, Kentucky.

Because Project 9 was designed as a self-contained fighting unit, Alison recognized a requirement for a light-cargo aircraft to provide unit support. The co-commanders selected Lieutenant Colonel Clinton B. Gaty from Wright Field to command the Light-cargo Section because, as an engineer, he could do more than just fly. Cochran related, "[He was a] guy to head up our whole maintenance-engineering function, to take care of [our] aircraft in the jungle, to practically rebuild them if we had to." (107:165) Captain Edward "Sam" Wagner was chosen to assist Lieutenant Colonel Gaty.

The Project 9 team recommended 35 C-47 Dakotas for the aircraft requirements of the Transport Section—13 were approved. The Glider Section requested 100 CG-4A Waco Hadrian gliders due to its 3,750-pound payload. Over 48 feet long with a wing span

Light Plane Section Commander
Major Andrew P. Rebori came to Project 9 from Panama. *Courtesy of 1ˢᵗ Air Commando Association*

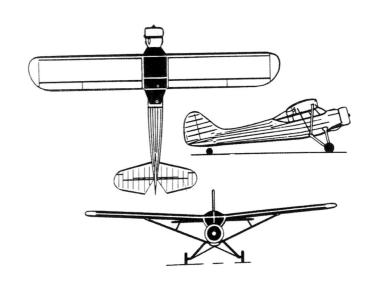

Vultee L-1 Vigilant
Built to carry two stretcher cases, the Vigilant's short takeoff roll was ideal for the jungles of Burma. *Courtesy of the Graphics Art Department, Maxwell AFB AL*

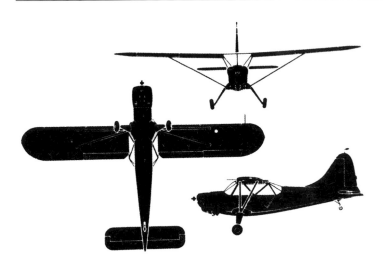

Stinson L-5A Sentinel
The Technical Order for the Sentinel stated the aircraft was designed for only one evacuee and required runways of 900 feet. *Courtesy of the Graphics Art Department, Maxwell AFB AL*

of 84 feet, the glider was capable of carrying 13 troopers, a jeep and five men, or two men and a 105 mm howitzer. Captain Taylor also selected 25 Aeronca TG-5 training gliders for use in remote sites. For unit support, Project 9 selected a little known bush airplane used extensively in Canada, the UC-64 Noorduyn Norseman. With a 17,000-foot operating ceiling, cruising speed of 160 mph, 2,000-pound cargo load, and runway requirement of no more than 2,000 feet, the requested 12 Norsemen were to be a bridge between the C-47 and the light planes planned for medical evacuation.

The light planes were not only to be used for the evacuation of wounded; they were also to provide liaison and transport of light supplies between India and the forward lines. The light planes would be flown almost entirely by enlisted pilots. At the recommendation of Captain Taylor, Major Andrew P. Rebori was chosen to command the Liaison Section, and he, in turn, brought along Captain Everett F. Smith as his deputy. Because Project 9 was to be a mobile unit, Major Rebori required volunteers to be trained in at least one usable craft other than aviation. Electricians, mechanics, and handymen were essential in the CBI because the pilots would be expected to fix their own planes.

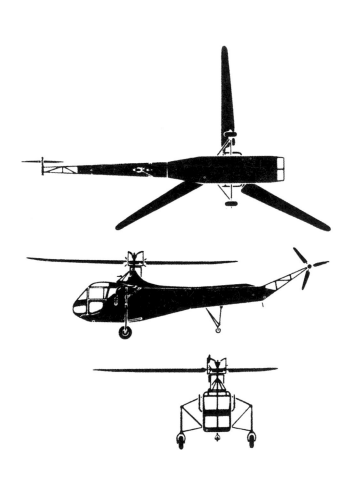

Sikorsky YR-4 Helicopter
Colonel Alison persuaded Wright Field to operationally test the unproven helicopters in actual combat conditions. Half of the helicopters came from U.S. Navy assets. *Courtesy of the Graphics Art Department, Maxwell AFB AL*

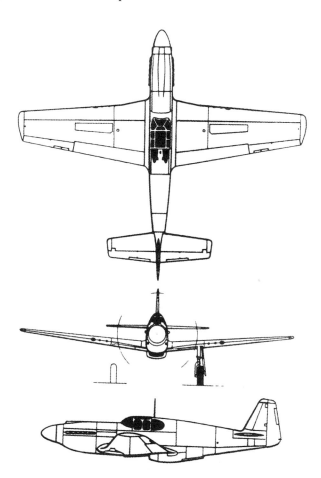

North American P-51A Mustang
For close air support, the Army Air Corps substituted Mustangs for P-38 Lightnings. *Courtesy of the Graphics Art Department, Maxwell AFB AL*

Project 9 Marksmanship Training, October 1943
Major Richard E. Boebel qualifies at the pistol range at Seymour-Johnson, North Carolina. *Courtesy of 1ˢᵗ Air Commando Association*

For the light plane force, Major Rebori selected the L-1 Vigilant. The plane carried two to three stretchers behind the pilot and had a short takeoff roll. Major Rebori required 100 L-1 Vigilants; however, when the number of serviceable aircraft could not be located, he augmented the L-1 with the newer L-5 Sentinel. The Sentinels were faster than the L-1; however, they were designed to seat only one evacuee. The L-5 was also less desired because its technical data called for a much longer runway—about 900 feet.

In addition to the light planes, Cochran and Alison decided to employ the newly developed Sikorsky helicopter in Burma. Lieutenant Colonel Cochran placed the diplomatic Alison in charge of securing the pre-production model YR-4 for rescue service in the jungle. Although he was initially turned down, Alison finally persuaded Wright Field to operationally test four of the unproven helicopters in actual combat. Arnold C. Podolsky, technical representative of Sikorsky Aircraft, traveled with the unit to India to assist with maintenance.

The organization, as far as equipment was concerned, was equal to a USAAF wing carrying a normal complement of about 2,000 men. Because of time constraints though, Project 9 personnel had to be completely air transported. Therefore, the requirements—including medical, engineering, supply, intelligence, and communication sections—were kept lean: 87 officers and 436 enlisted men.

Lieutenant Colonel Cochran and Lieutenant Colonel Alison sent their planned organization through channels to General Arnold who forwarded his approval to General of the Army George Marshall on 13 September 1943. The only alteration to the request involved the fighters; the Pentagon substituted P-51A Mustangs for the Thunderbolts. In less than 30 days, Cochran and Alison had built themselves a unit and gotten it approved. Their next job was to imbue the unit with life and prepare the personnel for deployment.

As the unit formed, the men seemed to sense they were exceptional and began acting accordingly. Gathering in North Carolina on 1 October—the fighters and gliders at Seymour-Johnson Field and the light planes at Raleigh-Durham—Project 9 began requisitioning specialized equipment. New ideas were encouraged. As a result, a new mobile hospital was included on the required equipment list and blueprints for experimental rocket tubes were ordered from Wright Field for the fighters. The Dakotas were to be equipped with the newest development in glider towing, the Model 80X Glider Pick Up System. Built by All American Aviation, Inc., the system was "designed for the non-stop launching ... of a glider." (120: —) For the gliders, Captain Taylor requested each Hadrian be equipped with gyro towing devices somewhat similar to an automatic pilot mechanism. It consisted of a small propeller on the right wing that drove a hydro-electric motor to move the ailerons and tail controls. Furthermore, Major Rebori designed bomb racks so parachute packs could be mounted on the wings of L-1 and L-5 aircraft. For the men, the co-commanders convinced the Army to issue weapons to all of the flyers in the unit—Thompson submachine guns, carbines, and .45 automatic pistols. So instead of the normal Port of Embarkation training given to overseas-bound soldiers, Project 9 spent spare time at the rifle range.

In North Carolina, some flight training was also conducted. While the Fighter Section assembled and began indoctrination courses on the P-51A and its Allison engine, the gliders got flying time. Major Cherry obtained the use of two C-47 tugs and crews, one each from the 436ᵗʰ and 439ᵗʰ Troop Carrier Squadrons. Daily the Dakota pilots practiced single, double, and automatic tow; flying in position below the C-47; and night operations. Captain Taylor emphasized double tow to maximize airlift capability. In this method, two gliders, one on a short rope and the other on a longer line, were towed by one C-47. Close coordination between glider pilots and a steady hand by tug pilots was required. Because of their demonstrated skills, two of the "loaned" C-47 pilots, Second Lieutenant Patrick Driscoll and Second Lieutenant Vincent L. Ulery, were asked to join Cochran and Alison's Project 9 team.

As Major Cherry's transport pilots arrived, they were taught glider pickup procedures—the art of *snatching* a Hadrian off the ground by an airborne Dakota. Developed under the oversight of Richard C. Du Pont, the snatch process was taught to Dakota pilots by Captain Norm Rintoul. Hidden inside each Project 9 C-47 was the heart of the Model 80X system—an energy absorbing drum, twin pulleys, torque tube, hydraulic cylinder, 950-foot nylon cable,

Project 9 Patch
Although Cochran and Alison adopted no official Project 9 emblem, this design or variations of it gained acceptance within the unit. Against a round dark blue setting was the multi-armed Hindu god Vishnu silhouetted in white, a gold chinthe, and nine gold stars. Collectively, they symbolized Southeast Asia, Special Force, and Project 9. *Courtesy of A. R. Van de Weghe, 1ˢᵗ Air Commando Association*

Transport Section Mascot
Just prior to deploying to India, First Lieutenant Frank M. Huxley adopted Roger in Miami, Florida. The dog logged time as part of Major Neil I. Holm's crew and became the mascot of the Transport Section. *Courtesy of 1ˢᵗ Air Commando Association*

and explosive cable cutter controls. Modifications evident from outside the Dakota included a plug-style access panel mounted within the aircraft's door frame and an exterior mounted wooden arm. At the end of the arm was a polished steel hook; nylon cable from inside the aircraft's cargo area was secured to the hook. In the stowed position, the hook, arm, and cable assembly was secured to the left side of the fuselage forward of the cargo door. Project 9 pilots were required to complete six simulated and four actual glider pick-ups prior to certification. Because procedures and equipment were new, All American Aviation provided a technical representative, Mr. William Burkhart, to the Cochran-Alison organization. He would accompany the unit to India.

Light plane pilots also worked with glider personnel by towing TG-5 training gliders, but primarily they busied themselves learning about their airplanes. Because the L-1 was obsolete and the L-5 was new to the USAAF inventory, most of the "flying sergeants" had not flown either and definitely not under the anticipated conditions in Burma. Major Rebori invited his men to brainstorm. As a result, Staff Sergeant Richard D. Snyder experimented by lashing two Thompson submachine guns to the struts of his aircraft. The vibration shook the Sentinel so badly the idea was rejected. Training emphasized speed and precision. One exploratory

tactic was for the light planes to act like a swarm of insects. Approaching from all points on the compass, light planes suddenly appeared over a crossroad and landed. Armed liaison pilots quickly blocked traffic and secured the roads. During training, Major Rebori began timing when the first plane appeared on the horizon and stopped as the last one parked. By constant practice, 18 airplanes were able to complete the exercise in 3 minutes or less. Another procedure simulated jungle obstacles. Major Rebori stretched ropes across the Raleigh-Durham runway and made the light plane pilots practice short-field landings and takeoffs over and over again. In fully loaded aircraft, the pilots began to routinely make takeoffs in 500-600 feet. While airborne, they trained themselves in low level flight. When the townspeople complained about planes flying at 100 feet, Major Rebori replied they should have been lower!

Originally scheduled to embark about 15 December, the group had to curtail the entire training program when the departure date was moved up 45 days. As the embarkation date neared, the enthusiasm of the unit soared. Flight Surgeon Cortez Enloe said, "They had the greatest morale of any outfit I ever saw, but not such strict discipline." (50:106) Armed with a transportation priority high enough to "bump" generals, the unit was scheduled to fly from Miami to Karachi, India, by way of Puerto Rico, Trinidad, British Guiana, Brazil, Ascension Island, Gold Coast, Nigeria, Anglo-Egyptian Sudan, Aden, and Masirah Island. When the men assembled for departure at Morrison Field, Florida, a last minute addition to the organization occurred. On 5 December, Second Lieutenant Frank M. Huxley persuaded Roger, a reddish-brown chow with a large ruff and fluffy tail, to join Project 9. Roger made the trip to India as a member of Captain Neil I. Holm's Dakota crew and instantly became the group's mascot. Ahead of the main unit and unaware, Colonel Cochran was already on his way, leaving Miami on 3 November 1943.

4

5318th Provisional Unit (Air)

True to his word, General Arnold had superimposed the organization on SEAC by forwarding a letter to USAAF Major General George Stratemeyer, a member of Mountbatten's staff and soon to be named commander of the Eastern Air Command. In the letter, dated 13 September, General Arnold stated, "...the Air Task Force will be assigned to the Commanding General of the United States Army Forces in the China-India-Burma [sic] Theater for administration and supply and operate under the control of the Allied Commander-in-Chief, South-East Asia." (80:Memo, Subject: Air Task Force Windgate [sic], 13 September 1943) Also General Arnold had carefully defined the purpose of Project 9. The unit was to fully support Wingate's Chindits by facilitating the forward movement of the columns as well as supply and assist in evacuating them if needed. Additionally, they were to provide a small air cover and strike force. Specifically, General Arnold wanted Project 9 to acquire air experience under the conditions expected to be encountered. Knowing the mission given him by General Arnold, Colonel Cochran wanted to discuss the latest developments with Admiral

Lord Mountbatten, find facilities for his personnel and aircraft, and continue unit training programs when he arrived in India.

Despite an engine change and a short delay en route, Cochran and a small group of his men arrived in Western India on 13 November. One of Cochran's first duties was to report to Delhi where Admiral Lord Mountbatten had temporarily set up his headquarters. When Colonel Cochran first talked to the SEAC staff, the facts of General Arnold's letter were not generally known and changes had been made to the Quadrant Conference plans. Colonel Alison later wrote of the situation in a Memorandum for General Giles on 10 April 1994:

When Colonel Cochran arrived in the theater, the general plan for Wingate's operation was to march into Burma initially three long-range penetration brigades. One to cross the Chindwin River from the West, one to march down from the North and a third to be flown to China and marched across the Salween to spearhead a Chinese advance. This unit would have to be moved by air to China, then re-supplied by air from Chinese bases. [USA] General Stilwell [Deputy Supreme Commander of SEAC] said that because of air lift limitations this would be impossible and the whole plan of offensive operations in Burma for this season were [sic] in danger of being abandoned. Colonel Cochran arrived at this meeting where [British] General Auchinleck [Command-in-Chief in India], General Stilwell, [USAAF] General Chennault [Commander, 14th Air Force], Admiral Mountbatten and General Stratemeyer's representative were present. At this time no-one in the theater, not even Admiral Mountbatten or General Wingate, knew what the 1st Air Commando Group in-

The dirigible hangar at Karachi, India *Courtesy of 1st Air Commando Association*

Crated UC-64 Norseman, Karachi, India, December 1943
Near the dirigible hangar, enlisted and officer personnel helped reassemble crated UC-64 Norseman aircraft. *Courtesy of 1ˢᵗ Air Commando Association*

Transport Section Marking
En route to India, Project 9 crews were asked about the strange hook and arm apparatus attached to the underside of their Dakotas. Unable to answer due to secrecy, the C-47 Section decided to unofficially call themselves the "Question Mark" Squadron. Major Cherry's men proceeded to paint a blue question mark over a white circular field on the tail surface of each Dakota. On the A-2 jacket, the design was brown on tan. *Courtesy of Chester Amedia, 1ˢᵗ Air Commando Association*

tended to do for Wingate's operation. Colonel Cochran was called upon to explain why we had been sent into the theater and at this meeting he explained to the Chiefs of Staff that it was not necessary to fly the third brigade to China, that the brigade should be streamlined and that the 1ˢᵗ Air Commando Force would move this brigade into the heart of Burma from bases in India. He was asked if this was possible and if it would be possible for the 1ˢᵗ Air Commando Force to move the brigade to the job in two weeks time. He stated that the 1ˢᵗ Air Commandos would do the job in one week or less. At this meeting Admiral Mountbatten made the statement, "Boy, you are the first ray of sunshine we have seen in this theater for some time." (80: Memo for General Giles, 10 April 1944)

To back up his claims, on 24 November, Colonel Cochran cabled Alison, still in the U.S., requesting an additional 50 CG-4A Waco gliders. Although the mission would remain a constant political football, for now, it was back on the front burner. By the following day, the additional Hadrian gliders had departed the United States for India.

When the unit's aircraft started arriving, Cochran began to arrange for facilities. To expedite the flow of equipment, the C-47 Dakotas were flown to India, using essentially the same course as the rest of the men. All other airplanes were shipped by sea. The P-51A Mustangs were deck-loaded on carriers; the gliders and all other airplanes were disassembled and crated. With the exception of the gliders ticketed for the East Indian port of Calcutta, everything was destined for Karachi. Colonel Cochran would have to put his airplanes back together before permanently locating the unit.

The Project 9 advance party secured stone barracks with wide shaded verandahs for the men. The Karachi Airport dirigible hangar acted as the reception and assembly area for the unit's airplanes. Unfortunately, just before Christmas 1943, two shipments of P-51A Mustangs were received in non-operational condition because of

Architect of Lalaghat and Hailakandi
As an artillery officer, Captain Andrew L. Cox could not be assigned to an Army Air Force organization. Colonel Alison convinced South-East Asia Command to place Cox on permanent detached service to Project 9. *Courtesy of Andrew L. Cox, 1ˢᵗ Air Commando Association*

saltwater corrosion and storm damage. Since no replacements were available in the theater, priority spares had to be ordered. The crated planes fared better. Because of limited personnel, officers and enlisted men pitched in to assemble the UC-64 and L-series planes as the crates were offloaded. Visitors to the site remarked on the unit's spirit of cooperation. Temporarily, Project 9 established a headquarters near Karachi at Malir Airfield. As the year neared an end, Cochran's newly christened 5318th Provision Unit (Air) began training exercises and theater indoctrination.

When the flight and maintenance crews completed assembly, they serviced and repainted the aircraft for operations. Colonel Cochran authorized unique markings for the unit's airplanes—five white diagonal stripes banding the fuselage, aft of the cockpit. Many stories were offered for the distinctive markings. Some remembered the stripes represented the five sections of the provisional unit; others said the five white strips and intervening spaces symbolized Project 9. For whatever the reason, the markings had a singular purpose. They were "to let the Japanese know who was dominating the skies of Burma." (131: 1995 Edition 1: 4)

On 1 December, the Glider Section joined First Lieutenant Vincent Rose and Second Lieutenant H. J. Delaney at Barackpore Field, near Calcutta, where they began rigging and testing their gliders. Shipped in wooden crates, five per CG-4A Waco, each flight officer fabricated his own airplane. Although all Hadrians were supposed to be shipped to Calcutta, on 23 December, Captain Taylor was forced to send four of his personnel back across India to assemble a glider inadvertently sent to Karachi. Without a tensionometer to determine the tautness of the control wires, the men tightened the rigging by ear, much the same as tuning a guitar. As each glider was assembled, pilots would test fly each for practice and evaluation. When Captain Taylor's men determined a Waco was operationally ready, Dakotas towed the glider from Calcutta to

Sick Inn, Group Hospital, Hailakandi, India
An Indian native stands in the road leading to the tea planter's cottage that served as the unit's hospital. The dispensary is located on the left side of the picture. *Courtesy of 1st Air Commando Association*

the unit's new bases in the Assam. The last assembled were the 3-place TG-5 training gliders.

On Christmas Eve, after Colonel Alison arrived, he, Colonel Cochran, Captain Taylor, and others flew to the Assam region of Northeast India to examine two airfields recommended for use, Lalaghat and Hailakandi. Major Robert C. Page, head of the Medical Section, described the airfields as grass strips "entirely British in construction. All barracks were basha [native bamboo hut] in

Indian Heavy Construction Equipment
To prepare Lalaghat and Hailakandi for operations, Captain Andrew L. Cox enlisted Indian laborers for the task. The natives used elephants for heavy construction equipment. *Courtesy of 1st Air Commando Association*

Hailakandi Commissary
The Tea Plantation Processing Building was converted to a commissary for Project 9. *Courtesy of James E. Eckert, 1st Air Commando Association*

Project 9 Medical Section
Sitting **(L-R): Captain Peter A. Rierson; Captain Weldon O. Murphy; Major Robert C. Page; Captain Donald C. Tulloch; Captain Cortez F. Enloe, Jr.** *Standing* **(L-R): Sergeant Nance; Staff Sergeant Robert J. "Red" Kendrigan; Technical Sergeant Leon S. Palmatier; Technical Sergeant Norman W. Wach; Technical Sergeant Carl K. Schmidt; Technical Sergeant Lloyd F. McClain; Technical Sergeant Edward LaFortune** *Courtesy of 1st Air Commando Association*

Night Glider Training
To prepare the Chindits for glider operations, Captain William H. Taylor, Jr., head of the Glider Section, conducted a series of exercises culminating in a night insertion. *Courtesy of 1st Air Commando Association*

type." (113:Medical History:19) Due to the dilapidated condition of the bases, the airfields had been previously designated for emergencies only. Colonel Cochran tasked Captain Andrew L. Cox to renovate the unit's new bases. One of the first officers recruited by the Cochran-Alison team, Cox was never officially a member of Project 9. Because he held a regular commission in the Coast Artillery Corps, he could not be assigned to the Army Air Force. An agreement was struck between Colonel Alison and General Albert C. Wedemeyer, SEAC Deputy Chief of Staff. Captain Cox was transferred to Mountbatten's Headquarters and, on arrival in India, placed immediately on "permanent" detached service to the 5318th Provision Unit (Air). Under Captain Cox's supervision, Indian laborers, using elephants as heavy construction equipment, began erecting additional living quarters, showers, latrines, and mess halls. He initiated engineering projects to build connecting roads, survey sites for ammunition dumps, dig drainage ditches, and establish administrative areas. While these projects were underway, the group decided the longer 6,300-foot strip at Lalaghat would be used by the transports and gliders. Hailakandi, some 8 to 10 miles away, would be for the fighters and light planes. Located on a tea plantation, Hailakandi was only 4,500 feet long.

Hailakandi was also designated home of the medical unit; sick bay was situated in a vacant tea planter's cottage. Under the watchful eye of Major Page, activities started immediately with much needed sanitation efforts. Operations began as soon as items of plasma, glucose, salt solutions, drugs, pharmaceutical supplies, and medical devices arrived in theater. Unlike the aircraft equipment,

not all medical shipments contained the latest technical innovations. Staff Sergeant Robert J. "Red" Kendrigan, medical technician, recalled unwrapping equipment shipped from Walter Reed Hospital to make medicinal alcohol for laboratory work-ups. Stenciled on the side of crates containing field distillery paraphernalia was the following: "Ship to American Expeditionary Force, France 1918." (120:—)

While unit operations began to take shape, the co-commanders decided Lieutenant Colonel Gaty would command Lalaghat, and Colonel Cochran would run Hailakandi. After Colonel Alison's

Field Cook
Through resourceful manipulations, Sandy McPherson, a British field cook, was assigned to Liaison Section of the 5318th Provisional Unit (Air). *Courtesy of 1st Air Commando Association*

P-51A Mustangs lined up at Hailakandi, India
Lieutenant Colonel Mahony did not want to be fired on by his own fighters so the distinctive combat markings were developed. *Courtesy of James Lansdale and the R. T. Smith Family, 1ˢᵗ Air Commando Association*

arrival in India, the two had decided that the co-command arrangement was awkward. To simplify matters, officially Colonel Cochran was deemed the commander and Colonel Alison took the title of his deputy. They were in such accord, however, that a decision by one automatically became the decision of the other.

Having found a permanent home, Cochran and Alison turned their full attention to supporting Wingate's 3ʳᵈ Indian Division, also known as Special Force. It was during this stage of evolution that the 5318ᵗʰ conducted training exercises with the Chindits, enlarged their own assault force, and exploited General Arnold's fourth purpose, "to acquire air experience under the conditions expected to be encountered."

While Captain Taylor's men were rigging gliders, they also conducted joint training drills. These operational tests with the Chindits helped cement the bond between the two units. Flight training practice began on 29 December. Ten days later, a 20-glider day exercise was conducted in which 400 men were landed on a mud field at Lalitpur. Even though four Hadrians did not release, the exercise was pronounced a success. However, there was one problem—the gliders got stuck in the mud and could not be moved by

ground personnel. To solve the problem and demonstrate his unit's capabilities, Colonel Cochran arranged with Major Cherry to have the Wacos snatched out the following morning.

In the dawn sunlight, the equivalent of shooting a glider out of a cannon promised to be a well-watched spectacle. To the attaching point on the rounded Plexiglas nose of the Waco, flight officers secured one end of a nylon tow rope; the other was clipped in a loop between two 12-foot poles spaced 20 feet apart. If required, night operations were also possible by placing flashlights on the ends of the poles; they marked direction and established height. Glider expert John L. Lowden described the procedures that followed.

[The] C-47 would fly in at treetop level [38.6 feet allowing only a 4-foot propeller clearance above the poles] and literally snatch the glider off the ground. A 20-foot rod hung down under the twin-engine transport, at the bottom of which was a hook attached to a steel cable that ran back up into the plane's cabin and wound around a motor-driven drum. When the rod struck the looped tow rope, the rope disengaged from

Fighter Section, 5318ᵗʰ Provisional Unit (Air)
Back Row (L-R) Captain Craig L. Jackson; First Lieutenant Robert W. Boyd; First Lieutenant Younger "Sonny" Pitts; Captain John A. Kelting; Captain Olin B. Carter; Captain Roland R. Lynn; Captain Hubert L. Krug; Captain Holly M. Keller; Captain Neil A. Bollum; Captain William R. Gilhousen; First Lieutenant John E. Meyer; Captain Mack A. Mitchell; Captain Lester K. Murray; Captain Erle H. Schneider *Front Row* **(L-R) First Lieutenant Ned Schramm, Jr.; Captain Paul G. Forcey; Major Robert L. Petit; Lieutenant Colonel Robert T. Smith; Lieutenant Colonel Grattan "Grant" Mahony; Colonel John R. Alison; Colonel Philip G. Cochran; Lieutenant Colonel Arvid E. Olson; First Lieutenant Robley B. Melton; First Lieutenant Martin O, Berry; Captain Duke Phillips** *Courtesy of A. R. "Van" Van De Weghe and James Lansdale, 1ˢᵗ Air Commando Association*

the clips on the upright poles, slid down to the hook, and the connection was made. At that moment, the C-47 pilot, flying in at an oblique angle, at 110 mph, poured on full power. The glider was in the air in three seconds. At the moment of pickup, the cable would pay out slowly to preclude ripping off the glider's nose or snapping off its wings. Then, the drum was braked gradually by a crew member to full stop and reversed to bring the glider, now 500 to 1,000 feet to the rear of the snatch plane, into proper position—350 feet back. This maneuver took incredible timing and coordination... (29:17)

Inside, the flight officer fought the glider through the slingshot effect of rapid acceleration and delayed deceleration with minimum instruments and controls. Grasping tightly to the control wheel during the snatch, the glider pilot had only airspeed, vertical speed, and turn and bank indicators to keep his position. Later, Flight Officer Earl C. Waller described a continuing problem which occurred while attempting to take up slack: "...the rope from time to time looped back far enough to slap on top of the outer right wing panel. I was deeply concerned about the rope looping over the end of the wing and tearing the wing off on the forward surge." (131: Winter

Glider Section, 5318ᵗʰ Provisional Unit (Air)
Standing **(L-R) Flight Officer Allen Hall, Jr.; Flight Officer Anthony J. Bracaliello; unidentified; Flight Officer Bernard P. McGaulley; unidentified; Flight Officer Earl C. Waller; unidentified.** *Kneeling* **(L-R) Flight Officer Bruce Williams; unidentified** *Courtesy of 1ˢᵗ Air Commando Association*

Chindit Training Exercise
On left, Major General Orde C. Wingate discusses the results of a glider training session with Colonel Philip G. Cochran. As was his custom, Wingate grew a beard before taking his command into action. *Courtesy of 1ˢᵗ Air Commando Association*

Glider Section Patch
On a blue background was a large gold numeral "1" imposed over a white letter "G". In the foreground was a gray mule's head with oversized winged ears. In its mouth, the mule gripped a kukri, the Gurkhas' surgically sharp knife-sword. The harness and mule's nostrils were red; the handle of the kukri, brown. *Courtesy of Chuck Noland, 1ˢᵗ Air Commando Association*

1991: 13) To avoid oscillations that occurred when entering the tug's prop wash, the pilot operated rudders, elevators, and ailerons connected by cable to the control surfaces via three overhead pulleys. As glider pilots perfected the maneuver, the success of these demonstrations instilled confidence and confirmed a capability that would be used often in the Burma jungles.

While working with Special Force, the light plane pilots discovered an excellent British cook named Sandy McPherson. Recognizing his culinary skills, members of the Liaison Section used their ingenuity to convince the British to place him on detached duty to "Cochran's Circus." Captain Moist, Pay and Personnel Officer, put him on an American payroll. When the paperwork was complete, McPherson was attached to the group although, like Captain Cox, he never appeared on the official unit roster. He continued to move with Colonel Cochran's units throughout their stay in India.

During one of the day training exercises at Lalitpur, the assault force allayed other fears expressed about the evacuation airplanes. First Lieutenant Paul G. Forcey, a former RAF pilot assigned to the P-51 section and one of the characters found in Milton Caniff's comic strip, demonstrated the survivability of the L-5 Sentinel. Chindits and light plane pilots alike watched with keen interest. With another fighter pilot of the Assault Force flying a Mustang and Lieutenant Forcey in a Sentinel, the planes squared off in a mock dogfight. Beer bets were made and covered. All eyes were on the two airplanes as they twisted and turned overhead. Using the smaller turn radius of the L-5 to advantage, Forcey continually outmaneuvered the faster aircraft. Gun camera film later verified the Sentinel had remained safely out of the Mustang's kill envelope.

These exercises helped Special Force and Colonel Cochran's men work out solutions to each difficulty. For instance, a problem Captain Taylor anticipated was the transportation of mules and bullocks. After many suggestions, including drugging the beasts, it was finally decided the night of 10 January 1944 to see if the animals could be transported without them kicking holes in the side of gliders. Mules were tested first. Hadrian floors were reinforced, the mule's legs were hobbled, their heads were tied down to keep the ears out of the control cables, and they were restricted in a sling-like contraption. Flight Officer Allen Hall, Jr., was selected to fly the Waco. Last minute instructions were given muleteers to shoot the animals if they became unmanageable. The worries were all in vain. Other than sanitation problems, the mules did well, reportedly even banking during turns. The heavier bullocks performed equally in flight.

Preparing the Helicopter for flight
Three maintainers work on the pre-production YR-4 helicopter. In the jungle heat, Mr. Arnold C. Podolsky, Sikorsky Aviation Technical Representative, had his hands full maintaining the underpowered "egg beater." *Courtesy of 1ˢᵗ Air Commando Association*

Following a night session, General Wingate decided to join in the activities and participate in a snatch. Admiral Lord Mountbatten, who had also attended the night exercise, was impressed with what he saw and discussed expanding the mission with General Wingate and Colonel Cochran. They agreed that an assault group of Chindits and an engineering unit could be towed in gliders to jungle clearings in Burma. Defended against attack by the Chindits, engineers could then cut out a landing strip for C-47 Dakotas. Once the strip was built, the remainder of General Wingate's brigades could be airlanded deep behind enemy lines. Captain Taylor agreed with the proposal and continued daily glider training.

The new idea required more than Colonel Cochran's 13 transports and crews, so SEAC Headquarters withdrew two troop carrier squadrons of Dakotas for glider tow and night formation training. Due to other demands in the theater, Admiral Lord Mountbatten sent a message to the U.S. Joint Chiefs of Staff requesting 38 additional C-47 Dakotas. The scheduled demand for airlift in the theater indicated a shortfall of 500 sorties; without more planes, British ground troop requirements could not be met. Air Transport Command responded by providing 25 C-46 Commando aircraft, the equivalent of 38 Dakotas.

Meanwhile, as the glider training progressed, Captain Taylor decided against the normal 360 degree overhead landing pattern in favor of a more rapid straight-in approach. A release point for the gliders was established 200 yards forward of the landing field. To accommodate two gliders, the field was marked with four lights configured in a diamond, 150 yards on a side. The top and bottom of the lighted diamond divided the landing zone in half. In effect, two parallel landing strips were marked—one on either side of the dividing line between the flanker lights.

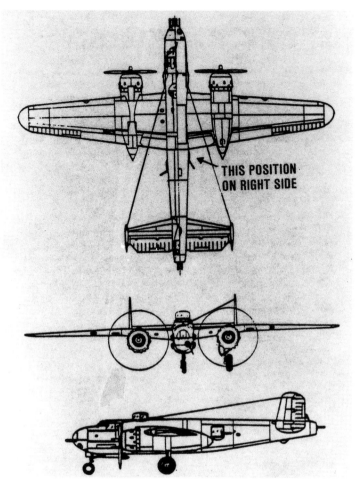

North American B-25H Mitchell
With four .50-caliber machine guns and a 75 mm cannon in the nose, the B-25H Mitchell functioned as the first gunship. *Courtesy of the Graphics Art Department, Maxwell AFB AL*

Then, on 15 February, a mishap occurred during a night double tow while working with Lieutenant Colonel D. C. "Fish" Herring's Dah Force that threatened operational unity. During takeoff, Lieutenant Kenneth L. Wells' glider on long tow moved forward and struck First Lieutenant Donald E. Seese's Waco on the short tow. Seese was able to recover, but Lieutenant Wells' glider plummeted, killing all. Also lost in the crash were Flight Officer Bishop Parrott, Private First Class Robert D. Kinney, and four British troops. The potential pall of the accident was lifted the following day when Wingate's unit commander sent the following note: "Please be assured that we will go with your boys any place, any time, anywhere." (50:155) This phrase captured the degree of teamwork achieved by the British and American groups and was adopted as the motto of the 1st Air Commandos.

By contrast, RAF support to the Chindits was not as well coordinated. That fact, along with the requirement for an engineering unit, was cause for the 5318ᵗʰ Provisional to grow one last time. The first enlargement occurred when problems developed concerning RAF bomber support to General Wingate's columns. The RAF

Assault Force, Bomber Section Commander
Colonel Philip G. Cochran selected Lieutenant Colonel Robert T. Smith to head up the Bomber Section. *Courtesy of Stan Zajac and R. T. Smith Family, 1ˢᵗ Air Commando Association*

had recently equipped their bombers with radios that were incompatible with those of the Chindits. In late January 1944, Colonel Alison wrote in a letter to General Arnold:

> At a conference with the RAF in the Imphal area it became clear that there were differences of opinion concerning the close support of Wingate columns and the mechanical feasibility of direction of assault from the ground. The RAF in this area is committed to the defense of an area, the support of an army and the support of Wingate and from the conversation

it appeared that assault support for Wingate would be limited. (80:Letter, Subject: History, Status and Immediate Requirements for 1ˢᵗ Air Commando Force, 21 January 1944)

General Wingate, faced with a repeat of the same slow response from the RAF during the first Chindit operation, appealed to Colonel Cochran. As a result, the commando commander used the circumstance to request 12 B-25H Mitchell medium bombers be diverted from the theater to the 5318ᵗʰ Provision Unit (Air). General Stratemeyer forwarded Colonel Cochran's request to General Arnold and by 21 January, Colonel Alison had a commitment from Washington.

Colonel Cochran got the planes in early February, but he was unable to secure "seasoned" crews. Given some "green" B-25 crews from the theater, Colonel Cochran assigned the pilots to other aircraft within the 5318ᵗʰ, primarily the UC-64 of the Light-cargo Section. He elected to man the Mitchells with fighter pilots. His reasoning was sound. The B-25H model was ideal for close air support as it was equipped with four .50-caliber machine guns and a 75 mm cannon in the nose. The cannon and the repositioning of the dorsal turret reduced the crew complement to only five people—pilot, navigator-bombardier, top-turret gunner (aerial engineer), radio waist gunner, and tail gunner. As configured, Mitchells could be flown much like fighters. This convinced Colonel Cochran that Major R. T. Smith should be the B-25H section commander and Major Walter V. Radovich should act as Smith's deputy.

A final section added to the 5318ᵗʰ was the 900ᵗʰ Air Borne Engineers Company. The purpose of this group was to build airfields behind Japanese lines. Complete with road graders, air transportable tractors, and bulldozers, the company mounted an imme-

Mongoose
Also drawn from the Fighter Section, Major Walter V. Radovich was named Bomber Section Deputy Commander. *Courtesy of Walt Radovich, 1ˢᵗ Air Commando Association*

Assault Force, Bomber Section, Hailakandi, India
Front Row (L-R) **Major Walter V. Radovich; Lieutenant Colonel Arvid E. Olson; Colonel John R. Alison; Colonel Philip G. Cochran; Lieutenant Colonel Robert T. Smith** *Middle Row* (L-R) **First Lieutenant Frank B. Merchant; Captain Daniel A. Sinskie; unidentified; First Lieutenant Frank W. Gursansky; First Lieutenant Robert A. Wink; First Lieutenant Wesley D. Weber; First Lieutenant Wesley D. Nielson** *Back Row* (L-R) **First Lieutenant Randolph K. Owen; First Lieutenant Brian H. Hodges; First Lieutenant Archie L. McKay; unidentified; First Lieutenant Murrell J. Dillard; Captain Carl E. Ziegler, Jr.; First Lieutenant William B. Burns; First Lieutenant Ralph K. Lanning; First Lieutenant Stephen A. Wanderer. The aircraft is Smith's** *Barbie III.* **The 75 mm cannon is visible over McKay's left shoulder** *Courtesy of James Lansdale, 1st Air Commando Association*

diate training effort by constructing a completely new landing strip east of Lalaghat. Commanding the 900th Engineers was First Lieutenant Patrick H. Casey.

Even before these final pieces completed the unit's organizational structure, 5318th personnel got a dose of combat. The light planes, gliders, fighters, and bombers were busy gaining experience before the main assault. During February, the light planes were divided into four sections and dispersed to forward locations in India. The "A" Flight was sent to Ledo to support General Wingate's 16th Brigade; "B", to Taro for General Stilwell's advance; "C", to Tamu in anticipation of the invasion of Burma; and 10 planes from "D" Flight were temporarily dispatched to support the Arakan front.

Like the light planes, the gliders also flew combat missions during the second month of 1944. On 28 February, a British patrol was loaded aboard a Waco glider piloted by Flight Officers John H. Price, Jr., and John E. Gotham. Encountering bad weather en route, Major Cherry and Lieutenant Ulery towed the glider east of the Chindwin River. Near Minsin, the Hadrian released from the Dakota. During the landing, the rutted sand bar damaged the glider; Flight Officer Price was badly injured. Major Cherry intended to snatch the Waco after disgorging the equipment, but the glider was unflyable. He was forced to return to Lalaghat alone. That night, the flight officers rested and Gotham pondered the options. The following day, he burned the Waco and decided to make his way back to India on foot. Flight Officer Gotham set out along with the impaired Price and three wounded British soldiers on 29 February. During the trek back, the small band killed two Japanese soldiers, floated 7 miles down the Chindwin River in a native boat, and walked 130 miles through Burmese jungles before safely reaching the Indian frontier 15 days later.

On 29 February, gliders again were called on to assist the Chindit's 16th Brigade. Led by Brigadier Bernard E. Fergusson, the columns had departed Ledo on 1 February and needed assistance in crossing the Chindwin River. Two Hadrians, piloted by Flight Officer James S. "Mickey" Bartlett and Flight Officer Vernon "Needlenose" Noland, landed on a sand bar in the Chindwin near Singkaling Khamti. The gliders carried two Mark 2 and four Mark 3 folding boats, two 9.2 HP and four 5.8 HP outboard engines, 20 bamboo poles, 36 paddles, and 80 gallons of gasoline. Although Flight Officer Noland's Waco was damaged on landing, all the materiel was successfully delivered. After offloading the equipment, the C-47 tug crew snatched the operational glider and returned to Lalaghat. The event marked the first time a glider had been snatched behind enemy lines. Captain Edwin J. Coe and First Lieutenant William W. Johnson, Jr., flew the C-47 Dakota; Flight Officer Bartlett was the pilot of the Waco.

Starting in February, 5318th crews also flew P-51 and B-25 missions into Burma for the first time. On 3 February, Colonel Cochran led five Mustangs on the unit's first combat mission. The B-25 section joined the fight on 12 February. During the mission, Major Smith demonstrated the effectiveness of the 75 mm cannon to General Wingate by blowing the roof off a large building. He later sheepishly admitted he was aiming at a railway switch roughly 200 yards in front of the warehouse.

From 3 February until 4 March, the 5318th Provision Unit (Air) flew 54 fighter and bomber missions. They concentrated their flights on attacking Japanese lines of communication and increasing their air-to-ground proficiency. From the beginning, fighter pilots and bomber crews laid their crosshairs on road and railroad bridges, warehouses, truck convoys, railroad locomotives, and river barges.

Glider Snatch
A C-47 Dakota pilot snags the nylon cable attached to a Waco CG-4A Hadrian glider. In 3 seconds, the glider was at full speed. The glider snatch procedures were a derivation of a system originally designed for rural mail service in the United States. *Courtesy of 1ˢᵗ Air Commando Association*

Supporting Brigadier Fergusson's Overland Thrust
Prior to Operation THURSDAY, the 1ˢᵗ Air Commando Group delivered boating supplies to the Chindit's 16ᵗʰ Brigade via gliders. *Courtesy of 1ˢᵗ Air Commando Association*

As the Assault Section attacked these targets, their accuracy, proficiency, and selection of ordnance improved. Lieutenant Colonel Smith later described the accuracy attained by his men:

> Our cannon and [machine guns] were boresighted for 1,000 yards and a typical pass would consist of three cannon rounds at [approximately] 1,500, 1,000, and 500 yards, interspersed with bursts of [machine gun] fire. This required making allowance for the different ranges by sighting slightly above, then on, and slightly below the target with the optical gun sight. Passes would be initiated at anywhere from 500 to 1,000 feet above ground, and terminated practically on the deck. Most attacks were made at between 200 and 250 mph airspeeds. Now, assuming the air was reasonably calm or only moderately turbulent, most of us could hit a target the size of a one-car garage 50% of the time or better with the 75 mm cannon. I know that I, and others in my squadron, scored many direct hits on targets as small as trucks and barracks-type buildings, and accuracy went up accordingly. (131:January/February 1982:4)

Equally important as the missions themselves was the intelligence gathered during each sortie. Many ranking Chindits flew on B-25 missions to locate and evaluate jungle clearings for possible use during the invasion. Helping them was a small detachment of men, the 10ᵗʰ Combat Camera Unit, using hand-held cameras. Lacking facilities in which to process film, the commander, First Lieutenant Charles L. Russhon (Charley Vanilla in Milton Caniff's *Terry and the Pirates* comic strip), was forced to improvise. He accomplished his task by developing pictures at night in the open. To keep the area dark, a sentry stood guard on the road leading to the camp. A nearby well furnished the necessary water.

Besides the pictures, pilots reported enemy defenses, troop movements, and noted supply lines. This information, when com-

First C-47 Dakota Crew to Accomplish a Combat Glider Snatch
(L-R) Technical Sergeant Wayne Hoffman; Private First Class Salvatore Canale; First Lieutenant William W. Johnson, Jr., copilot; Captain Edwin J. Coe, pilot. The non-standard stripes on the tail were redesigned after Operation THURSDAY to look more like those of the Assault Section. *Courtesy of 1st Air Commando Association*

bined with the aerial photographs, would be used by General Wingate's staff to plan for his proposed offensive, named Operation THURSDAY. During discussions with Chindit commanders, Colonel Cochran realized once operations began the Assault Force raids and photographic intelligence would be ineffective without

the ability to talk to the columns. While operating behind the lines, General Wingate planned to use encoded signals. To maintain contact with the Chindits, Major Bonham sent Staff Sergeant Leslie F. Ghastin and four others to the British Cipher School in Gwalior. The men were the first Americans to be taught Britain's secret code. The classes were very strict; every scrap of paper was burned at the close of daily instructions. In addition to code, the Americans became familiar with a new language, one that included vehicle windscreens, jeep bonnets, and cannons called 20-pounders. After completion of training, each graduate received a personal emergency code and returned to Hailakandi and Lalaghat in time to support the upcoming invasion.

As Operation THURSDAY neared, Colonel Cochran's unit was set for action. The organization had mushroomed from a light plane operation into a sizable assault force. While it grew, the concept of mission support changed also. The use of gliders was a prime example. Originally included for re-supply, Colonel Cochran proposed they be used to air transport one of General Wingate's brigades. Later, the idea of building a fortified airstrip was advanced, and the mission of the gliders changed accordingly. By 5 March the training was over, and the 5318th Provision Unit (Air) was poised to fulfill its part of the Quadrant Conference plan. The next step, the Allied invasion of Burma, would test General Arnold's dream. But even up to the scheduled launch, events suggested the execution of Operation THURSDAY was in jeopardy.

Air Commandos
Because he knew so much about Operation THURSDAY, Colonel Cochran rarely went into Burma after the 3 February raid. Although his airplane is seen behind Major Robert L. Petit's *Mrs. Virginia*, **the pilot is probably Second Lieutenant Aurele R. Van de Weghe.** *Courtesy of James E. Eckert, 1st Air Commando Association*

5

Operation THURSDAY

Throughout the time the 5318th Provisional Unit was training, Southeast Asia Command was developing alternative actions that were not in accord with the Quadrant plan. Admiral Lord Mountbatten proposed several operations to the Allied strategic planning staff: BULLFROG, an attack on Akyab Island; CULVERIN, an assault on Sumatra; PIGSTICK, a landing on the Mayu Peninsula; BUCCANEER, an amphibious offensive on the Andaman Islands in the Bay of Bengal; TARZAN, the airborne capture of the Indaw airfield; and finally, AXIOM, a scaled down version of the "dusty" ANAKIM plan. All were either disapproved or abandoned. Brigadier Derek D. C. Tulloch, General Wingate's Chief of Staff, became convinced Admiral Lord Mountbatten did not want the mission to be conducted.

Colonel Cochran felt otherwise, but did note some clumsy attempts to misdirect his unit. During the early part of January 1944,

General Stilwell had attempted to conscript the 5318th Provisional Unit into his camp. After a clarifying letter from General Arnold, that idea was scotched, but other CBI units attempted to draw off the unit's resources. Colonel Cochran later stated Admiral Lord Mountbatten was not at fault; instead, it was the Admiral's staff that was constantly trying to absorb the airplanes, men, and materiel of the 5318th Provisional Unit into existing SEAC organizations. Finally, Colonel Cochran produced a letter from General Arnold to Admiral Lord Mountbatten with the salutation "Dear Dickie." Although it no longer exists, a summary of that 16 January 1944 letter quotes General Arnold. He unequivocally stated to Mountbatten that Colonel Cochran's unit was to "solely support the long range penetration operations for which they are now being trained." Later stipulations by General Arnold indicate the following principles were established for their use:

Windshield Tour

In a jeep driven by his brother, Colonel Philip G. Cochran delivered General Arnold's "Dear Dickie" letter. Dickie was Mountbatten's family nickname. The letter limited the use of Cochran's organization to the support of General Wingate's Special Force. *Courtesy of 1st Air Commando Association*

Corporal Joseph L. Cochran

Colonel Cochran's younger brother was a member of the 5318th Provisional Unit (Air). It was not unusual for Joe to borrow clothes, vehicles, and even airplanes from his brother. *Courtesy of Andy Cox, 1st Air Commando Association*

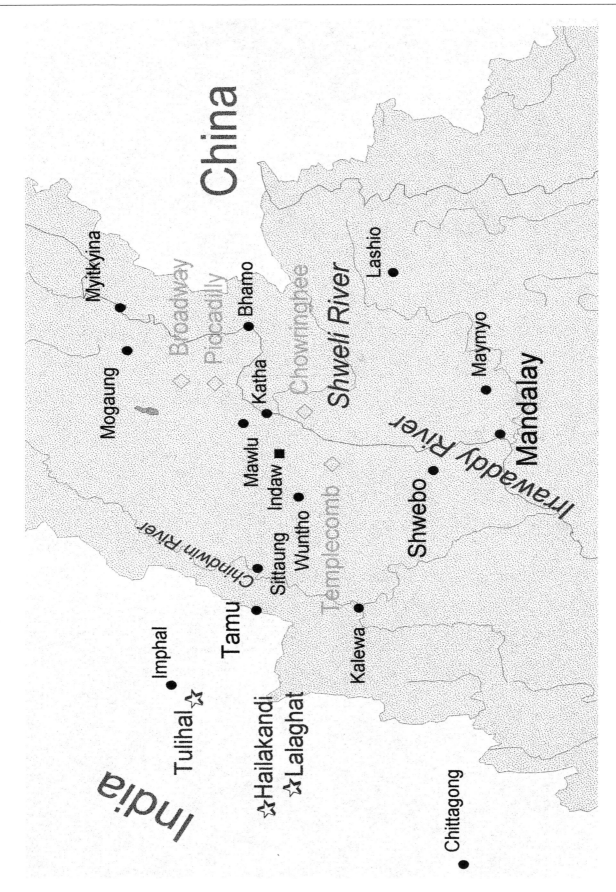

China

India

Myitkyina

Mogaung

Broadway

Piccadilly

Bhamo

Katha

Chowinghee

Shweli River

Lashio

Maymyo

Mandalay

Irrawaddy River

Mawlu

Indaw

Sittaung

Wuntho

Templecomb

Shwebo

Chindwin River

Tamu

Imphal

Tulihal ☆

☆Hailakandi

☆Lalaghat

Kalewa

Chittagong

Map 6- Northern Burma1944: Operation THURSDAY

Transport Section, C-47 Pilots
Front Row (L-R): First Lieutenant James E. Richmond; First Lieutenant Richard T. Gilmore; First Lieutenant Fred P. "Plaster of" Paris; First Lieutenant John K. "Buddy" Lewis, Jr.; First Lieutenant Vincent L. Ulery; Captain John C. Sanichas *Center Row* (L-R): First Lieutenant Stanley Pelcak; Captain Nelson E. Eddy, Jr.; First Lieutenant Ralph C. Bordley; Captain John E. "Jack" Lewis; First Lieutenant Jesse B. Hepler; First Lieutenant William W. Johnson, Jr.; Captain Neil I. "Nipper" Holm; Captain Edgar L. Barham *Back Row* (L-R): Captain Richard E. Cole; Captain John M. DeHoney; Captain Thomas R. Baker; Major Jacob P. Sartz; Major William T. Cherry (with cigar); First Lieutenant Albert T. Ward; Captain Edwin J. Coe; First Lieutenant Patrick J. Driscoll; First Lieutenant Leo S. Tyszecki *Courtesy of 1ˢᵗ Air Commando Association*

Glider preparations for Operation THURSDAY
Ground crews make ready the glider tow ropes. Each line was 350 feet long, 15/16 inches in diameter and had enough nylon to make 1,620 pairs of stockings. *Courtesy of 1ˢᵗ Air Commando Association*

Warrant Officer James W. Tate in front of a Waco CG-4A Hadrian Glider prior to Operation THURSDAY. *Courtesy of 1ˢᵗ Air Commando Association*

Last Minute Instructions prior to Operation THURSDAY
Under the wing of a Waco CG-4A Hadrian glider, Major General Orde C. Wingate (in pith helmet and beard) addresses the Chindits. *Courtesy of 1ˢᵗ Air Commando Association*

Briefing Operation THURSDAY
Colonel Philip G. Cochran briefs transport and glider personnel prior to Operation THURSDAY. To his left is Captain William H. Taylor, Jr., who would fly the first glider into Broadway. The maps behind Cochran depict the clearings of Broadway on the left and Piccadilly on the right. They were made from bedsheets stained with ink. *Courtesy of 1ˢᵗ Air Commando Association*

(1) The unit be employed only for special operations, such as airborne operations, or for supply and support of LRP Groups for limited periods only.

(2) For planning purposes the unit shall only be included as a unit and in their specific role.

(3) Command and control of the Air Commando Group should be under the Commanding General, USAAF, India-Burma Sector, in conformity with the Supreme Allied Commander's operational directions to the Allied Air Commander-in-Chief.

Operation THURSDAY Glider Briefing
On the extreme right, Captain William H. Taylor, Jr., discusses Operation THURSDAY with Glider Section personnel. *Courtesy of Harry McKaig, 1ˢᵗ Air Commando Association*

For whatever reason, under whomever's direction, the net result of SEAC's indecision was evident. Admiral Lord Mountbatten had lost the support of Generalissimo Chiang Kai-shek's Chinese Army, General Slim's 14ᵗʰ Corps was not committed to the invasion, and Major General Wingate was irate. Apart from General Wingate's own 16ᵗʰ Brigade, only General Stilwell was advancing into Burma. Even General Wingate's hand was involved in this assault. Assisting General Stilwell were two American LRP units trained by General Wingate; established as the 5307ᵗʰ Provision Unit, they were more commonly known as Merrill's Marauders. Originally intended to augment the Chindits, General Wingate had released the Marauders to General Stilwell in January.

By 4 February, General Stilwell was marching down the Hukawng Valley when General Wingate received instructions that indicated his mission had been changed. His orders now were to accomplish the objectives below. As in the first Chindit operation, General Wingate's command again was being sent into Burma without a major offensive or a strategic objective.

(1) To help the advance of General Stilwell's combat troops by drawing off and disorganizing the enemy forces opposing them and by preventing the reinforcement of the enemy forces.

(2) To create a favorable situation for Chinese forces to advance Westward.

(3) To inflict the maximum confusion, damage, and loss on the enemy forces in North Burma.

First considering resignation, General Wingate soon learned through intelligence information the Japanese were massing troops

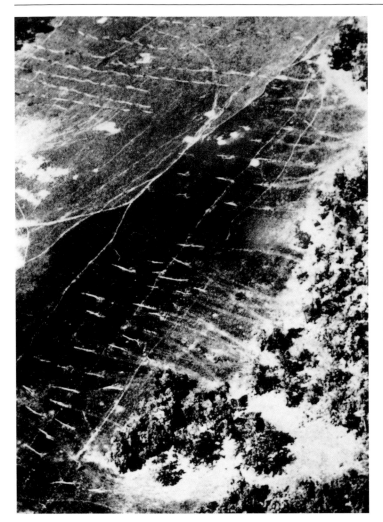

Piccadilly
First Lieutenant Charles L. Russhon's photograph of Piccadilly just prior to Operation THURSDAY. *Courtesy of 1ˢᵗ Air Commando Association*

Waco CG-4A Hadrian Glider Interior
Raised visor shows provisions and stores loaded on Waco CG-4A Hadrian. After Operation THURSDAY was revised, Chindits grossly overloaded gliders. *Courtesy of 1ˢᵗ Air Commando Association*

for an invasion of India. He then realized the Japanese would provide the frontal action needed, so he recanted and continued planning Operation THURSDAY. In doing so, General Wingate committed Colonel Cochran's organization to Operation THURSDAY and to Special Force until the monsoons began.

The plan for the Allied invasion of Burma was straightforward. Under cover of darkness, two small columns of General Wingate's Special Force, airborne engineers, and air transportable equipment would be moved by gliders into selected jungle clearings near Katha. Engineers would then prepare landing strips during the day, and transport planes would bring in the remainder of the Chindits on succeeding nights. To cause confusion the night of the operation, equipment that simulated ground fires would be airdropped at a variety of places behind Japanese lines. Despite the seeming simplicity, during the planning, preparation, and execution of the plan, adjustments to Operation THURSDAY were constantly required.

Before SEAC published the operating procedures of the mission, the fluid situation around the Indo-Burman border brought

about the first changes. Prior to D-Day, the commandos were scheduled to tow 52 gliders to the area of Tamu to test the plan. The majority of the operation would then be launched from this forward location. Unfortunately, in view of possible Japanese activity in the area, the idea of using Tamu was discarded. Denied the use of this base meant the mission would have to be conducted from Lalaghat, Hailakandi, and Tulihal (Imphal). Additionally, it required Dakotas to climb to 8,000 feet over the Imphal Plateau and cross the Chin Hills before heading into Burma. When the revised plan was finalized, the impact of the additional altitude requirement was not fully recognized.

General Wingate released the execution orders for Operation THURSDAY on 29 February. The plan stated on Sunday, 5 March, C-47 Dakotas would tow 40 gliders each to Broadway (24-45N 96-45E) and Piccadilly (24-29N 96-46E), two jungle clearings named after the major streets of New York City and London. Takeoff time was set for 1700 so the Pathfinder gliders would reach the objec-

Operation THURSDAY
After everything was redirected to Broadway, Operation THURSDAY was delayed only 72 minutes. A C-47 Dakota lifts off with two gliders in tow. In the distance, another double tow can be seen. *Courtesy of 1ˢᵗ Air Commando Association*

tive areas just after dark. The main force would take off 40 minutes later with the interval between aircraft being one minute apart.

Formally, Colonel Cochran received the unit's mission taskings from Air Marshall Sir John Baldwin, commander of Third Tactical Air Force. Operational Instruction No. 5/44 charged the 5318th Provisional Unit with assisting in the operations of the 3rd Indian Division. In particular the organization was to provide a small covering and striking force, facilitate forward movement by the LRP columns, and conduct re-supply and evacuation for the columns.

The units involved in Operation THURSDAY were from both British and American organizations. British Brigadier Michael Calvert, a veteran of Wingate's first campaign, would lead the 77th Brigade into action on D-Day; Brigadier W. D. A. Lentaigne's 111th Brigade would be injected into combat three days later. General Wingate would hold the 3rd West African Brigade, 14th Brigade, and 23rd Brigade in reserve and release them as the situation dictated. Seven air force units were to provide aircraft and crews; these

included the 5318th Provisional Unit (USAAF), 315th Troop Carrier Squadron (USAAF), 27th Troop Carrier Squadron (USAAF), 31st Squadron (RAF), 62nd Squadron (RAF), 117th Squadron (RAF), and 194th Squadron (RAF).

The 5318th Provisional Unit would spearhead the airborne requirements. Based on the double tow experience of his C-47 crews, Colonel Cochran recommended all 26 of his transport pilots be designated aircraft commanders for the mission. With some reluctance, General Old agreed to supply the remaining requirement for 13 aircraft and 26 co-pilots. In addition to the Dakotas and Hadrians, 4 days before the mission, UC-64 Norsemen were added to airdrop 1,000 pounds of concertina wire and other material needed to establish perimeter defenses around the Chindit strongholds at Piccadilly and Broadway.

The mission was projected to continue for 7 days. The second and third days, 6 and 7 March, were dedicated to airlanding the Chindits at Broadway and Piccadilly clearings. On 8 March, the

111th Brigade would be towed to Chowringhee (23-57N 96-24E), a clearing south of the Shweli River named for Calcutta's major thoroughfare. Duplicating the procedures at Broadway and Piccadilly, the entire operation was to be completed by 11 March.

A fourth clearing, Templecombe (approximately 23-48N 96-10E), was also to be used, but the procedures varied from the others. Intended for a very small unit, Dah Force, the strip was to be cleared by native Burmese labor under the supervision of a special operations agent. Once inserted, Dah Force was responsible for raising Kachin levies in the hills of Northern Burma and annoying the Japanese in the area between Bhamo and Myitkyina. The date and time of the glider lift of Dah Force was flexible; the mission would be cued by a signal that Templecombe was secured. As events were to prove, the execution of the entire Operation THURSDAY plan was a demonstration in flexibility.

On the day of the mission, Air Marshall Sir John Baldwin, senior air commander in SEAC, sent the signal that weather conditions were right and Operation THURSDAY was on. Lalaghat was

Broadway

First Lieutenant Russhon's photographs indicated Broadway was clear. Japanese opposition was anticipated from the lower right quadrant so Colonel John R. Alison landed his glider near the spit of trees. *Courtesy of Frank Davis, 1st Air Commando Association*

teeming with activity as loud speakers barked out instructions. Tow ropes—each about 350 feet long, 15/16 inches in diameter, with enough nylon for 1,620 pairs of hose—were stretched out across the ground. Colonel Cochran and General Wingate would stay behind that night, but many others would participate. Colonel Alison, with a bare minimum of glider flights, would pilot a CG-4A to Piccadilly; Lieutenant Colonel Olson was headed toward Broadway with the communications gear; and Captain Taylor would fly the Pathfinder Waco. Most of the SEAC staff was present. Admiral Lord Mountbatten was absent, recovering from an eye injury, but General Slim, Air Marshall Baldwin, General Stratemeyer, and Brigadier General William D. Old, Commander of Troop Carrier Command, were on hand.

This entire command structure would be called on when the sudden necessity for change occurred during the execution phase. While General Wingate busily directed activities out of a tent at the west end of the runway, Colonel Cochran, on a hunch, ordered Lieutenant Russhon to take last-minute photographs of the clearings from a B-25. Later, nearing scheduled departure time, the solemnity of the operation was brought home when escape kits were issued—90 silver rupees and a small block of opium. Colonel Cochran added to the moment by concluding his mission briefing saying, "Nothing you've ever done, nothing you're ever going to do, counts now. Only the next few hours. Tonight you are going to find your souls." (71:9) Fifteen minutes before scheduled takeoff time, a light plane flew into Lalaghat with Lieutenant Russhon aboard. With wet print blowups of Piccadilly, Broadway, and Chowringhee, he rushed to show them to Colonel Cochran and Colonel Alison. Broadway and Chowringhee were clear, untouched since the last look, but Piccadilly was scattered with logs in a somewhat regular pattern. Two days before, it had been clear. The pattern effectively

Jungle Trek after Operation THURSDAY Invasion

When his glider broke a tow line over Burma, Major Richard W. Boebel, unit intelligence officer, led a band through Japanese lines and across the jungle. *Courtesy of Harry McKaig, 1st Air Commando Association*

Glider wreckage at Broadway
Teakwood logs (lower left) were not visible in aerial photographs. Colonel Alison attempted to control the bedlam as waves of gliders plummeted to the jungle clearing. *Courtesy of 1st Air Commando Association*

made Piccadilly a potential death trap for gliders. The commanders gathered round the photos to discuss the implications and options.

Two plausible arguments were offered to explain the conditions at Piccadilly. First, the Japanese may have penetrated the plan. If this were true, then Broadway and Chowringhee may have been left open as a trap. The second reason given involved the previous Chindit operation. Piccadilly was the same clearing that British Major Scott had used in 1943 to air evacuate his men. Since photographs of the area had been published in the 28 June 1943 edition of *Life* magazine, the Japanese did not necessarily have to know about the mission. If they had felled the trees, Japanese soldiers

may have done so for precautionary measures. The latter was accepted as most probable. Hindsight later attributed the condition to Burmese teakwood farmers. Regardless of the cause, Piccadilly was ruled out.

The most logical solution was to transfer the Piccadilly troops to Chowringhee; however, it was not the best under the circumstances. Brigadier Calvert opposed this recommendation because the Shweli River ran between the two landing zones, thus cutting his brigade in half. The commanders ruled out cancellation because of the negative effect on morale. Airlifting the entire brigade to one location was the only other option. General Slim reduced the requirements to 60 gliders and committed the entire mission to Broadway. Colonel Cochran took the responsibility for breaking the news to the C-47 and CG-4A crews previously ticketed for Piccadilly. With typical aplomb, General Slim wrote, "He sprang on the bonnet of a jeep. 'Say fellers,' he announced, 'we've got a better place to go to!'" (44:228-229) For such a major decision to be made, the British and American commanders delayed the mission only 72 minutes.

Given the green light, the Dakotas took to the runway. Due to overloading of the gliders, a problem occurred. When the C-47 put tension on the nylon tow ropes, the Hadrians pitched forward—nose down, tail up. To make takeoff possible, ground crews provided ballast by running as far down the grass strip as possible leaning on the tail assembly. When the first C-47 with two gliders in tow lifted off at 1812, the mission was out of the hands of General Wingate and Colonel Cochran. It belonged to the Dakota crews, the Waco pilots, and the forgotten UC-64 section.

For the C-47 aircraft commanders and glider pilots, the climbout phase was an indication of future problems. Each C-47 pilot was to fly a left-hand box pattern to achieve altitude. The procedure was to immediately turn after takeoff and climb for 10 minutes, turn left for a base leg of 10 minutes, then left for another 10 minutes, and finally left again to fly back over the field. If the Dakota was at or above 4,000 feet while passing over the runway, the

Light Cargo Section, UC-64 and YR-4 Pilots
Front Row **(L-R): First Lieutenant Frank M. Bowman; First Lieutenant Frank N. Davis; First Lieutenant Julius Goodman; First Lieutenant David C. "Buck" Beasley; First Lieutenant Frank M. "Pete" Turney** *Back Row* **(L-R): First Lieutenant Elbert E. Davis; First Lieutenant Fred H. Van Wagner; Lieutenant Colonel Clinton B. Gaty; Captain Edward "Sam" Wagner; Captain Leon R. "Mac" McMullen; First Lieutenant Carter Harman** *Courtesy of 1st Air Commando Association*

Light Cargo Section, UC-64 Flight Engineers
Front Row **(L-R): Staff Sergeant Lawrence N. Poepping; Corporal Silas H. Rhodes; Staff Sergeant Felix C. Lockman, Jr.; Sergeant Francis H. Marshall** *Back Row* **(L-R): Corporal William B. Ringwood; Staff Sergeant Clarence F. Ripple; Corporal Kenneth J. Powell; Sergeant John A. Stroebeck; Corporal Allen H. Canter; Staff Sergeant George C. Gregson; not shown is Technical Sergeant John C. Pink** *Courtesy of 1ˢᵗ Air Commando Association*

pilot continued to Broadway. Some pilots experienced a lower climb rate than anticipated and had to circle over Lalaghat. As this happened, Lieutenant Ulery related, he barely avoided a midair collision.

Unfortunately, additional glider-related problems occurred during the climb to cruise altitude. Four Hadrians crashed shortly after takeoff; two were cut loose over Lalaghat when their Dakota developed electrical problems; and two more were released over Imphal when their tug experienced such high fuel consumption that Broadway was unattainable. All eight of these gliders landed west of the Chindwin.

For other Waco pilots, there were problems after crossing the Chin Hills—tow ropes began to fail. Colonel Cochran later described the difficulties to General Arnold:

The moon was almost full but was partially offset by bad haze conditions. Gliders were overloaded, average gross load for each glider being approximately 9,000 lbs. [Technical Data limited gross weight with cargo to 7,500 pounds]... Most of the difficulties were encountered after altitudes of above 8,000 ft. had been reached and mountain ranges and turbulent air had been crossed. As the tow planes started their descent poor visibility over the Chindwin area and the tendency of gliders to overrun the tow plane (accentuated by heavy loads) created a surging of the gliders which was extremely difficult for the pilots. In the worst cases the tow ropes broke. The part in the ropes invariably was caused when both gliders surged at the same time and the shock of the tow rope was taken up simultaneously by the one lead rope. (96:8)

Morning Scene of Broadway
Glider wreckage at Broadway. *Courtesy of 1ˢᵗ Air Commando Association*

Glider Carcass
Visor of wrecked glider among the trees at Broadway. *Courtesy of 1ˢᵗ Air Commando Association*

River, Corporal Estil I. Nienaber, a non-swimmer, was swept away from Major Boebel's escape party by the strong currents. Rather than call for help and possibly give away the group's position to Japanese patrols, he silently drowned—grimly determined not to utter a sound. Seven of the nine crews eventually made the harrowing journey back to India or on to Broadway.

In another instance, the glider transporting Captain Murphy and 19 others was forced to land nearly 100 miles short. Setting out from near Katha, the men moved east, crossed the Irrawaddy River, and finally limped into Broadway 10 days later. The group told of extreme deprivation; they had exhausted their food supply long before reaching the landing zone. In desperation, one resourceful member tossed a hand grenade into a pond. That day the men voraciously gorged themselves on the fish that floated to the surface.

By coincidence, the gliders seemed to go down near Japanese headquarters. Two Hadrians landed in the immediate vicinity of the 31st Divisional Headquarters, two more came down near 15th Division Headquarters, and three Wacos landed close to a Regimental Headquarters area. The Japanese interpreted these landings as raiding parties in support of General Slim's IV Corps. In the confusion, the tow rope problem had created a diversion. SEAC reported, "It is probable that this diversion assisted for over a week in keeping Japanese attention focussed [sic] away from the area of the main landings..." (110:87)

Problems encountered by the gliders at Broadway were just as grim. By 2200, Captain Taylor, in the lead Hadrian, touched down on Broadway and the Chindits fanned out to intercept any Japanese. There were none. Captain Taylor ordered the green flare lit and positioned the smudge pots. As succeeding gliders established

Informal Conference
While walking through camp, Colonel Philip G. Cochran, Major General Orde C. Wingate, and Major Walter V. Radovich discuss Operation THURSDAY in an impromptu meeting. *Courtesy of 1ˢᵗ Air Commando Association*

Nine gliders were lost east of the Chindwin River. Lieutenant Colonel Olson was aboard one of those Wacos, as were Captain Weldon O. Murphy, a medical officer; Major Boebel; and others. The treks back to safety for the downed crews were marked by the heroism of a glider mechanic. During a crossing of the Chindwin

Light Plane Ambulance
Fearing mass casualties, Major Andrew Rebori dispatched nine L-1 Vigilants to Broadway. The L-1 was preferred for aeromedical evacuations. *Courtesy of 1ˢᵗ Air Commando Association*

L-5 from Taro
L-5 Sentinels arrived at Broadway at first light. En route they flew at tree-top level to avoid detection. *Courtesy of 1ˢᵗ Air Commando Association*

themselves on the lights, pilots cut loose at 1,000 feet and began their descent toward Broadway. Extreme overweight conditions caused glider approach speeds to be much higher than planned.

The resulting landings were unpredictable and hazardous. The second Waco pilot had to crash land his CG-4A to avoid hitting Captain Taylor's glider, while Colonel Alison, third into the clearing, landed without incident. Colonel Alison immediately took over command of Broadway. A quick inspection of the ground showed the strip was not as suitable for the assault as photographs had shown. The clearing was traversed with deep ruts from dragged teakwood trees. Tree trunks and water buffalo holes were also masked from aerial photographs by tall elephant grass. With Hadrians though, there was no way to turn them back. When they touched down, the speeding gliders caromed off the tree stumps and furrows, ripping

off landing gear and smashing to a stop. Without landing gear, the men could not move the crippled gliders out of the path of the incoming waves. One Waco pilot, Lieutenant Seese, avoided a disaster by "jumping" his glider over an inert tangle of canvas, steel, and wood.

To mitigate the congestion, Colonel Alison and his men rearranged the smudge pots to disperse the landings. The glider assault continued as pairs of gliders plummeted toward the interior of the diamond. For Colonel Alison, the pace was exhausting; after each pair landed, the pots were repositioned. Most gliders touched down within the landing zone; two did not. They undershot the field and crashed in the jungle, killing all on board; included on one of those gliders was the commander of the engineers, Lieutenant Casey. Medical Officer, Captain Donald C. Tulloch began treating the

Follow-on Dakota
After receiving word Broadway was completed at 1630 on 6 March, Cochran and Wingate launched six Dakotas with equipment, supplies, and personnel. *Courtesy of 1ˢᵗ Air Commando Association*

Chindit Transportation
Among the most important item shipped to Broadway were mules. The Chindits needed mules, horses, and bullocks to carry heavy communication gear, rations, and ammunition through the jungles. As a precaution, the mule's vocal cords were surgically removed. *Courtesy of 1ˢᵗ Air Commando Association*

wounded during the ongoing assault while other personnel tried to extricate trapped men from the twisted wreckage. Complicating Colonel Alison's problems was an inability to communicate with Colonel Cochran and General Wingate in India; his one radio was damaged during landing.

Back at Lalaghat, the launch of Dakotas had been followed by a 10-ship formation of UC-64 aircraft led by Lieutenant Colonel Gaty. Not adequately equipped for night flying, the wing airplanes soon lost visual contact with lead. Unfortunately, members of the flight had been briefed to simply stay in formation and follow. Captain Wagner and his crew chief, Staff Sergeant Felix C. Lockman,

Jr., became separated from the others; they continued the mission but were unable to locate the objective area. Returning to India and running low on fuel, they were forced to make an emergency landing at an unknown strip. Luckily it was held by the British. The debrief from First Lieutenant Julius Goodman and his mechanic, Staff Sergeant George C. Gregson, was much the same. Another UC-64 did not reach Broadway because the crew had not been properly briefed about the change of landing sites. When they lost sight of the formation, Second Lieutenant Fred H. Van Wagner and his co-pilot Captain Leon R. McMullen flew on to Piccadilly. Seeing no lights, they turned back, not dropping their stores. They too ran short of fuel. Unable to locate Lalaghat because of similar navigation radio frequencies in the area, the two pilots had to bail out. One other UC-64 crew landed on a sandbar in Burma while another returned to base. In total, only two free-fall bundles were dropped near Broadway and three Norsemen were lost during the night invasion. This portion of Operation THURSDAY was considered a failure.

Meanwhile, the Dakotas had begun returning to Lalaghat just after 2300; one was unable to return and had to land at Imphal for fuel. After a limited debrief, the crews prepared to fly again. Based on the tow rope difficulties, General Old recommended crews no longer pull two gliders. Believing double tow still feasible, Colonel Cochran launched some Dakotas with two Wacos in trail, but after reconsidering, he agreed to cut back to single tow. Including those released in the Assam area, a total of 63 gliders was dispatched to Broadway.

Finally, at 0227 on the morning of 6 March, Colonel Cochran and General Wingate received a coded message from Broadway. Repairs to the damaged radio set had been slow and risky. Periodically dodging the incoming gliders or falling tow lines, Corporal Robert E. True, the communication specialist, worked feverishly to

Glider Section, Broadway, Burma
Front Row **(L-R) Flight Officer Samuel F. Steinmark; Second Lieutenant H. J. Delaney; unidentified; First Lieutenant Vincent J. Rose; unidentified; Captain William H. Taylor, Jr.; First Lieutenant Jackson J. Shinkle; First Lieutenant Patrick H. Hadsell; Flight Officer John L. "Jackie" Coogan** *Back Row* **(L-R) Flight Officer Francis L. Randall; First Lieutenant Soloman Schnitzer; Flight Officer James S. "Mickey" Bartlett; unidentified; unidentified; unidentified; Flight Officer Leo Zuk; First Lieutenant James E. Sever; First Lieutenant Steve T. Uminski** *Courtesy of 1ˢᵗ Air Commando Association*

make it operable. At last able to transmit for a limited time, Brigadier Calvert sent the single code word, "SOYA-LINK." Before the mission, Brigadier Tulloch had established only two code words, "PORK-SAUSAGE" and "SOYA-LINK," for the mission. The former would indicate all was well; the latter, named for a meat substitute hated by the British, meant trouble—no more gliders should be dispatched. Due to atmospheric conditions, the message was not received directly from Broadway. Passed through two intermediaries, Colonel Cochran and General Wingate could not know the circumstances at Broadway. Brigadier Tullock wrote, "Those at Lalaghat had a mental picture of parties of men in close contact with an undetermined number of enemy." (97:4-5) They assumed the worst had happened and the landing field was under attack. Wrestling with the situation, Colonel Cochran ultimately decided to recall the second wave. When the recall was broadcast, all aircraft except one responded. The Dakota that continued had a glider tow of engineering equipment.

An exhausted and discouraged Colonel Alison was almost asleep when he heard the last Waco release. To Colonel Alison's horror, the glider flew beyond the landing field and pranged between two trees. The noise of the crash was deafening; the silence that followed, foreboding. Colonel Alison was sure everyone on board was dead; however, he was wrong. Auspiciously, the pilot, Flight Officer Gene A. Kelly, had rigged the bulldozer to the hinged nose of the glider. As the equipment broke its mooring and shot forward, the visor raised the pilots out of the way as the bulldozer cleared. When the nose slammed shut, the only mishap was a broken thumb—the equipment was not even damaged. Significantly, on board the last Hadrian was Second Lieutenant Robert R. Brackett of the airborne engineers, a man who would play an influential role in the completion of Broadway.

Glider Pilots
(L-R) Flight Officer Harry L. McKaig, Flight Officer Edward G. Scott, Flight Officer Vernon "Needlenose" Noland, and Flight Officer Charles Hahn. Noland already had distinguished himself in combat before Operation THURSDAY. *Courtesy of 1st Air Commando Association*

When dawn brought slivers of light to the darkness of the jungle clearing at Broadway, the losses to equipment and personnel became a grim reality. In all, 37 Wacos had arrived; almost all, 34 gliders, were damaged and could not be towed out. The injuries to personnel were not as bad as originally thought; only 33 were injured severely enough to require evacuation. Fortunately, the number killed was also low, much lower than Colonel Alison had anticipated. A total of 31 men was originally reported killed—4 Americans and 27 Chindits. Later this figure was reduced to a total of 24. The number dead was almost totally comprised of the personnel in the two gliders that crashed into the jungle; only four persons were actually killed on Broadway. The Chindits dug a simple grave in the trees at the edge of the clearing and a Burmese chaplain conducted a eulogy for the lost comrades in arms.

Balanced against the losses were the accomplishments. During the night, General Wingate's staff figured 539 personnel, 3 mules, and 29,972 pounds of stores were delivered to Broadway. Captain Taylor's report showed a total glider payload of 221,648 pounds on the manifests. These figures did not include the supplemental supplies added by the Chindits that never appeared on any official documents, nor did it reflect the changes to the loading plan because of Piccadilly. Colonel Alison later attested to the fact that Wingate's figures were somewhat in error. While he had been frantically directing the glider landings and running from one smudge pot to another, a Chindit had offered him use of a horse flown in on a Waco glider!

At 0630 on 6 March, Brigadier Calvert was able to get a message through requesting evacuation planes for the injured. Major Rebori quickly responded by launching nine L-1 Vigilants, one from Tamu and eight from Taro, and six L-5 Sentinels from Taro. Flying at treetop level, the light planes arrived over Broadway by early morning. They planned to stay and operate out of this forward base. Rather than expose all the light planes to the enemy, only six patients were evacuated that day. The remainder would be airlifted aboard a C-47 Dakota when the airfield was finished.

Alison, seeing the mass of twisted gliders and undulated surface, talked to the surviving engineering officer about preparing the strip. Asked how long it would take to make an airfield, Lieutenant Brackett replied, "If I have it done by this afternoon will that be too late?" (106:7) And he did it. Personnel not essential elsewhere were put on the job. Using manual labor and the undamaged equipment, the men began the backbreaking work of filling the ruts and flattening the ground. Improvising with teakwood logs between tractors to make crude graders, engineers began to level the field.

Finally, at 1000 General Wingate established direct communications with Brigadier Calvert at Broadway. The 77th Brigade commander informed General Wingate and Colonel Cochran the field was secure, they had been unopposed by Japanese, and the airfield should be ready to receive transport planes by nightfall. General Wingate was beside himself with relief and joy! By 1630, the good

Prowling the Skies
When Staff Sergeant Shyojiro T. "Tom" Taketa reported heavy enemy traffic in Central Burma, Lieutenant Colonel Mahony led a highly successful 21-plane sweep at Anisakan. *Courtesy of R. T. Smith Family, 1st Air Commando Association*

news was better. A report was forwarded, saying by evening a 4,700-foot strip would be completed and lit.

The first flight of six Dakotas took off at 1730 with General Wingate aboard and General Old in the lead airplane. Told to approach from the South, General Old chose to land from the North due to traffic. He reported the field was narrow but usable. Troop Carrier Command sent 62 C-47 sorties into Broadway that night, departing from both Lalaghat and Hailakandi. Colonel Alison related that Broadway was as busy as any civilian airport, punctuating his remark with "La Guardia has nothing on us." (3:182) During the peak of activities that night, a transport arrived or departed every 47 seconds. The only accident reported was to two RAF transports; the damage was slight and the planes were flown out two days later.

With the good news about Broadway, General Wingate decided to move the 111th Brigade into Chowringhee 2 days earlier than planned. Based on the previous night's experience, Colonel Cochran had approved single tow operations and prepared 12 C-47 Dakotas for the job. Like the assault on Broadway, the first CG-4A contained Chindits and engineers. Unexpectedly, the first Hadrian pilot released early while Major Cherry maneuvered the tow plane prior to its final lineup over the clearing. The glider was flown by motion picture actor Flight Officer John L. "Jackie" Coogan. As Chowringhee began receiving gliders, Flight Officer Charles B. Turner felt the jolt as he cut loose from the tow aircraft. Flying a one-of-a-kind modified Hadrian, he plunged his craft toward the jungle below anticipating the worst. He later explained:

Flight Officer Harry L. McKaig and I conceived the idea that gliders should be armed since we were supposed to fly in the face of resistance behind the enemy lines. We, therefore, set about requisitioning, either officially or by night, .30-caliber plug-in machine guns and the other necessary hardware. The first unit to be completed was Harry's, and on test firing the entire windshield exploded in pieces. Not to be deterred, we secured heavier Plexiglas and installed it in my glider for use in the Chowringhee landing. Unfortunately, the gun was

Breaking up after Anisakan Mission Debriefing
First Row **(L-R) Captain William R. Gilhousen; Lieutenant Colonel Grant Mahony; Major Robert L. Petit; Captain Mack A. Mitchell** *Second Row* **Unidentified; Major Walter V. Radovich; Captain Roland R. Lynn; Captain Olin B. Carter; Unidentified** *Courtesy of A. R. Van de Weghe, 1st Air Commando Association*

Multi-talented Air Commando
In a rare shot, Lieutenant Colonel Robert T. Smith leans against his P-51A Mustang *Barbie*. **He had been assigned to the Bomber Section because he was considered too large for the small Mustang cockpit. Nevertheless, Lieutenant Colonel Smith, along with Major Walt Radovich, flew Mustang and Mitchell sorties during the 8 March raid over Central Burma.** *Courtesy of R. T. Smith Family, 1st Air Commando Association*

never fired as my copilot that night was a Lance Corporal in the Royal Gurkha Rifles. (120:—)

Colonel Cochran launched 12 Hadrians into Chowringhee that day; all gliders made it to destination. However, one Waco overshot the jungle clearing, killing all on board. The ill-fated glider contained the only bulldozer slated for Chowringhee. Plans for the following day were based on landing transports at Chowringhee the night of 7 March 1944. That day, at about 1200, Lieutenant Colonel Gaty, commander at Chowringhee, radioed that without the bulldozer, the strip would not be prepared on schedule. Colonel Cochran immediately dispatched a C-47 to Calcutta to obtain another bulldozer. The load was transferred to a glider that departed for Chowringhee at 2100. At Broadway, Colonel Alison also responded by loading one of his bulldozers on a serviceable glider. A C-47 then towed the glider, piloted by Flight Officer Noland, to Chowringhee; the glider touched down at 2100. Due to the late arrival, Lieutenant Colonel Gaty estimated the strip would not be available until after midnight.

Delayed preparation of Chowringhee required Colonel Cochran to change plans again, diverting some C-47 sorties to Broadway until Lieutenant Colonel Gaty was ready. Without Japanese resistance, the landing strip at Broadway had been improved during the day. Based on handling 16 aircraft per hour, Colonel Cochran ultimately launched 92 C-47 aircraft to Broadway that night. At 2330 the code word "ROORKEE" was received indicating Chowringhee was serviceable for C-47 Dakotas. A 6-ship wave was airborne for

Chowringhee by 0029. By the time 24 Dakotas had taken off, Chowringhee reported that only 2,700 feet were lit and approved for use. With 4,500 feet required for night operations, Brigadier Tulloch issued the recall order. Of the seven that did not respond, none experienced landing difficulties.

Even while the airlift into Broadway was being conducted, the men of Colonel Cochran's assault force were prowling Burma looking for the Nippon Air Force. No Nippon action was observed until 8 March when Staff Sergeant Shojiro T. "Tom" Taketa, Japanese-American intelligence technician, intercepted increased Nippon "line talk." It was between pilots and ground controllers at an airfield code-named "Nagoya." Able to break down the communication using Allied Intelligence information, he made an educated guess the enemy was massing aircraft in the Shwebo area of Central Burma. Without delay, Sergeant Taketa notified Cochran who ordered the Assault Section into immediate action. Deciding to arm each aircraft with a single 500-pound bomb, Lieutenant Colonel Mahony led a 21-plane fighter sweep over the enemy airfield at Anisakan, Burma. Observing about 17 fighters on the ground, Mahony's formation attacked. After dropping their bombs and auxiliary fuel tanks on antiaircraft positions, the Mustang pilots set up a strafing pattern, making as many as eight or nine passes.

On the way back to Hailakandi, Lieutenant Colonel Mahony led his flight over the airfields of Onbauk and Shwebo. There the formation found about 60 aircraft—fighters, bombers, transports,

Barbie III Crew
Standing **(L-R): Sergeant John D. Fitzgerald, Crew Chief; Sergeant Leonard J. Miller, Tail Gunner; First Lieutenant Wesley D. Weber, Navigator; Master Sergeant Charles N. Baisden, Armor Gunner; Lieutenant Colonel Robert T. "Tadpole" Smith, Aircraft Commander; Sergeant Stanley G. Zajac, Engineer-Gunner** *Kneeling:* **Staff Sergeant Richard M. Dixon, Radio-Gunner. Earlier on a demonstration flight, Smith had multiple problems while flying his original B-25H Mitchell,** *Barbie II*. **When she was scrapped, Smith christened the replacement aircraft** *Barbie III. Courtesy of R. T. Smith Family, 1st Air Commando Association*

and trainers—in the process of landing or already on the ground. Instructed to go for the bombers, the air commandos duplicated the procedures used in the raid at Anisakan. Diving on the airfields, the assault force continued to make iterative passes until all their ammunition was spent.

The pilots had used their bullets wisely. Destroyed on the ground at all the airfields were 27 fighters, 7 bombers, and 1 transport; in the air, the Mustang section added another fighter. Tragically, after shooting down the Japanese fighter, Captain Erle H. Schneider accidentally ran into the Oscar and both were killed. As Lieutenant Colonel Mahony departed the area, he alerted the bomber section at Hailakandi to be prepared to launch as soon as the fighters returned.

Within 45 minutes of landing, Lieutenant Colonel Smith and Major Radovich, who had been flying in the fighters, changed planes and flew back to the Onbauk and Shwebo area. Moonlight helped the formation of nine B-25H aircraft identify ground targets. Reaching the fields at 2000, the Mitchells pattern-bombed the revetments with fragmentation and incendiary loads, claiming an additional 12 aircraft. Even though his formation returned to Hailakandi after night fall, Smith easily located the runway; Colonel Cochran had ordered his men to line the runway with burning oil drums. At the informal debriefing, Lieutenant Colonel Smith reported the enemy airfields were last seen ablaze—buildings, gasoline trucks, and an oil storage depot in flames.

During the one day, the assault force destroyed a total of 48 enemy aircraft. A single squadron equivalent of fighters and 12 bombers accounted for more than 40 percent of all the Japanese aircraft destroyed by the Allies in the CBI during the month of March. General Stratemeyer stated, "In one mission [the unit has] obliterated nearly one-fifth of the known Japanese air force in Burma." (113:8) Intelligence reports also acknowledged the importance of the raid to Operation THURSDAY by observing the mission "...no doubt nullif[ied] enemy air opposition to the original fly-in." (98:4)

With this assistance, the operations continued into Chowringhee and Broadway. By 9 March 1944, General Wingate decided the location and capacity of Broadway exceeded the value of Chowringhee. Therefore, he sent Brigadier Tulloch to Burma to detail the planned evacuation with the 111th Brigade Commander, Brigadier Lentaigne. The evacuation of Chowringhee was completed by 0600 on the following day—just in time; the Japanese bombed the strip of wrecked gliders at 1300. With the emphasis now on Broadway, General Wingate poured in materiel and men. The signal from Templecombe was not received by 11 March, so General Wingate transferred Dah Force from Waco gliders to Dakotas and flew them into Broadway. There was still no Japanese opposition against Broadway when Operation THURSDAY was completed on 11 March.

Figures compiled from various sources show the magnitude of THURSDAY. From 5 March to 11 March, the 5318th Provisional Unit (Air) transported 2,038 personnel, 16 horses, 136 mules, and 104,681 pounds of stores. Including the glider dispatched from Broadway, 80 gliders were launched—63 to Broadway and 17 to Chowringhee. Personnel sent to the two strips by glider totaled 971. The C-47 effort, which included Troop Carrier Command and RAF flights, amounted to 579 sorties. For the entire operation, the following table indicates the amount of men, animals, and equipment airlifted.

TABLE 1
Operation THURSDAY Summary

Location	Personnel	Horses	Mules	Weight of Stores
Broadway	7,023	132	994	444,218 pounds
Chowringhee	2,029	43	289	64,865 pounds
Grand Total	9,052	175	1,283	509,083 pounds

Although these are impressive figures, the most momentous feature of the operation was the establishment of an airfield and the delivery of fresh troops more than 200 miles behind enemy lines. By landing soldiers beyond those lines, the Allies, for the first time, used air power for the backbone of an invasion. As soon as the Chindits landed, they formed columns and disappeared into the shadowed jungles. Their purpose was to strangle the supply lines of the Japanese by controlling choke points. As they stalked their way across the jungle floor, the 3rd Indian Division would continue to call on Colonel Cochran's men to be their artillery armada for close air support, their umbilical cord for supplies, and their airborne ambulances for the evacuation of casualties.

Lethal Firepower
Normally, Lieutenant Colonel Smith's men flew echelon formations. The geometry allowed for a left hand turn over the target for identification prior to beginning the bomb run. *Courtesy of 1ˢᵗ Air Commando Association*

6

Air Power

As elements of the 3rd Indian Division arrived at Broadway during Operation THURSDAY, they formed into columns and set out into separate areas of Northern Burma. Brigadier Calvert's 77th Brigade drove west toward the railroad line between Mandalay and the enemy airfield at Myitkyina. Near Mawlu, the brigade was to establish a roadblock and keep supplies from reaching General Stilwell's opposition in the Hukawng Valley, the Japanese 18th Division. Brigadier Lentaigne's 111th Brigade was to push west-south-west toward Wuntho to cut off Japanese replacements going north by rail and road. Brigadier Fergusson's 16th Brigade, exhausted from the trek across the Chin Hills, was expected to capture the Nippon supply hub of Indaw before the monsoons. There, General Wingate hoped to use the two all-weather enemy airfields of Indaw

East and Indaw West. A fourth LRP unit was also injected into Burma; General Wingate committed his reserve 3rd West African Brigade to Broadway for garrison support.

The tempo before, during, and after the invasion was exhausting. As D-day neared, Colonel Cochran's unit was required to stock Lalaghat and Hailakandi with equipment, supplies, and munitions from Indian warehouses in Eastern Assam. The last consumables to arrive were petroleum, oil, and lubricants. To meet the requirements of Operation THURSDAY, the men of the 5318th Provision Unit (Air) repeated the egalitarian procedures established at Karachi. Officer and enlisted personnel labored side by side to transfer oil and fuel drums from the Dimapur railhead to Lalaghat and Hailakandi. Due to the poor quality of petroleum product, Cochran's

Chindits
After landing at Broadway, the Chindits receded into the jungle to set up strongholds at key Japanese lines of communications. *Courtesy of 1st Air Commando Association*

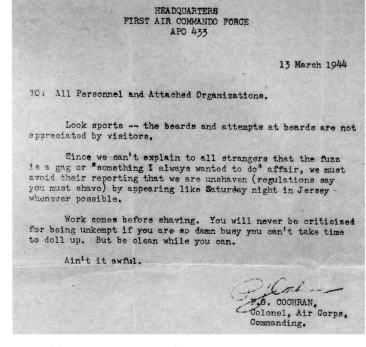

HEADQUARTERS
FIRST AIR COMMANDO FORCE
APO 433

13 March 1944

TO: All Personnel and Attached Organizations.

Look sports -- the beards and attempts at beards are not appreciated by visitors.

Since we can't explain to all strangers that the fuzz is a gag or "something I always wanted to do" affair, we must avoid their reporting that we are unshaven (regulations say you must shave) by appearing like Saturday night in Jersey whenever possible.

Work comes before shaving. You will never be criticized for being unkempt if you are so damn busy you can't take time to doll up. But be clean while you can.

Ain't it awful.

P.G. COCHRAN,
Colonel, Air Corps,
Commanding.

Order of the Day
Colonel Cochran's "Ain't it awful" directives is one of the most unusual in air power history. Date of order indicates this may not be the original. *Courtesy of 1st Air Commando Association*

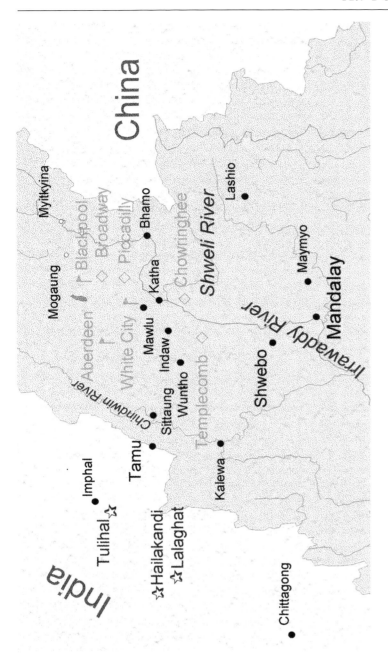

Map 7- Northern Burma 1944: March-May

Broadway Under Air Attack
When the RAF placed Spitfires on Broadway, the Japanese attacked the behind-the-line citadel daily. *Courtesy 1ˢᵗ Air Commando Assoc.*

Provisional Unit (Air) as an emergency airfield when Captain Daniel A. Sinskie bellied-in *Burma Baby* at Broadway on 8 March. Following Operation THURSDAY, Cochran planned to use Norsemen and Dakotas to flow supplies into the heartland of Burma at night through the airfield. Additionally, nearly 30 light planes were to operate daily out of this behind-the-line bastion.

Without consulting Cochran, the British insisted on positioning Spitfires at Broadway to act as interceptors. The six fighters of the 81 Fighter Squadron, RAF, proved to be a magnet. On 13 March, 2 days after the completion of Operation THURSDAY, Japanese fighters discovered the Spitfires and tried to dislodge them from Broadway. Although an SCR 602 radar was installed at the air strip, limited range put the RAF at a disadvantage. Japanese attacks were too swift and offered little reaction time. During the first encounter, Squadron Leader "Babe" Whitamore and his flight were still trying to takeoff when the Rising Sun arrived.

Believing General Wingate had been instrumental in the RAF decision, Cochran angrily confronted the Chindit commander. Disarmed by Wingate's candor, Cochran soon realized his only recourse was to dispatch air commando fighters to the field. To avoid detection, the airplanes were pushed under the trees out of view of Japanese reconnaissance aircraft. Despite these precautions, 2 days after arrival, Broadway came under attack. The Spitfires were first off the deck. Then Lieutenant Colonel Mahony, Major Petit, Captain Roland R. Lynn, and Captain Hubert L. Krug scrambled for an intercept. Mahony and Petit's airplanes created so much dust, Lynn and Krug had to hold for clearer vision. While waiting, a Japanese bomb hit Krug's aircraft, causing a small fire and knocking him unconscious for a short time. He had to be taken to the hospital for severe burns. Colonel Cochran immediately ordered the Mustangs back to Hailakandi.

men worked virtually around the clock. Although the process was manpower intensive, the unit strained fuel through chamois skins to remove rust and other impurities. Wearily the men continued the work, disregarding physical hygiene. When General Old made a remark about the slovenliness of the unit, Colonel Cochran posted one of the most unusual Orders of the Day. The beards came off, the work went on, and reportedly, General Old got as greasy as the rest when he pitched in to help. As a result, flights into Broadway never slowed down due to fuel.

Colonel Cochran and General Wingate agreed to retain Broadway as a supply site and a harbor for the light planes. Strategically, Broadway was invaluable. The strip had already served the 5318tʰ

Natural Revetments
Light Planes were pushed back into the jungle at Broadway to avoid detection by the Japanese. *Courtesy of 1ˢᵗ Air Commando Association*

Broadway: Emergency Airfield
Captain Daniel A. Sinskie lost an engine over Burma and was forced to divert to Broadway. *Burma Baby* **was later stripped for parts and pushed into the jungle.** *Courtesy of James E. Eckert, 1ˢᵗ Air Commando Association*

The Nippon air arm returned the following day. Only Whitamore and Flying Officer Alan Peart got off before the Oscars arrived over the field. During the attack, the RAF lost four Spitfires on the ground. Squadron Leader Whitamore managed to get airborne. He downed one Oscar before he was killed in a fiery dual. That evening, the surviving British pilots were evacuated. Japanese interest in Broadway waned after it was stripped of its air cover. One final air assault damaged the early warning radar set, radio equipment, and a few light planes. Personnel casualties were low.

The jungle citadel remained firmly in the hands of the Allies. Later, Japanese ground forces engaged Colonel Claude Rome and his Chindit garrison troops; however, they were repulsed. Like frustrated children, the Japanese slashed at the canvas skin of the light planes with bayonets before receding into the jungle. The airfield was never overrun and was protected enough to eventually include

amenities—maintenance shops, a dispensary, a small garden, and even a chicken farm.

Meanwhile, Colonel Cochran's men and Troop Carrier Command supplied the Chindits. Constantly reconnoitering the area for possible drop zones, brigades literally lived and functioned from one drop to another. When General Wingate's troops passed a message to India that a clearing was available, C-47 Dakotas would be scheduled to takeoff after dark and fly to the coordinates given. As they neared the site, Dakota pilots searched for a L-shaped row of lights to pinpoint the Chindit position. This was always a critical time because of the exposure of the C-47 and Special Force.

At first, drops were made using parachutes, but results were spotty. The Chindits reported loads landing anywhere near the zone to some distance away because of winds. To lessen the drift effect, only delicate loads were rigged with chutes; the remaining cargo

Burma Baby
Captain Daniel A. Sinskie's B-25H Mitchell took part in the 8 March 1944 attack on Anisakin, Burma. Note the outlined armor plate under the pilot's side window. *Courtesy of 1ˢᵗ Air Commando Association*

was pushed out the door to free fall to the awaiting troops below. Special Force would then gather the stores and disappear into the undergrowth. The supplies contained anything and everything consumable for the Chindit columns—rations, ammunition, medicine, and fodder for the animals. Bundles of hay were delivered via the free fall method. During a light plane re-supply mission, while flying into Burma, Staff Sergeant Rodney E. Petty, Jr., became curious about the large oat sack next to him. Feeling around in the bag, he discovered a bottle of *Three Feathers* Whiskey nestled in the rice straw packing; then he found another. Sheepishly, he admitted the sack was somewhat lighter when it was delivered, but no one dared complain. Despite such contraband, the most common parachute-pack contained 5-days rations for five men and a 30-pound sack of mixed grain for the animals. The following account describes the normal contents of supply bundles:

The basic ration was the American K-type, but in order that the troops might have some variety in their diet, one "luxury meal" was delivered with each drop. The luxury meal consisted of 14 ounces of bread, a 7.5-ounce can of fruit, 2 ounces of margarine, 2 ounces of rum, and 1 raw onion per man. Usually the Chindits ate this meal at the dropping zone. In addition to the luxury meal, 6.5 ounces of tea, sugar, salt, and powdered milk per man were provided in each drop. The salt was, of course, needed for seasoning and to prevent heat exhaustion; the other items made possible the hot tea which was so essential to British troops. (131:—)

Although supply drops were normally conducted at night, light plane functions required actions during broad daylight. Precautionary measures were necessary. If the Chindits had injuries, casualties, or jungle sicknesses, they requested evacuation support, provided the location of a suitable clearing, and established an arrival time. To locate the ever-moving brigades, the light plane pilots (commonly called L-pilots) attempted to establish a signal system to assure positive identification. Codes were tried and soon abandoned except when used in conjunction with map coordinates and time over target; decoding caused response time to be too slow and required centralized control. In short order, satisfactory results were attained by using aerial mosaic photographs and setting aside one frequency, 4530 kHz, for all ground-to-air radio traffic. Combining the mosaics and direct communication, a Chindit RAF liaison officer could describe ground locations from the perspective of the pilot flying overhead. As a final precaution, before attempting to land or drop supplies, the L-pilots also looked for predetermined visual signals such as "Very" flares, smoke, or panels.

Unlike the debilitating effect on the 1943 LRP expedition, treatment of casualties by this time became a source of high morale. Under normal circumstances, the wounded were brought back to Broadway and transferred to a UC-64 Norseman or a C-47 Dakota. When a soldier required immediate attention, the L-pilots would fly directly to hospitals in India if possible. Also, the air commando UC-64 pilots augmented the L-series planes by flying to larger clearings to evacuate up to 10 litter patients at a time. Even though the L-1 was supposed to carry only a maximum of three patients, Chindits reported it was not uncommon to see a Vigilant stagger skyward with five to seven casualties on board. Colonel Alison later gave a testimonial to the effectiveness of the commando air evacuation effort by saying, "A man could be wounded anywhere in the battle area and that night he would be in a hospital in India." (76:9)

Light Plane Damage
Unable to dislodge the Allies from Broadway, a Japanese patrol resorted to slashing the canvas exterior of an L-1 Vigilant. The canvas cover was doped and the airplane was quickly flightworthy again. *Courtesy of 1ˢᵗ Air Commando Association*

Ubiquitous
Flying alone at low level, L-5 Sentinel pilots covered the countryside. The enlisted pilots accomplished a variety of missions never before envisioned for light planes. *Courtesy of 1ˢᵗ Air Commando Association*

Precision Ordnance
The Japanese respected the accuracy of the 1ˢᵗ Air Commando Mustang pilots. Often fire support was so exact, the Chindits could move about with impunity after an attack. The two broad strips and tail number indicate the plane belonged to Lieutenant Colonel R. T. Smith. *Courtesy of R. T. Smith Family, 1ˢᵗ Air Commando Association*

It was not long before the air commandos recognized the versatility of the L-5 Sentinel; they expanded the role accordingly. Husbanding the L-1 Vigilants for air evacuation, the light plane section found a number of uses for the ubiquitous L-5. Often these aircraft were the vital backup supply link to the stealthy Chindits. Rigged with a 75-pound parachute pack on each bomb rack, the Sentinels made emergency airdrops of ammunition or food to brigades who had been missed during normal C-47 re-supply missions. One light plane pilot described these emergency airdrops: "Our method of getting the drops on target was to dive on the prescribed location and at an altitude so low that the chute would open just before it hit the ground. We could put the drops exactly on the spot and we followed each other in a close line astern formation. This always worked out real[ly] well because it did not expose us to ground fire for a very long period of time." (131:—)

Besides dropping food supplies, the pilots used their imagination to develop new applications for the light planes. Ultimately the Sentinels performed a variety of functions in support of Special Force that were never envisioned when the unit formed. Aside from medical evacuations, L-5 aircraft were used to accomplish the following:

(1)   Transport headquarters personnel to and from Burma,
(2)   Drop critically needed medical supplies,
(3)   Airland replacements directly to Chindit columns,
(4)   Evacuate captured prisoners of war,
(5)   Provide transportation for glider personnel,
(6)   Return captured documents and materials,
(7)   Transport official orders,
(8)   Deliver mail,
(9)   Make reconnaissance flights,
(10) Gather intelligence information,
(11) Spot targets for the assault sections, and
(12) Search and rescue operations.

Never before used on this scale or in this fashion, the light planes performed spectacularly. General Wingate personally wrote a commendation to the light plane pilots of Broadway. It was posted for all to see on one of the derelict Hadrians used as a medical room. Later, a Japanese bombing attack destroyed the well-earned tribute. Publicly, General Wingate often spoke of his debt to the light plane section. Early in the operation, he expressed his appreciation of the L-pilots by saying, "Without you men and your aircraft, this campaign could not have hoped to be a success." (99:5)

Buoyed by the actions of the air commandos, General Wingate felt confident about his air power theory. By the third week of March, the Chindits were crouched in four locations preparing to leap on the logistics tail of the Japanese dragon. While waiting for Special Force to deploy, the P-51A Mustangs and B-25H Mitchells had roamed the skies of Northern Burma striking supply lines, roads, bridges, airfields, and more. When Brigadier Calvert radioed that his brigade was entrenched on a hill overlooking the railroad line outside Mawlu, the assault force refocused its attention on close air support.

Although a semi-permanent stronghold defied the original LRP principles of speed and mobility, the addition of air power made it possible. The need for precision was satisfied by intelligent use of the RAF liaison officers assigned to each column. The following account illustrates the degree of cooperation achieved between

White City
Brigadier Calvert established a light aircraft strip between the road and railroad tracks. Daily his men received the mail, supplies, equipment, and munitions needed to withstand Japanese assaults. *Courtesy of 1ˢᵗ Air Commando Association*

Lightning Struck the Chindits
In the foreground, *Sweet Sue* (First Lieutenant Brian F. Hodges' aircraft) is shown in formation with *Barbie III*. *Sweet Sue* had been damaged just days before General Wingate's fateful flight. Lieutenant Hodges flew a replacement B-25H Mitchell, tail number 34242, the night of the crash. *Courtesy of 1ˢᵗ Air Commando Association*

Chindits and air commandos and their combined effectiveness against Japanese ground troops:

> Most often the liaison men gave the command "Smoke!" by telephone, and mortars would fire a smoke-shell to mark the target. If the shell did not burst precisely where intended, pilots were told by radio and, as soon as the targets were re-duced, succeeding aircraft in the flight were diverted to the next objective. After a little while the system worked so supremely well that no Japanese artillery would fire while aircraft were near in case they gave away their position, and soon the same fear restrained Japanese infantry. Chindits found that after treatment by fighter-bombers they could sometimes walk in the open within a hundred yards of the enemy and stay immune. The almost total absence of enemy air opposition made possible a leisurely and orderly destruction of enemy positions. (131:—)

Brigadier Calvert installed his roadblock on 17 March and immediately began using the 1ˢᵗ Air Commando Group (officially as of 29 March 1944) to dig in. The following day, although they were unable to establish radio contact, the air assault force dove on enemy positions marked by smoke and dropped depth charges and fragmentation bombs. As a result, the Japanese remained quiet for 3 days and then rushed the stronghold under a volley of mortar fire and machine guns. The attack was turned back. Using antitank guns and ammunition supplied by gliders, Calvert's men had fortified the position, established the perimeter with concertina wire, and hunkered down for a long siege. To keep the Chindit blocking action continually supplied, consumables had to be airdropped into the citadel on a daily basis. The stronghold soon took on the name White City because of the plethora of parachutes hanging from the trees. Brigadier Calvert's roadblock withstood the repeated attacks and caused a serious supply and munitions problem for the Japanese 18ᵗʰ Division.

While the air commandos helped White City fortify their stranglehold on Japanese lines of communication, Hadrian pilots were silently aiding Brigadier Lentaigne's 111ᵗʰ Brigade. The operation was typical of glider missions. On the night of 19 March and morning of 20 March, six Hadrians carrying 10 sappers each

Aberdeen, Burma
With equipment flown in on gliders, civil engineers put the finishing touches on the C-47 airstrip at Aberdeen. *Courtesy of 1ˢᵗ Air Commando Association*

First on the Scene
Staff Sergeant Lloyd I. Samp located Wingate's wreckage. Little was left of the Mitchell bomber—one wing and a strut were the only parts of any size. While directing a British search party, his engine iced over and he was forced to crash land near the scene. *Courtesy of Evelyn Samp, 1ˢᵗ Air Commando Association*

were flown single tow to a point northwest of Tigyaing. Approaching the objective area, Dakota pilots identified two columns of three fires marking the landing area. Moments before the release of each Waco, Lentaigne's Chindits flashed a green light. One by one the Wacos plunged to the jungle below. For unreported reasons, the sixth aircraft was given a red light and did not release his glider. The last Dakota, with Hadrian in tow, silently turned westward toward India.

Just five days after Calvert had begun setting up his stronghold of White City, the 16ᵗʰ Brigade was in position to begin an attack on Indaw. Because of the long march from Ledo, General Wingate decided to assign the 14ᵗʰ Brigade to help Brigadier Fergusson's weary men. Therefore, on 22 March, General Wingate signaled the 1ˢᵗ Air Commando Group to begin construction of another airstrip northwest of Indaw. Using the same techniques as Broadway, C-47 Dakotas towed six Hadrians with construction equipment to level the new strip, christened Aberdeen. The Chindits' second airfield

was not a clearing like Broadway; instead, it was surrounded by hills.

While Aberdeen was being built, the enemy fought fiercely to keep the Chindits from severing the key supply line through Indaw. One of General Wingate's columns was pinned down during the fighting and requested a strike to aid their retreat. The P-51A Mustangs responded by making shallow dive-bombing and strafing attacks while Special Force ground troops directed the action. The fighter pilots purposely conserved their ammunition by interspersing numerous dummy runs with live approaches. Special Force and the air commandos carefully coordinated procedures—enemy positions were marked with mortar smoke and friendly positions with Very flares. Before takeoff, munitions experts had hung a pair of drop tanks filled with a combination of crankcase drainings and gasoline under the wings of the lead Mustang. Rolling in on the Japanese position, lead dropped the tanks while his wingman fired incendiary tracers into the area, setting the mixture ablaze. Before the advent of napalm, this highly accurate firepower enabled Wingate's men to disengage from the Japanese. As a result, the Chindits ultimately worked their way back to safety.

The withdrawal was a success but casualties were high. By the end of the first week of the operation, over 150 light plane missions had been flown, over 200 casualties had been evacuated, and almost 75 supply drops had been accomplished in support of Aberdeen. The enemy desperately needed Indaw because the supply hub now played a major role in the Nippon strategic plans for the conquest of India.

As Chindits were being flown into Burma during Operation THURSDAY, Lieutenant General Renya Mutaguchi, commander of Japan's 15ᵗʰ Army, launched his own invasion. It was a 3-pronged attack into India called Operation U-GO. The Japanese 33ʳᵈ Division advanced from south of Tamu; 15ᵗʰ Division, from east of Imphal; and 31ˢᵗ Division, through the Tuza Gap east of Kohima. The Japanese 18ᵗʰ Division in the Hukawng Valley was also in-

Egg Beater
Colonel Cochran considered flying to the wreckage in a YR-4 Helicopter, shown here piloted by First Lieutenant Frank M. "Pete" Turney. The idea was discarded due to the elevation of the crash site. *Courtesy of Harry McKaig, 1ˢᵗ Air Commando Association*

Erotic Edna
First Lieutenant Ralph K. Lanning's *Erotic Edna* helped the Assault Force compile impressive statistics for March 1944. The 1ˢᵗ Air Commando Group accounted for 42.7 percent of the Japanese aircraft destroyed during the month. *Courtesy of 1ˢᵗ Air Commando Association*

volved; they were to block General Stilwell's Chinese troops from joining in the fight. The genesis of the plan could be traced to Operation LONGCLOTH. As a result of General Wingate's first expedition, General Mutaguchi realized the Japanese defensive posture in Burma was vulnerable. Therefore, he decided to cut off the British from their supply depot at Imphal and interpose Japanese troops on India soil prior to the monsoons. From this "toehold," the Japanese 15ᵗʰ Army commander would increase his outer perimeter of defense.

Additionally, General Mutaguchi planned to use the operation to generate favorable propaganda for a "March to Delhi" by Indian

National Army leader Chadra Bose. General Mutaguchi hoped the U-GO offensive would be swift, lasting less than a month, as the invading troops were provided only a 21-day ration of supplies. Each division would furnish its own provisions along the avenue of advance until the invasion; after that, the Japanese would move stores by the Shwebo-Imphal Road as well as the previous supply routes. The only all-weather artery was between Shwebo and Imphal. Inauspiciously, the "dry season only" routes were near the area of the Chindits.

With the required major offensive now in being and knowing the poor supply conditions of General Mutaguchi's army, Wingate

Air Commando B-25H Mitchell Destroyed
Before the end of March, *Erotic Edna* was destroyed. On 29 March 1944, she burned after a pancake landing at Hailakandi. The pilot on that day was First Lieutenant Frank W. Gursansky. *Courtesy of James E. Eckert, 1ˢᵗ Air Commando Association*

Rockets in Combat
At Aungban, Burma, on 4 April 1944, the 1ˢᵗ Air Commando Group became the first unit to fire rockets in combat. Lieutenant Colonel Clinton B. Gaty obtained the design from Wright Field and Major Frank Fazio installed the bazookas on 1ˢᵗ Air Commando P-51A Mustangs. *Courtesy of 1ˢᵗ Air Commando Association*

felt he was on the verge of proving LRP theory. He immediately dispatched an optimistic letter to Winston Churchill concerning the situation. Tragically, within days of reading the news, the British Prime Minister was shocked to learn the circumstances in Burma had changed.

For Special Force, lightning struck on 24 March and the direction of the wind forever shifted against the Chindits. General Wingate flew to the front lines in an L-5 on 23 March to observe the operations and discuss strategy with his brigade commanders. After the conferences, he proceeded to Broadway where he boarded an air commando B-25H. General Wingate normally flew with either Colonel Alison or Major Radovich; on this flight, First Lieutenant Brian F. Hodges was the Mitchell aircraft commander. Following an intermediate stop at Imphal, the aircraft headed west for General Wingate's headquarters at Sylhet. It never arrived. On the last leg of its journey, the bomber inexplicably exploded into the side of a hill, killing all on board.

Mystery and intrigue accompanied the crash. Air commando Staff Sergeant Lloyd I. Samp was the first to find the wreckage. He reported that strangely, despite the flight path, the aircraft impacted sharply into the west side of the mountain range—it was heading east! Questions were raised about engine trouble, weather, and even sabotage; none of the answers were conclusive. The aircraft nosed-in and the wreckage was severely confined. The only recognizable clue to the passengers on board was located near the crash site— the familiar pith helmet of the Chindit commander. Those who died along with General Wingate were Captain T. G. Borrow, his adjutant; Stewart Emeny and Stanley Wills, war correspondents; Lieu-

Forward Air Controller
Air Commando L-5 pilots like Staff Sergeant Richard D. Snyder helped define the role of light planes. While primarily moving casualties, Sentinel pilots also acted as spotters to pinpoint Japanese positions. Later, Colonel Gaty expanded the process by marking enemy targets with smoke for fighters and bombers. *Courtesy of 1ˢᵗ Air Commando Association*

tenant Hodges, aircraft commander; Second Lieutenant Stephen A. Wanderer, navigator; Technical Sergeant Frank Sadoski, Staff Sergeant James W. Hickey, and Staff Sergeant Vernon A. McIninch, crew members. Interestingly, according to the rules of war, all the bodies, including that of Major General Orde C. Wingate, were buried at Arlington Cemetery outside Washington, D.C.

General Wingate's death came in the midst of the most complicated operation ever attempted in that theater and robbed the Allies of a colorful and dynamic commander. Prime Minister Churchill sadly spoke of the blow to Allied operations by saying of Wingate's death, "... a bright flame was extinguished." (13:485) Admiral Lord Mountbatten understood the Chindit commander's contribution to the theater and issued the following Order of the Day to Special Force:

General Wingate has been killed in the hour of his triumph. The Allies have lost one of the most forceful and dynamic personalities that this war has produced. You have lost the finest and most inspiring leader a force could have wished for, and I have lost a personal friend and faithful supporter. He has lit the torch. Together we must grasp it and carry it forward. Out of your gallant and hazardous expedition into the heart of Japanese-held territory will grow the final re-conquest of Burma and the ultimate defeat of the Japanese. He was so proud of you. I know you will live up to his expectations. (120: —)

In selecting a successor, General Slim did not choose an original Chindit, such as Brigadier Calvert or Brigadier Fergusson. Neither did Slim pick General Wingate's Chief of Staff, Brigadier Tulloch; instead, he opted for the most orthodox officer within General Wingate's former command—Brigadier Lentaigne. The Special Force commander's credentials were beyond reproach; he was a competent and heroic officer. However, he did not endorse LRP theory, nor was he favorably impressed with the late General Wingate. Although Colonel Cochran's mission did not change, events soon showed than under General Lentaigne, the ideals of LRP were discarded. By mid-April the Chindits began to form large formations and attack fortified positions. For the time being, though, operations continued with air commandos providing direct ground support to columns protecting the White City stronghold, at the C-47 airfield of Aberdeen, along supply roads west of Wuntho, and to a splinter unit of the 77ᵗʰ Brigade cutting traffic lines between Lashio and Myitkyina.

All the air commando sections helped the Chindits, not always in the most conventional way possible. The Japanese communication system proved particularly vulnerable to one of the air commandos' maverick schemes. The tactic required an unapproved modification to the fighters. Laying a 450-foot cable around the rear of a Mustang, ordnance specialists connected the ends to each of the wing bomb racks. Attached to this cable was a weight that

P-51B Mustangs

Second Lieutenant Charles J. Vagim stands before a B-model Mustang—note the 4-bladed propeller. The increased power and range of the new Mustang allowed for deeper attacks into Burma. On 21 April, Major Robert L. Petit scored a direct hit with two 1,000-pound bombs and collapsed the Shweli River bridge. *Courtesy of A. R. Van de Weghe, 1ˢᵗ Air Commando Association*

made the device drag behind during takeoff; once airborne, it hung like a pendulum beneath the cruising P-51. The assault force pilots would use the cable assembly to cut Japanese communications by diving on telephone and telegraph lines, pulling up just in time to wrap the weight around the wires like a bola. Normally, the lines snapped, but occasionally, pilots reported uprooting telephone poles and dragging them for miles before jettisoning the cable. Once, Major Petit overzealously resorted to using his plane like a flying wire cutter after losing his cable assembly—slicing through several telephone lines with his wings before heading back to Hailakandi.

But the assault force was not the only offensive arm of the air commandos. Toward the end of the first month of the invasion, a frustrated Dakota crew—Captain John C. Sanichas, First Lieutenant John E. "Jack" Lewis, and Private First Class Morris H. Zalmonovich—supplemented its airland re-supply missions by try-

ing a hand at bombardment. On 25 March, while making a supply run into Broadway, Zalmonovich dropped two mortar shells on some Japanese trucks. Three days later, the same crew spotted another convoy of mechanized transport and dropped incendiary devices followed by 25-pound fragmentation bombs from the side door of the C-47. Captain Sanichas explained, "We may not have done any damage but I'll bet we scared the hell out of them." (113:12)

March closed with two important personnel changes. During the month, command of the L-1/L-5 section changed hands. The need for the change came to light when one light plane section moved up to an airfield called Dixie, inside the border of Burma. Shortly after flying operations had begun, intelligence reports said the enemy was advancing in the area and would soon overrun the strip. Acting on short notice, the unit's hasty departure from Dixie was not accomplished well. Code books and reports were left behind. More seriously, Staff Sergeant Raymond J. Ruksas and Staff Sergeant Bruce H. McCormick were not informed the field had been abandoned. When they returned, luckily the enemy had not penetrated the camp. In the aftermath of the debacle, Colonel Cochran decided to alter the organization of the light plane section because the operations of four separate sections could not be tracked adequately. As a result of the change, the L-series aircraft were placed under the command of Lieutenant Colonel Gaty.

The other personnel move left Colonel Cochran without his right hand man. On 28 March, General Arnold called Colonel Alison home to help establish more air commando units. At Broadway when summoned, Alison wasted no time getting back to India. Commandeering an RAF Dakota with a badly damaged wing, Alison flew the crippled plane out. Because he had never flown the C-47 before, he requested help from a pilot in the tower at Hailakandi during the approach. By the time he touched down, Colonel Alison had a second message requesting he brief General Dwight D. Eisenhower's European Theater Staff on Operation THURSDAY. He departed India on 1 April for Washington by way of the British Isles.

Under the dual leadership of Colonels Cochran and Alison, the air commandos had accumulated an impressive set of statistics. The C-47 Dakotas had flown in over 450,000 pounds of supplies during March, and the CG-4A Hadrian gliders had delivered an additional 310,000 pounds. The light planes estimated they evacuated 1,200 to 1,500 casualties before the end of the first month of the operation. Damage inflicted by the assault force during March is shown in Table 2.

During the critical month of action, the Allies established air superiority over Burma for the first time. USAAF records show the Japanese lost 117 airplanes in the third month of 1944. (9:511) Significantly, the 1ˢᵗ Air Commando Group—only a single squadron of fighters and 12 bombers—accounted for 42.7 percent of the total Japanese aircraft destroyed. And the following month would be equally impressive.

TABLE 2
Assault Force Damage Report
March 1944

Category	Destroyed
Aircraft	50
Trucks	29
Rolling Stock	48
Locomotives	4
Bridges	8
Warehouses	38
Bashas	55
Ammunition Sites	7

YR-4 Helicopter Ground and Air Crew
Back Row (L-R) First Lieutenant Carter Harman, First Lieutenant Frank M. "Pete" Turney *Front Row* (L-R) Sergeant Alexander Zalman, Sergeant Warren C. MacArtney, Staff Sergeant John A. Manter, Sergeant James D. Phelan. During training at Sikorsky, Carter Harman ran out of fuel and accomplished one of the first helicopter auto rotations. *Courtesy of 1st Air Commando Association*

Early in April, the air commandos reprised the Anisakan-Onbauk-Shwebo mission; only the location changed. Acting on intelligence information of Japanese movement in the area of Rangoon, the commando assault force took off at 0800 on 4 April heading for Aungban, Burma. Slung under each wing of the Mustangs were three loaded rocket tubes. Just before the arrival of the fighter section, the Japanese had scrambled their flights from Heho to parry a P-38 attack from the USAAF 459th Squadron. Shortly after the enemy fighters recovered to Aungban, Lieutenant Colonel Mahony's P-51A Mustangs arrived over the airfield. Finding the Japanese aircraft parked next to and in revetments, the commandos kept the antiaircraft batteries at bay with rockets while strafing the field on continual passes. The assault force destroyed 4 medium bombers and 20 fighters on the ground. In the air, Captain Forcey dove on an enemy aircraft, making a pass within 200 yards before pulling off; the Japanese fighter poured smoke and exploded. On the way home, air commando fighters also destroyed an enemy bomber on the ground at Anisakan. Total enemy losses were 26 verified kills, and the air commandos did not lose any P-51A Mustangs during the mission.

The raid marked the first time rockets had been fired from an American airplane in combat. The unit's use of the airborne bazookas almost did not happen, though. Originally the shipment of 1,000 rockets was mishandled and delivered to 14th Air Force in China. Major Frank Fazio, an engineer sent from Eglin Field to install the rockets, learned of the mistake and caught a flight to Kunming. Colonel Cochran sent him to talk General Chennault's logistics chief out of the shipment. The cost to correct the error was merely three bottles of *Haig & Haig* Scotch Whiskey valued at about $200 per bottle. Corporals Jack Curtis, Milan J. Urbanic, and Jennings B. Rader worked out the installation. Corporal Rader, armament technician, described the design:

> The mounts we installed were a bracing rig on either side of the bomb racks. The rockets were fired from regular 4.5-inch bazooka tubes. These tubes were about 8 feet long and banded together in groups of three, two lower and one on top. The top tube had lugs that fit the regular bomb rack, this way they could be dropped after firing. Firing was accomplished by an electrical hookup at the rear of the projectile, and triggered from the cockpit by a switch … They made a hell of a noise when in flight, like blowing into a giant coke bottle. (131:—)

Sharknose P-51B Mustang
This unusual Air Commando P-51B Mustang was believed to have belonged to Captain William R. Gilhousen. Shot down over Burma in late May, Gilhousen died in prison camp less than 2 months later. *Courtesy of James E. Eckert, 1st Air Commando Association*

As the Allies asserted air superiority over Burma, the work of the air commandos showed dramatic results. The situation at White

City illustrated this aspect. The Japanese continued their pressure on White City, storming Brigadier Calvert's position almost daily after the block had been established. In response, the fighters and bombers of assault force frequently pounded the Japanese positions around the stronghold. Throughout, the light planes removed casualties from a small strip constructed next to the railroad line. Because there was no enemy air opposition, a Sentinel pilot offered to fly Calvert over the surrounding area to locate and record enemy concentrations.

To dislodge the Japanese, Calvert used this new information to request bombing runs within 50 yards of his own position. The accuracy of the air commando attacks and the incessant bombing finally proved too much for the Imperial troops. On 15 April, a Chindit wrote in his dairy, "... air action on this occasion against the enemy has been consistent and destructive. Amongst other things it has been shown that aircraft alone can force the enemy to move or leave his artillery." (98:Appendix B:1) The air attacks had caused the Japanese to break ranks and run, leaving behind everything—dead, documents, equipment, and weapons. With this kind of help from Colonel Cochran's men, Special Force effectively blocked the rail line into Myitkyina for nearly 2 months. As a result, the holding action by the Japanese 18th Division was impossible.

Meanwhile at Aberdeen, 16th Brigade continued to use the 1st Air Commando Group and Troop Carrier Command to re-supply their attempt to secure Indaw. On the night of 7 April, a Nippon fighter pilot sent a shudder through the transport organizations when he intercepted an RAF Dakota on approach at Aberdeen. First Lieutenant Leo S. Tyszecki's C-47 suffered damage to the landing gear and lost one engine, but the pilot was able to land without casualties. Nevertheless, the effect of this incident was profound. The Allies could no longer assume flights into behind-the-line airfields would be conducted with impunity. Thereafter, C-47 Dakota sorties were synchronized to arrive and depart stronghold airstrips at dusk and dawn. Additionally, fighter escorts were assigned to patrol the area. Fortunately, the attack was not repeated and future transport flights were conducted without incident.

The attack on the Dakota did not affect the L-pilots though; they continued flying unescorted while establishing a reputation for courage and skill. In supporting the Chindits, the air commandos were known for their ability to fly out of places others could not. For example, when Merrill's Marauders were pinned down by fierce Japanese resistance at Nhpum Ga, their own L-4 Grasshoppers were unable to extricate the sick and wounded because of the small landing strip. General Stilwell immediately ordered the air commando L-1 Vigilants to transport the casualties to front line hospital aid stations. Flying into the 700-foot strip, Staff Sergeants John J. Hyland, Joseph H. Sparrow, Thomas E. Purcell, Jr., and Ray Ruksas evacuated over 350 hospital cases. Tragically, Sergeant Purcell lost his life during the operation when his airplane failed to clear the trees that ringed the air strip.

In other ways, the light plane pilots enhanced their prestige by developing a novel method of air support which proved to be very effective. During the construction of Aberdeen, one of Brigadier Fergusson's RAF liaison officers became separated from his column and discovered a large supply dump in the jungle around Indaw. When he finally returned to his brigade, the officer requested the air commandos destroy the site. L-5 pilots took to the skies to establish the supply location for the fighters and bombers. Frustrated because he was unable to locate the site using maps or aerial mosaics, Lieutenant Colonel Gaty asked the RAF officer to fly with him in a Sentinel to reconnoiter the area. Pinpointing the position, he returned to Aberdeen to set up a rendezvous with the assault force. As the P-51A Mustangs and B-25H Mitchells arrived at the prearranged point, Lieutenant Colonel Gaty had the RAF liaison officer mark the target with smoke bombs as the L-5 cleared the tree tops. The Mustangs and Mitchells delivered their ordnance on the smoke. Due to the success of this coordinated mission, the light plane pilots continued to use "forward air controller" methods and occasionally even dropped grenades on small targets themselves.

In support of all the Chindit brigades, Colonel Cochran's men were also employed in a more orthodox role. Targeted against Japanese surface and river lines of communication, the air commandos were equally effective. Flying replacement P-51B Mustangs, the assault force attacked the Shweli River bridge, a target that had on numerous occasions withstood Eastern Air Command bomber attacks. The bridge controlled a major supply route to Northern Burma. On 21 April, Major Petit proved the accuracy of the dive-bombing Mustang when he scored a direct hit with two 1,000-pound bombs and collapsed the span. This is only one example. By the end of the campaign, the road and railroad system of Burma was so confused, the Japanese were unable to move supplies from Northern Burma to their only usable traffic artery—the Shwebo-Imphal road.

Helicopter Rescue
Lieutenant Harman moved forward to Aberdeen in April 1944. During subsequent operations, he conducted the first helicopter combat rescue in military history. *Courtesy of 1st Air Commando Association*

Replacement Bomber Pilot and Airplane
First Lieutenant Daniel B. Mitchell in his B-25H Mitchell, *Dangerous Date,* **tail number 34472, did not lack for combat missions. The markings show 26 bombing sorties.** *Courtesy of Dan Mitchell, 1st Air Commando Association*

While the assault force hammered on the Japanese lines of communication, the light plane force concentrated on the evacuation of casualties. In April, the 1st Air Commando Group made military history by placing the YR-4 helicopter into combat. Unfortunately, the helicopters Colonel Alison worked so hard to secure proved to be less useful than hoped. Of the original four rotary-winged aircraft, two were lost before they had flown a successful mission in the CBI Theater. En route to India, a C-46 transport crashed while carrying one of the untested craft and killed Master Sergeant Peter D. Kelly and Corporal Emmit R. Sommers. A helicopter pilot flew a second one into a power line on a training mission and crashed, killing a passenger. As training continued, how well the "eggbeater" was suited for operations became questionable. The YR-4 had a service ceiling of only 4,000 feet density altitude and a pilot, passenger, and fuel allowance of only 515 pounds. In Southeast Asia's steamy climate, Cochran's unit discovered in the heat of the day the craft's 180-horsepower engine was inadequate—the YR-4 could barely lift itself above the trees.

Despite these difficulties, on 21 April, First Lieutenant Carter Harman flew a YR-4 on a rescue mission into Burma to evacuate a light plane pilot forced down on a Japanese-controlled road. Staff Sergeant Edward F. "Murphy" Hladovcak, the downed L-pilot, and his three wounded British passengers were directed to seek shelter in the hills while awaiting the rescue. Because of overheat problems, the helicopter flew by stages to Aberdeen. When he arrived on 23 April, Lieutenant Harman was immediately pressed into action. Dispatched to a British-held staging area behind enemy lines, Harman flew 10 more miles over Japanese-held territory to the rescue site. Due to performance limitations, he had to extract one passenger at a time. Although the YR-4 was barely able to hover under the additional weight, Harman was able to "jerk" the helicopter almost 20 feet in the air. By immediately lowering the nose, he gained enough forward airspeed to clear the trees. Only able to make two lifts before the engine overheated, Harman returned to the staging area and waited overnight for cooler morning temperatures. To keep Sergeant Hladovcak informed, Staff Sergeant Robert J. Fiske dropped him a note. Always a practical joker, Fiske impishly included a retroactive 3-day pass.

On the following day, Lieutenant Harman successfully transferred the pilot and casualties to awaiting L-1 Vigilants and returned to Aberdeen on 24 April. He continued to fly combat missions until 4 May. When Aberdeen came under heavy Japanese bombardment, Lieutenant Colonel Gaty ordered Lieutenant Harman and his craft back to India. In the 23 combat sorties performed, the concept of the helicopter was proved; however, the YR-4 was grossly underpowered and maintenance-intensive. Eventually it was withdrawn after the engine failed due to overheat.

TABLE 3
Assault Force Damage Report
April 1944

Category	Destroyed
Aircraft	35
Trucks	4
Rolling Stock	6
Bridges	3
Barracks	45
Bashas	130
Ammunition Sites	5
Anti-aircraft Positions	11

The month of April again provided some impressive statistics for the 1st Air Commando Group. United States Army Air Force records indicate during April the Japanese lost 107 planes. For the second month in a row, the contribution of the 1st Air Commando Group was staggering; the Mustangs and Mitchells accounted for 32.7 percent of the total Japanese aircraft destroyed within the CBI Theater. Table 3 shows damage inflicted by the air commando assault force during April.

May marked the sixth month that the air commandos had been in India. According to General Arnold's plan, on 1 May Colonel Cochran's men were scheduled to be relieved of duty and sent back to the United States. The plan was altered because, as Colonel Cochran said, "… we kept wanting to protect those troops that were still there." (107:258) As of 17 May, the 3rd Indian Division officially came under operational control of General Stilwell, but even before the Infantry General had ordered the 111th, 14th, and 3rd West African Brigades to move north toward Mogaung. General

Stilwell wanted the three brigades to link with Brigadier Calvert's men to assault the Japanese garrison.

The 16th Brigade had already been sent back to India in early May. In Burma longer than the other units, Brigadier Fergusson's men showed signs of sickness, exhaustion, and strain. General Slim ordered their withdrawal. Because Aberdeen was open to Japanese attacks, most of 16th Brigade had to march from the Meza Valley to Broadway for evacuation. The other four brigades were in equally bad shape, but General Stilwell would not allow them to be relieved. He feared their retreat would attract Japanese troops toward his position. After "salting" Broadway, Aberdeen, and White City with land mines, the Chindits abandoned their strongholds and began working their way north through jungles and rice paddies.

They fought on, worn and weary from the effects of months in close contact with the dragon. The men's resistance was gone. Mild malaria cases made war-hardened soldiers helpless and chills took others. Despite the appalling condition of the men, medical attention was refused, so Special Force continued its sleepwalk to Mogaung. Encountering savage resistance, the Chindits resorted to clearing the village house-by-house, room-by-room because they had no heavy artillery—monsoon rains often grounded Cochran's fighters and bombers. On the last day of fighting, the Chinese crossed the Mogaung River and entered the northwest section of the town. In press releases, General Stilwell gave all the credit to the Chinese though the Chindit loses were almost 30 times greater. One of the Chindit 1,300-man columns was clearly left in the field too long; as it was relieved, only 30 men remained in fighting shape. Exhausted and out of patience, Brigadier Calvert sent Stilwell a wire objecting to the injustice by saying, "AS THE CHINESE HAVE TAKEN MOGAUNG, 77 BRIGADE WILL PROCEED TO TAKE UMBRAGE." (30:276) His protest fell on deaf ears; General Stilwell's staff reportedly searched in vain for Umbrage on the Burmese map.

Meanwhile, Stilwell gave the 111th Brigade, now commanded by Colonel John Masters, responsibility for applying further pressure on the logistic lines that fed the Japanese 18th Division. On 9 May, Colonel Masters selected a site and requested gliders to build an airstrip. Known as Clydeside, the block was re-designated Blackpool when the original name was compromised. Despite valiant fighting, the 111th Brigade never fully secured the stronghold, in part because General Mutaguchi released some of his U-GO reserve soldiers to fight the Chindits. The full brunt of these fresh troops flushed Special Force from Blackpool after only 2 weeks. Throughout, the air commandos continued to operate into Blackpool under extreme hazard. While maneuvering on base leg to the block, Flight Officer Hadley D. Baldwin's Waco was subjected to withering fire and he was killed. Another part of the problem at Blackpool was weather—the monsoons broke before the brigade could get entrenched. Flying during the intervals between squall lines, the assault force shelled and bombarded the perimeter of the bastion, but the support lacked continuity.

Just before the monsoons, the Air Force of the Rising Sun made a last ditch attempt to regain control over Burma by bringing up large numbers of replacements. It was too little, and it was too late. On 19 May, the fighter section had just arrived at Blackpool when a flight of 16 Nippon warplanes was spotted. Salvoing their bombs on Japanese positions around the stronghold, the air commandos attacked the enemy fighters and bombers. During the dogfight, P-51 pilots shot down one bomber and two fighters. There was no damage to the seven Mustangs.

Deadly Guns
The front end of a B-25H Mitchell is raised to reveal belts of ammunition for the .50-caliber machine guns. The Mitchell also carried as many as 21 shells for the 75 mm cannon mounted in the nose. *Courtesy of 1st Air Commando Association*

Pending Monsoons
Colonel Cochran wanted to stay and help the Chindits, but he almost stayed too long. A B-25H Mitchell kicks up water after a downpour at Hailakandi in May 1944. *Courtesy of James E. Eckert, 1ˢᵗ Air Commando Association*

This was the air commandos' last hurrah; weather was now critically hampering the effectiveness of the group. Colonel Cochran tried to operate out of the airfields in Eastern India as long as possible; it was a dangerous gamble. The rains soaked the grass strips at Hailakandi and Lalaghat, turning them into quagmires. At one point, Colonel Cochran believed he had waited too long. He related, "We had one tough rain where actually there was a couple of feet of water on the landing strip." (107:288) Unable to avoid the pending torrent, Colonel Cochran ordered the air commandos back to Asansol, an abandoned British airfield 120 miles northwest of Calcutta. On 23 May, a UC-64 raised a "rooster tail" as it slogged down Hailakandi's rain-drenched strip for the final time. The pilot's log read, "Beat bad storm by inches." (136:Pilot's Log)

Lieutenant Colonel Boebel ordered all the light planes back to India; however, he was unaware part of his section stayed in Burma to fly casualties to hospitals. Without the strength of their air artillery, the 111ᵗʰ Brigade had retreated from Blackpool on 24 May and fled westward toward Lake Indawgyi. Colonel Masters described the support he received during the withdrawal as follows: "The American pilots of the Light Plane Force came, hour after hour, day after day, to the little patch of swamp we had made into a

strip, and shuttled back through the heaving skies." (30:234) With Gurkhas guarding their planes at night, Master Sergeant Charles M. Lee, Staff Sergeant John D. McNamee, and Sergeant Hyland led five other light plane pilots as they evacuated Colonel Masters' sick and wounded. The L-pilots continued until an alternative solution was found. Colonel Masters finally convinced General Lentaigne to divert a Sunderland seaplane from the Bay of Bengal to Lake Indawgyi to assist the effort. Altogether, nearly 400 casualties were airlifted to hospitals northeast of Dimapur. When Lieutenant Colonel Boebel located the group, the light plane commander immediately ordered them to return to India.

This was the 1ˢᵗ Air Commando Group's final action in support of Operation THURSDAY and the campaign that followed. General Arnold had sent Colonel Cochran and Colonel Alison to Burma to support General Wingate's Chindits. That mission was now completed. The operation breathed new life into the China-Burma-India Theater, and the air commandos had been promised a return to the United States. Yet, as the group began moving to the rear, desperate fighting on the plains of Manipur would give them no respite. Many did not go home following the Chindit Campaign. Those who stayed would write a new page in air commando history.

7

Imphal and Kohima

Earlier, on the plains of Manipur, Lieutenant General Mutaguchi's gamble, Operation U-GO, struggled to establish the flag of the Rising Sun on Indian soil. The Imperial General Headquarters emphasized the operation was to move the Japanese defensive line forward, forestall any British attack into Burma, and gain the political capital of occupying free India. War Minister Tojo's approval stated the operation's narrowly defined objective: "For the defense of Burma, the Commander in Chief Southern Army shall destroy the enemy on that front at the appropriate juncture and occupy and secure a strategic zone in North-East India in the area of Imphal." (1:167)

However, General Mutaguchi, commander of the Japanese 15th Army, had bigger plans than a strategically limited offensive with partisan overtones. He proposed to define the future of the war by betting heavily on the Japanese Army's ability to surround, demoralize, and destroy the British garrisons guarding the Assam supply hubs. The most lucrative target in 15th Army's plans was the Bengal-Assam Railway terminus at Dimapur—storehouse for IV Corps in the south, munitions railhead for offensive operations into Burma, and warehousing center for Hump supplies. Once the supply hub on the banks of the Brahmaputra River was in Japanese hands, 15th Army was prepared to continue into the heartland of India. Geography dictated the task. Connecting Dimapur to the British Army was a mountain road through Kohima to Imphal. General Mutaguchi intended to overpower these vital nodes by designing his Operation U-GO offensive to include four objectives:

(1) To encircle, starve, and destroy IV Corps.
(2) To sever at Dimapur, the Bengal-Assam railway, which was ...the lifeline to Stilwell's force, so the General would be compelled to return to his base at Ledo, leaving his road behind for Japanese use.
(3) To seize the Hump airfields and so dry up finally the supplies to China.
(4) To march on Delhi.

The operation started well for Mutaguchi but soon showed the weakness of Japanese planning. The first step, a diversionary offensive called Operation HA-GO, began on 4 February far to the south in the Arakan. Its primary purpose was to pin down British forces, thus preventing them from influencing the Assam offensive. Major General Tokutaro Sakurai crossed the Mayu Range, caught Major General Frank W. Messervy in his pajamas, and sealed off the 5th Indian Division headquarters at the supply dump in Sinzweya—a place known as the Admin Box. Relying on the successful 1942 tactics of encirclement, sudden night attacks, and cut communications, Sakurai anticipated quick victory. Instead, the British dug in, called for air re-supply, and exhausted the Japanese initiative.

Light planes from "D" squadron became embroiled in the Battles of Admin Box. From 4 February until the end of the month, the British fought back. During that time, "D" squadron, flying in and out at treetop level, kept the British spirits high by delivering mail and newspapers, bringing in replacement, and evacuating the wounded. In all, the squadron removed nearly 700 British to a rear airfield called Reindeer 2 near Ramu for transfer to C-47 Dakotas. Impressed by the light plane pilot's courage and proficiency, Air Marshal Baldwin made a personal visit to offer his congratulations.

With air commando light airplanes flying medical support missions and transport aircraft providing constant food and munitions lines of communication, British tanks and guns determined the outcome of the battle. Operation HA-GO ended far ahead of Japanese Burma Area Army's intended schedule, before the end of February, with more than 5,000 of the Emperor's soldiers dead on the field. General Slim later wrote, "A British force had met, held and decisively defeated a major Japanese attack...its effect, not only on the troops engaged, but on the whole XIV Army, was immense." (44:213) Despite the setback, 15th Army's offensive continued to march down the time line. Lieutenant General Motozo Yanagida's 33rd Division, the first Japanese troops involved in Operation U-GO, moved out on 7 March 1944.

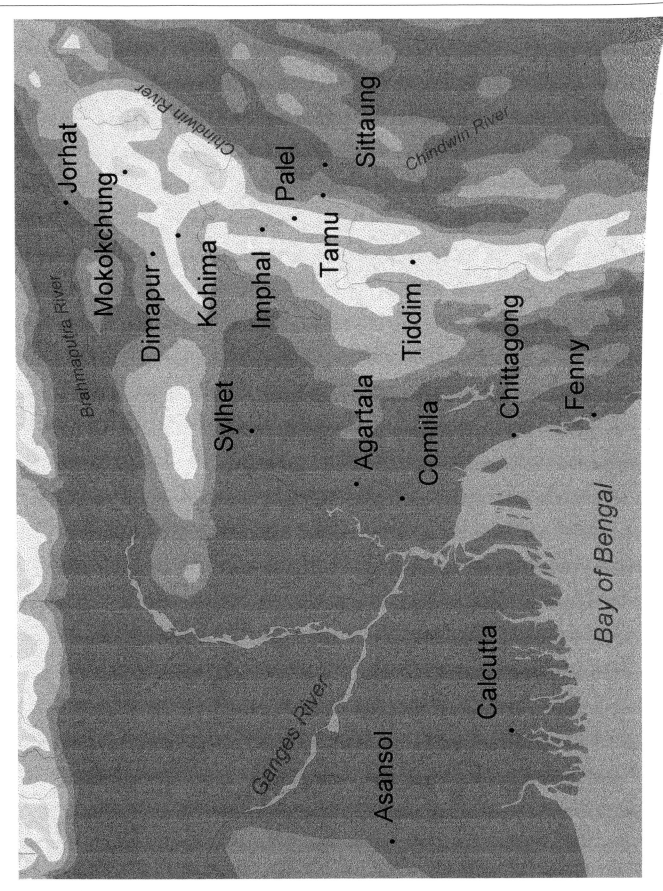

Map 8-East India and Burma 1944: Operation U-GO

The Japanese Imperial Army's 1942 conquest of Burma had been steeped in maneuver and mobility, and during the early Imphal battle, the savage fighting appeared to favor 15th Army. What Mutaguchi could not know was General Slim had decided to meet the Japanese army on the Imphal Plateau because the territory favored his XIV Army. Slim later wrote, "I was tired of fighting the Japanese when they had a good line of communications behind them and I had an execrable one. This time I would reverse the procedure." (44:250) Admiral Lord Mountbatten concurred and took action outside normal channels. Rather than ask U.S. permission through his deputy, General Stilwell, Admiral Lord Mountbatten directly wired the British Chief of Staff and British Joint Staff Mission in Washington. He stated his intention to divert 30 C-47 Dakota-equivalents from Hump missions unless contrary orders were received in 2 days. The bold action was approved the following day; at once, 20 C-46 Commandos began flying cargo into Imphal. As Mountbatten and Slim waited for the drama to unfold, they ultimately hoped a defeat of the Rising Sun in India would propel a counteroffensive to dislodge all Japanese troops from Northern Burma. The next move belonged to Japan.

It came faster than expected. Avoiding early detection, Yanagida's 33rd Division rushed two tank battalions and artillery into India along the Tiddim Road. If able to advance quickly, 15th Army hoped to cut off British troops operating south of Imphal and capture a major supply site established at mile marker 109. After preliminary success, General Yanagida received a garbled message from a subordinate concerning a negligible setback and slowed to a *controlled advance*. Inexplicably, he then dispatched a signal recommending the operation be aborted. While Yanagida delayed, the British slipped through the Japanese noose, destroyed the supply site, and withdrew to Imphal. Enraged, General Mutaguchi spurred his reluctant division commander to restart the offensive. There were more problems.

On 18 March 1944, Major General Masafumi Yamauchi's 15th Division launched what was intended to be a coordinated attack on the Imphal citadel. His objective was to cut the main northern route connecting Imphal to Dimapur via the summit pass of Kohima. As his division advanced, Yamauchi's 58th Regiment commander, Major General Shigesaburo Miyazaki, became distracted with dislodging British troops occupying the out-of-sector village of Sangshak. After nearly a week of fierce fighting, Sangshak finally was cleared, but the tariff was dear—time, more than 500 men, and most of the experienced company commanders in Miyazaki's regiment.

Finally able to get both 15th Division and 33rd Division reengaged, General Mutaguchi watched Operation U-GO begin to show results. In measured steps, the garrison approaches, resembling a spoked wheel with roads radiating from Imphal in all directions, were either cut or occupied by Japanese soldiers. The surprise and strength of the attack left Lieutenant General Geoffrey A. P. Scoones, IV Corps commander, and the men inside Imphal isolated. But as long as the munitions and supplies of the citadel were still held by British troops, sand continued to run out of Japan's fragile hour glass.

Alongside the British at Imphal were members of the 1st Air Commando Group. Communication specialists Master Sergeant Thomas Gibbons, Technical Sergeant Andrew M. Ternosky, Private First Class John J. Miller, and Private First Class Henry Galbraith were caught inside the city during Operation U-GO. Operating *Uncle Bud One*, a forward air warning control center established at Imphal before Operation THURSDAY began, they were bolstered by the arrival of two fellow air commandos. Captain Lewis S. Smith and Master Sergeant John H. Porter drove into the city just days before the 15th Army invasion began. Although neither Smith nor Porter intended to stay, their return route was cut by the Japanese advance.

Enveloped by Japanese, General Scoones became concerned about evacuating injured or wounded personnel. At the request of the British, the 1st Air Commando Group sent Dakotas and Waco gliders into Imphal to join other aircraft in a massive airlift. Flying daily missions, transport pilots flew 7,360 sorties bringing cargo and supplies into the village while returning to hospitals in Comilla, Chittagong, and Ledo with the sick and wounded. Also sent to Imphal was Staff Sergeant Ben T. Harris, Jr., an air commando liaison pilot. Throughout the siege, he and others flew medical evacuation and supply missions in and out of the surrounded citadel. During the first month of the airlift, 744 sick and wounded men were removed from Imphal, but as the fighting intensified, the number of troops requiring hospital care increased steadily. Medical

Light Planes at Admin Box

Members of the Liaison Section's "D" Flight at Cox's Bazar in the Arakan. *Seated* **(L-R) Staff Sergeant Daniel G. Claus; Staff Sergeant Russell L. Parrott, Jr.; Staff Sergeant Edward F. "Murphy" Hladovcak; Technical Sergeant Joe L. Cunningham; Staff Sergeant John C. "Jack" Gallagher** *Standing* **(L-R) Staff Sergeant Hugh A. Coll; Staff Sergeant Bernard P. Dole; Staff Sergeant John A. "Nick" Nickolson; Staff Sergeant Clarance A. Lingle, Jr.; Staff Sergeant Arthur E. Burrell; Staff Sergeant Woodrow W. Reynolds** *Courtesy of Art Burrell, 1st Air Commando Association*

evacuations for May spiraled to 4,400, and by the height of fighting in June, the monthly figures showed 5,295 casualties were moved.

As the siege extended into weeks, SEAC commanders and staff recommended a variety of options. Debunking suggestions to use tanks as battering rams, General Slim relied instead on Allied air superiority. Noting the success of General Wingate's jungle lines of communication, General Slim proposed supplying IV Corps by airdrop. He was prepared to continue even into the impending monsoon season, if necessary. By borrowing 70 aircraft intended for the Mediterranean campaign, diverting 20 C-46 Commandos from Hump missions, and re-tasking the 76 Dakotas already in Northern Burma, Admiral Lord Mountbatten used every available aircraft in the CBI to save the beleaguered city. It was to be the largest air supply operation in World War II up to that time.

The airlift was aptly called Operation STAMINA, and the results were spectacular. Despite limited all-weather airfields and frequent cloudbursts between April and June, 12,000 reinforcements and 21,600 tons of supplies were flown into the garrison at Imphal. At the same time, 43,000 noncombatants and 14,927 casualties were evacuated. Beginning 29 March, 28,000 British and 90,000 Indian troops were wholly sustained by air supply. Airmen delivered more than 14,000,000 pounds of rations, nearly 1,000,000 gallons of fuel, roughly 40,000,000 cigarettes, and over 1,000 bags of mail to Imphal. Toward the end of June, the warehouses of the fortress even began to show a slight surplus. Drawing materiel from Sylhet, Fenny, Agartala, Comilla, and Chittagong, whatever IV Corps requested, within reason, was delivered.

Most supplies were flown into either Palel or Imphal Main— the only two all-weather strips available. Both airfields were located within the British perimeter, but isolated units relied on parachute drops. Among the items airlifted to the waiting troops were live mules, sheep, and goats, and also more conventional equipment and provisions. Even prefabricated bridging material was delivered to the British via the overhead lines of communication. Standardized loads were attempted to meet the mounting demands of IV Corps. Chittagong was established as the primary airfield for shipping ammunition, Fenny specialized in petroleum, oil, and lubricants (POL), and Sylhet handled supplies. Other airfields overlapped each other's supplies to ensure commodities were always available. The airfield at Agartala was the hub for multiple stocks, such as supplies, ordnance, signal stores, and mail. Comilla was responsible for reinforcements, medical, ordnance, and ammunition. Jorhat controlled canteen stores, mail, reinforcements, and ordnance. With respites only for aircraft servicing and repairs, transport pilots flew day after day. There was no lull for maintenance crews.

While Imphal was under siege, Kohima, astride the vital mountain pass connecting Manipur and the supply-rich Assam region, was teetering. General Mutaguchi realized Japanese success depended on the third prong of his offensive. Ordered to seize the village "with the speed of wildfire," Lieutenant General Kotoku

Sato's inexperienced 31ˢᵗ Division clumsily applied pressure in a deadly pincer movement on Kohima. Systematically, the redoubt was reduced to a triangle of ground no more than 500 yards on a side. Admiral Lord Mountbatten, anticipating the crisis, decisively ordered the mountain village be re-supplied by air and flew in reinforcements. Instead of the workhorse Dakotas, C-46 crews conducted the bulk of the operation because the Commando had twice the carrying capacity of the more nimble C-47. In time, the Commando pilots were up to the task as British troops reported complete loads of bagged rice were dropped into areas no more than 100 yards in diameter. The besieged Kohima garrison thus stood, a stubborn obstacle between the Japanese and the food, ammunition, and weapons of Dimapur.

Lieutenant General Montagu G. N. Stopford's XXXIII Corps was immediately flown and railed to Dimapur to relieve Japanese pressure on Kohima. Despite heavy commitments behind the lines in Burma, the Chindit's 23ʳᵈ Brigade and liaison pilots from the 1ˢᵗ Air Commando Group also relocated to Northern India to aid the British counterattack. On 1 April 1944, Staff Sergeant Julian Chiml and Staff Sergeant Hugh A. Coll began supporting the Chindits from Jorhat. Weather permitting, they flew rations and medical supplies from Jorhat south through the Naga Hills to fair weather air strips outside Kohima. When Chiml suffered a malaria attack, Staff Sergeant Howard L. Smith joined the operation. Later, just as Brigadier Lancelot E. C. M. Perowne prepared to lead the 23ʳᵈ Brigade south, Coll suffered from the same illness. The Chindit commander requested a replacement for Coll and additional light planes to support his march. In response, Colonel Cochran sent Staff Sergeants Lemuel A. Davis, Alfred J. Lieto, Harold C. Mendelson, and McNamee to augment Smith. On 23 April 1944, the small group was enlarged again. The L-5 pilots were joined by Staff Sergeant William E. Bussells, Jr. who flew medical evacuation missions in an air commando L-1 Vigilant.

Pre-monsoon rains began early in 1944 and the British hastily had to prepare light plane airfields as they moved south. Small clearings soon dotted the landscape. From a former rugby field at Mokokchung in Naga Hill country to Kezoma, and finally Chakhabama, British engineers carved out flat strips. As the rains increased, the rutted runway and deep mud at Chakhabama made landings perilous. Under the direction of a well-meaning RAF flight lieutenant, bamboo matting was laid on top of the runway to keep the light plane's wheels from sinking in the mud. The solution was almost as bad as the problem.

By word of mouth, the Flying Sergeants advised others to use their brakes sparingly because the matting tended to roll up. Unprepared for this precaution, Lieutenant Colonel Boebel flew into Chakhabama to discuss how long the missions could be continued. After he applied brakes, the Sentinel's landing gear caught on the mat and Boebel's L-5 swung into another aircraft. Fortunately the light plane commander could fly out; the damage was not severe— merely pride, a propeller, both struts, and his flying hat.

Operation STAMINA
Between April and June 1944, transport crews flew 12,000 reinforcements and 21,600 tons of supplies into Imphal. It was the largest air supply operation in World War II up to that time. *Courtesy of 1ˢᵗ Air Commando Association*

After considering the pending monsoons and lack of all-weather airfields, the air commandos and Brigadier Perowne decided the light planes would have to shut down in June. The last L-5 departure closed the book with the operational records showing the liaison pilots flew more than 300 hours and evacuated 154 casualties. The 23rd Brigade's defensive campaign was critical to XXXIII Corps' successful relief of Kohima.

Throughout the battle for Imphal and Kohima, the Wingate and Cochran team gnawed away at the hindquarters of the dragon. Their actions at White City and Aberdeen disrupted General Mutaguchi's anemic logistics system and occupied troops intended for Operation U-GO. Dakotas from the 1st Air Commando Group continued to provide rations and supplies to the Chindits and the light plane sections worked with Merrill's Marauders and Stilwell's advancing Chinese. Air commando C-47 and GC-4A pilots also evacuated the wounded and typhus-ravaged troops fighting in the Kabaw Valley. To relieve over-tasked C-47 crews, USAAF Mitchell and RAF Wellington bombers began flying ammunition and bombs into Imphal. Crewmen from other multi-engine aircraft supplemented the exhausted Dakota crews. Thus, pressure continued to be applied to 15th Army's precarious Tiddim Road line of communication. Meanwhile, Japanese soldiers were instructed to consume only one-third normal rations and eat foraged food as much as possible. With irony the Emperor's Finest watched from the hills overlooking Imphal as their encircled British counterparts received more

than 400 tons of rations, munitions, petroleum, and medical supplies each day.

Time had become an enemy to the Japanese forces. The fate of the 33rd Division is illustrative of the bloodshed that resulted. General Yanagida's slow pace threw off all time tables and hampered the offensive. After many attempts, General Mutaguchi was convinced 33rd Division's commander lacked spirit and drive. On 22 May 1944, the 15th Army commander replaced Yanagida with Lieutenant General Nubuo Tanaka. As the new commander of 33rd Division, Tanaka found himself at the head of a retreating army. By the end of the operation, the division strength would wither from almost 17,000 troops to little more than 3,000 effective soldiers. Replacement units planned for the offensive never arrived on Indian soil; instead soldiers were thrown against the marauding Chindits in the rear area and Stilwell's troops advancing down the Hukawng Valley.

Japan had launched Operation U-GO with sparse provision; success was dependent on a quick, decisive victory. As the siege persisted, Nippon troops were exhorted, "The struggle now has developed into a fight between the material strength of the enemy and our spiritual strength.... Continue in the task till all your ammunition is expended, till all your strength is exhausted. If your hands are broken, fight with your feet. If your hands and feet are broken, use your teeth.... Lack of weapons is no excuse for defeat." (14:470) Grasping for victory, General Mutaguchi ordered the 31st Division

Light Plane Operators
Maintaining a British defensive campaign that extended from Johrat to Chakhabama, Technical Sergeant Howard L. Smith and seven other Air Commando light plane pilots evacuated 154 casualties. In a lighter moment, Sergeant Smith and Staff Sergeant Bernard P. "Bernie" Dole feed an India monkey named Bongy. *Courtesy of 1st Air Commando Association*

to "Advance on Dimapur at once," but General Sato withdrew to seek supplies instead. When General Sato argued that his men had not received food or ammunition and were too weak to fight, the initiative was lost. Burma Area Army followed his action by countermanding Mutaguchi's order. Accused of being mentally unstable, General Sato was relieved and sent elsewhere.

Likewise was General Yamauchi's fate. His bold soldiers were met by British tanks as the 15th Division tried to advance on Imphal. Here General Slim used his tank's mobility and firepower to decimate Yamauchi's division. General Mutaguchi, directing from 15th Army Headquarters in Indainggyi, Burma, implored the division to advance. When 15th Division fell back in retreat, General Mutaguchi ordered them to maintain position unless authorized by higher headquarters. But General Slim's coordinated attack had depleted division strength. Commanding less than four combat battalion equivalents and physically racked with malaria, General Yamauchi elected not to reply to such impossible demands. Mercilessly, General

Mutaguchi dismissed the ailing division commander. General Yamauchi would die in a rear area of Burma within months.

Allied endurance paid off on 22 June 1944 when IV Corps from Imphal and Kohima's XXXIII Corps met at mile marker 109. The siege was over. In General Slim's order of the day, he said, "What you owe to your comrades in the Allied air forces I need not remind you. Our whole plan of battle was based on their support. There would have been no success had they failed us. Their share in our combined victory was magnificent and historic." General Sir George Giffard, Command in Chief of Eastern Army, echoed those sentiments in a letter dated 28 July. The correspondence was addressed to General Slim but intended for all who paved the way to the successful Imphal relief effort:

> In writing this I have not forgotten the immense debt which the Army owes to the Air. It is no exaggeration to say that without the really magnificent assistance given by the Eastern Air Command, the Army could never have won its victories. I am sure no one who watched them is likely to forget the courage, determination and skill of the aircraft pilots and crews who have flown through some of the worst weather in the world over appalling country ... to deliver reinforcements, supplies, ammunition, etc., to the troops isolated in the Arakan, Imphal and Central Burma. (25:301)

The ability of General Slim's commanders to hold Kohima and Imphal and the Chindits' interruption of replacements, rations, medical supplies, and munitions progressively frustrated the resolve of Japan's most seasoned troops. Unable to win swiftly, General Mutaguchi hoped to regroup during the monsoons; instead, he discovered the Commoner General elected not to disengage. A gored and exhausted dragon, the Japanese continued to fight with rabid passion, but by late June, the backs of 15th Army's field commanders were broken. The end finally came on 5 July when the Japanese Imperial Headquarters ordered Burma Area Army to close down General Mutaguchi's gambit.

As indicated in Table 4 below, the officially reported Japanese losses were staggering—and these were conservative estimates. Japanese historians quote General Mutaguchi's end strength of combat units at less than 12,000. Nippon support units suffered as well. Their number before the offensive was placed at 50,000; afterwards, General Slim calculated there were no more than 35,000 soldiers in Mutaguchi's staff, transportation, and supply organizations. Imperial General Headquarters' estimates included casualties categorized as sick or wounded, but in truth, a far greater than normal percentage were deaths since medical care for Japanese wounded was almost negligible. On the other side of the ledger were 40,000 British casualties; included in that number were 15,000 dead. Although the figures were somewhat similar, the notable difference between British and Japanese combat loses was many of General Slim's sick and wounded recuperated in hospitals throughout India.

TABLE 4
Imphal and Kohima: Japanese Army Losses

Organization	Commander	Before	Killed	Missing	Disease	Medical	After
15 Division	Yamauchi	16,804	3,678	747	3,843	3,703	3,309
31 Division	Sato	15,000	3,700	500	2,064	2,800	5,936
33 Division	Yanagida	18,000	5,065	405	2,500	4,500	5,530
Total		49,804	12,443	1,652	8,407	11,003	14,775

Note: Of the 14,775 soldiers, Japanese sources stated "The great majority of those on duty were sick, suffering from wounds and malnutrition"

The havoc wrought on the Plains of Imphal and in the tiny mountain village of Kohima was evident as General Slim pursued the Emperor's 15th Army down the Tiddim Road. The amount of carnage suggested to General Slim and his corps commanders that continued pressure would open Burma like an overripe watermelon and crush the reeling Nippon war machine. Former SEAC Intelligence Officer Louis Allen described the surreal scene as XIV Army pursued the remnants of the Japanese army into the Chin Hills of Burma.

The tatterdemalion divisions staggered back along the mountain roads. Weapons gone, clutching a stick in one hand and rice tin in the other, the Japanese stumbled painfully through the torrential rain. The lucky casualties were taken to the Chindwin on horse-drawn sledges, others bounced to and fro on sodden stretchers. The more seriously wounded lay by the side of the tracks. The pain from untended wounds, the frantic hunger, and the inward racking of malaria and dysentery pushed

them inexorably to the moment when they would beg passersby for a hand grenade with which to finish themselves off.

Some were too weak even to ask for that and lay with the maggots of putrefaction squirming and wriggling in eyes, noses, mouths. Even the walking wounded were too exhausted to brush off the white worms that gathered in their long matted hair, so that they gave the odd appearance of hoary sages tottering down the jungle tracks...They were soldiers no longer. As the historian Kojima Noboru writes, "15 Army, once released from battle, was no longer a body of soldiers, but a herd of exhausted men." As they pressed on down the Kabaw Valley, a trap for every bacillus of dysentery, typhus, and malaria, their generals tried to keep a semblance of organized movement.

At Sittaung, they waited to be taken across the Chindwin, and British planes swooped down on them. The river banks were heaped with corpses, and it was impossible to tell whether the piles of mud and blood, eaten up by maggots, were the corpses of human beings, or heaps of earth. Some were already picked clean, and as the British planes flew off, their place was taken in the sky by hovering flocks of vultures. (1:313)

When the curtain of rain finally lifted from the China-Burma-India Theater, the wall of water had washed away more than General Mutaguchi's three divisional generals. As the ragtag remains of the Imperial Army fled across the Chindwin River, the ramifications of the Rising Sun's worst defeat reached into the highest echelons of the Japanese Army. Among the collateral victims was the Japanese War Minister himself. Two days after the order to halt Operation U-GO, Tojo's Cabinet fell. General Kuniaki Koiso was named War Minister on 7 July 1944. In rapid succession other dominoes began to fall. General Kawabe, Burma Area Army Commander, was sacked and transferred to the mainland on 30 August 1944. In his place, the Japanese Imperial General Headquarters selected General Hyotaro Kimura, a Tojo-protege known for shrewdness, strategic planning skill, and flexibility. On the same day as Kawabe's removal, Lieutenant General Shihachi Katamura took command of the Japanese 15th Army. Unceremoniously, a nondescript position

Air Evacuation
Despite being encircled by Japanese soldiers, C-47 Dakota crews transferred litter patients from Imphal and Kohima to surrounding British hospitals. On 1st Air Commando Dakotas a plug hatch fitted into the left door frame for easier access to the aircraft's snatch equipment. In this picture, the plug has been removed. *Courtesy of 1st Air Commando Association*

on the General Staff in Tokyo awaited General Mutaguchi. Both Burma Area Army and 15th Army staffs suffered as well.

Operation THURSDAY is rarely cited for its strategic value by Allied historians; in some cases, evaluation of the Chindit operation is so obviously biased, the report fails reliability. Despite such mistreatment, the Japanese acknowledge the contribution of the air commandos' protection and support of the 3rd Indian Division to the abortive Operation U-GO offensive. After the war, the Japanese Imperial Army generals spoke of the failed offensive and pointed out very succinctly their assessment of the impact of Operation THURSDAY and the LRP phase that followed: "The penetration of the airborne force into Northern Burma caused the failure of the Army plan to complete the Imphal Operations...the airborne raiding force... eventually became one of the reasons for the total abandonment of Northern Burma." (105:61) In a monograph, General Mutaguchi admitted, "The Chindit invasion did not stop our plans to attack Kohima but they had a decisive effect on these operations, and they drew off the whole of 53rd Division and parts of 15th Division, one Regiment of which would have turned the scales at Kohima." Others of the 15th Army staff affirmed the operation had the following impacts:

(1)   The [15th] Army was unable to advance its headquarters until the end of April because it was forced to provide measures against the airborne force. Consequently, communication with various groups became inadequate and eventually caused a hostile attitude between the Army and its divisions in later operations.

(2)   Transportation of supplies to units engaged in the Imphal Operations became very difficult because of damage to roads which prevented the transfer of vehicles from the rear preparation area to the Shwebo-Tiddim Road.

(3)   Elements of the 15th Division, 24th Independent Mixed Brigade, and 53rd Division scheduled for the Imphal operations, were involved elsewhere.

(4)   The 5th Air Division was forced to operate against the enemy airborne units.

(5)   The 18th Division which was fighting desperately in the Hukawng area had to deal with an increasingly difficult situation due to interception of the supply route.

Furthermore, Lieutenant General Takazo Numata, Chief of Staff of the Japanese Southern Army, affirmed the impact by saying, "The difficulty encountered in dealing with the airborne forces was ever a source of worry to all the headquarters staffs of Japanese army and contributed materially to the Japanese failure in the Imphal and Hukawng operations." (7:289) Apparent from the remarks of Lieutenant General Eitaro Naka, Chief of Staff, Japanese Burma Area Army, is the effectiveness of the air commandos' *forward air controller* raids on the supply dumps at Indaw. He certified the Indaw lines of communication became useless as they were "wiped out by bombing and ground raids." (7:289)

Because actions speak louder than words, the most telling argument for the operation can be found in Lieutenant General Sato's actions during Operation U-GO. By late April, his unit, the 31st Division, was feeling the effects of Operation THURSDAY; they were very short of ammunition, provisions, and food. In May, General Sato sent a message to General Mutaguchi stating, "Since leaving the Chindwin we have not received one bullet from you, nor a grain of rice." (48:230) Food was in such short supply, some men subsisted on grass and black slugs; sickness, such as beriberi, was sapping the 31st Division's fighting ability. Finally, General Sato radioed General Mutaguchi that he was withdrawing from Kohima. When threatened with a court martial, General Sato replied, "Do what you please. I will bring you [General Mutaguchi] down with me." (48:230) Ordered back into the fray, he refused again, saying, "The 15th Army has failed to send me supplies and ammunition since the operation began. This failure releases me from any obligation to obey the order—and in any case it would be impossible to comply." (35:156)

The successful execution of Operation THURSDAY had caused the pendulum to swing in favor of the Allies. Clearly from the testimony, the Allied air invasion was directly instrumental in defeating the Imperial Japanese Army. Additionally, General Wingate's LRP theory was completely substantiated. The air commandos and the Chindits had caused widespread confusion and uncertainty behind the enemy's forward areas that led to a progressive weakening and misdirection of the Japanese main forces. Heavily influenced by the actions of the 1st Air Commando Group and the 3rd Indian Division, a nation known for fanatical obedience suffered the ultimate shame of having a general breakdown in combat and abdicate. Colonel Cochran and General Wingate had accomplished their task. They helped bring the Nippon war machine to its knees and made it possible for XIV Army to unleash the Allied hounds on the badly mauled Japanese dragon. At Imphal and Kohima, General Slim picked up the scent of victory. Until the end of the war, the Nippon aggressor of 1942 would become a hounded prey.

8

Monsoons

Even before the beginning of the 1944 monsoon rains and the crushing defeat of the Nipponese Army at Imphal and Kohima, General Arnold recognized the impact of his vision on the Japanese. Shortly after Operation THURSDAY, he began planning the creation of more air commando units. In the 1st Air Commando Group, General Arnold created a means of projecting air power without dependence on ground transportation. Applied fully in an area such as Burma, additional air commando units could spare ground forces long, tedious marches where surface lines of communication were sometimes impractical, if not altogether impossible. He planned to deploy four more air commando groups and associated cargo support to the China-Burma-India Theater to airlift the British Army further into Central and Southern Burma. Commitment dates for the air commando and combat cargo group activations were established as 15 July, 15 August, 15 September, and 15 October 1944. General Arnold intended for the United States to retake that Southeast Asian country from the air!

As he formulated his Air Task Force strategy, General Arnold saw each of the air commando groups and a counterpart organization, combat cargo groups, as two pieces of the same puzzle. Lieutenant General Barney M. Giles, Deputy Commander of the Army Air Forces, described the interrelated missions of the two types of organizations by explaining that they were similar to the island-hopping tactics of the Pacific Theater. Air commando groups would team with British Chindits to initially seize and defend landing sites. In turn, combat cargo groups were to provide large-scale air transport of ground troops and their supplies to enclaves established by air commando groups. Once Special Force was positioned and provisioned to advance, the columns would need fire power. Using fighters, the air commando groups were to clear the skies and provide close air support to columns engaged in combat operations.

In General Arnold's scheme, the two separate but related organizations were essential to placing troops behind enemy lines and keeping them supplied. Therefore, he proposed to use them in combination as a single Air Task Force. As each air commando group was activated, a combat cargo group would mushroom alongside.

By the time Colonel Alison had returned to the United States in April 1944, General Arnold had activated two each air commando and combat cargo groups. Colonel Alison was to direct the training of the air commando units and monitor the activation, organization, and training of two additional groups sometime in the near future.

General Arnold modeled the newly formed 2nd and 3rd Air Commando Groups after the Cochran-Alison original except sec-

Second Commander of the 1st Air Commando Group
Colonel Clinton B. Gaty shortly after he assumed command of the 1st Air Commando Group. *Courtesy of 1st Air Commando Association*

1ˢᵗ Air Commando Group Headquarters, Asansol, India **The plaque at the base of the flagpole reads, "Dedicated to the men of the 1ˢᵗ Air Commando Group who have given their lives."** *Courtesy of 1ˢᵗ Air Commando Association*

tions were given squadron designations. Each activated air commando unit consisted of the following four components:

(1) Two P-51 squadrons of 25 aircraft each with long-range equipment and suitable armament for ground neutralization of the enemy air force.
(2) One Troop Carrier Squadron, highly trained and specialized in glider operations—the squadron was equipped with 16 C-47 aircraft and 32 CG-4A Hadrian gliders.
(3) Three liaison squadrons, each with 32 litter-carrying L-5 [Sentinels] and a small complement of UC-64 Norsemen, and
(4) Support organizations—one company of airborne engineers, a service group for each two Air Commando Groups, four airdrome squadrons, and one Air Depot Group common to both Air Commando Groups and Combat Cargo Groups.

Thus, the air commandos were self-sustaining units, equipped to establish island-airfields in the heart of enemy-held territory. Once Chindit units were deployed in the field, General Arnold would use the combat cargo group to keep the logistic lifeline open. Each combat cargo unit was made up of two elements:

(1) Airlift forces consisting of four C-47 squadrons of 25 aircraft each: Although equipped for double tow, their main job was to move in troops and re-supply them once they began operating in enemy territory.

(2) Various service organizations: There would be a special service group for each three Combat Cargo Groups, four airdrome squadrons, and an Aerial Re-supply Depot for packing supplies to be delivered by air.

If all four air commando and combat cargo organizations had been activated, General Arnold's commitment to the re-conquest of Burma would have been staggering. In excess of the air assets already in the CBI Theater, General Arnold intended to allocate an additional 200 P-51 Mustangs, 464 C-47 Dakotas, 128 CG-4A Waco gliders, 384 L-5 Sentinels, and approximately 50 UC-64 Norsemen! As the planning progressed, the makeup of the combat cargo group was changed to C-46 Commandos. But General Arnold's plan was never fully enacted.

After General Arnold related his intentions, Colonel Alison stated he did not believe the British intended to invade Central and Southern Burma. Alison later explained, "In this campaign the only two activist officers arguing for the recapture of Burma were General Wingate and General Stilwell who was fighting to reestablish the Burma Road. The British General Staff apparently had other ideas, and with the death of General Wingate...the momentum for retaking Burma died with him." (120:9 July 1986 Letter from John R. Alison) General Arnold immediately recalled Colonel Cochran from the field for confirmation; later, the Chief of the Army Air Corps visited Sir John Dill, the senior British officer stationed in Washington. Colonel Alison's evaluation of British intentions was affirmed. Although General Arnold fought tenaciously to keep his Air Task Force idea alive by appealing to Admiral Lord Mountbatten, he was rebuffed.

The matter was turned over to Eastern Air Command in an attempt to keep the plan's faint hopes energized. During the summer, General Stratemeyer wrote General Arnold noting, "In effect the operations being conducted in Burma by British, American, and Chinese [are] all one big air commando action as regards air supply." (113:25 June 1944 Letter) As late as 20 June 1944, Eastern Air Command organizational blueprints still included Arnold's vision. The command's infrastructure consisted of six components: Strategic Air Force, Third Tactical Air Force, Photographic Reconnaissance Force, Tenth Air Force, 293 Wing, and Arnold's Air Task Force. However, the Air Task Force alternative was not earnestly considered because the unit was not constituted until late in the planning season nor had General Stratemeyer's staff adequately defined its responsibilities. In part this was because of the following factors:

(1) From the outset, staff support of long-range penetration was noticeably cool;

(2) Establishing the air task force, if not at the bottom of SEAC priorities, was far enough down to have the effect of a dead letter; and

(3) SEAC staff plans continued to emphasize amphibious operations.

Without Lord Mountbatten's full support, General Arnold turned elsewhere to keep his idea intact. At General Stratemeyer's urging, he offering General Stilwell both the 2nd and 3rd Air Commando Groups. Unlike Admiral Lord Mountbatten, the Infantry General did not equivocate but just as surely declined when he replied:

To take full advantage ... I must have troops as competent and as well organized to do the job as your specially trained and organized [Air] Commandos and Combat Cargo units.... If you will secure for me one or more American Division, I will prove the value of Air Commando units and I think I can make Buck Rogers ashamed of himself.... If you can get me a few good American troops, we can go to town. P. S. "A few good American troops" is two divisions. (80:26 June 1944 Letter)

Shortly after General Arnold conceived his Air Task Force idea, Colonel Cochran moved the 1st Air Commando Group to the drier climate of Northeast India. Upon arrival in Asansol, the number of men began to thin out. Cochran convinced General Stilwell to send personnel back to the United States if they had completed two tours of duty in the war. Falling into that category were most of the section commanders and their deputies—Lieutenant Colonel Mahony, Lieutenant Colonel Smith, Major Radovich, Major Cherry, Captain Sartz—as well as Colonel Cochran himself. Before answering Arnold's request to conference in Washington and continuing on to a subsequent assignment to General Eisenhower's staff, he relinquished the 1st Air Commando Group to Colonel Gaty on 20 May 1944. As Colonel Cochran departed the theater, some crews of the C-47 transport section and a handful of light plane pilots were still active in Northern Burma.

Colonel Gaty immediately set out to prepare his new command for the anticipated follow-on action in Burma. During the monsoon season, several fighters, commanded by Major Duke Phillips, Jr., were placed on detached service with 20th Bomber Command. As B-29 Superfortresses were forward staged to Eastern India, a dozen air commando pilots, flying a mix of A and B model P-51 Mustangs and reconditioned P-40N Tomahawks, were stationed at Kalaikunda to provide airfield protection. Six more fighter crews

Terry's Tavern, Asansol, India
The tail section of a Japanese Oscar rests in front of the Non-Commissioned Officers Club. *Courtesy of 1st Air Commando Association*

Asansol Officers Club
The interior of the Asansol Officers Club was decorated with characters from Milton Caniff's *Terry and the Pirates* **comic strip.** *Courtesy of 1st Air Commando Association*

Interior of Asansol Officers Club
Continuation of the Interior of Asansol Officers Club. The artwork was done by First Lieutenant Steve T. Uminski, glider pilot. *Courtesy of 1ˢᵗ Air Commando Association*

pulled alert at another Indian airfield, Chakulia. While carrying out these missions, Second Lieutenant John M. Ferron, a replacement pilot, was killed when his airplane crashed into a brick revetment at Kalaikunda. Two other pilots died during training missions—Second Lieutenant Leonard D. Waters lost control during a practice dive bombing run and Second Lieutenant Merle E. Reed's aircraft got too low.

For those at Asansol, Colonel Gaty initiated a physical conditioning program, formed work details to repair all usable equipment, and opened the supply channels to secure any needed new materiel. Camp repairs were also required. Asansol was a deserted Royal Air Force Base of plastered brick barracks and thatch-covered tile roofs. During the coming spring, rice grains, embedded in the straw, sprouted on the roof; the shoots momentarily turned green only to fade to yellow in the intense heat of summer. The barrack windows were screened with wooden shutters, but there was no glass to protect the men from the mosquitoes. When the camp was renovated, it included an outdoor theater, chapel, NCO Club called Terry's Tavern, mess hall named Ye Old Greasy Spoon, and post exchange. Staff Sergeant John M. Gourley, a light plane pilot, described the living conditions:

> In the hot humid weather, leather turned green overnight from mildew, so our shoes needed attention every day. Drinking water was kept in an unglazed clay jug. The slight evaporation through the jug wall kept the water cool. We slept on [charpoys] (Indian beds). Our [charpoys] were the size of a single bed, only lower. They had a wooden frame and legs, with hemp rope stretched inside the frame to support an Indian mattress...At each corner, a bamboo pole about 5 feet high was attached, then a mosquito net was tied to the poles. When go-

ing to bed we would crawl under the net, tucking it under the mattress, then spray inside with a mosquito bomb in case any mosquitoes had gotten in.... At times we would sleep outside hoping to get a breeze. (127:69)

The still air was stifling. Temperatures during midday in Central India parched the land. One pilot reported the outside air gauge in his airplane read 135 degrees Fahrenheit and the men began driving with the windshield up on jeeps so the wind would not burn their skin. Ever inventive, the air commandos devised a unique method of cooling the large 4-room office building at the camp. In the center of each room, 9 feet above the floor, was a large piece of burlap attached to a bamboo rod. The rods were coupled to a long rope running the length of the building; the line exited the exterior wall of the building at the end. Outside on the ground, an Indian boy was hired to pull the cord making the burlap fans move back and forth to provide a cooling breeze to the rooms inside.

The primitive base water supply suffered in the heat along with the men and required the air commandos to work around the very poor system of piping. Staff Sergeant John C. "Jack" Gallagher, a liaison pilot, described it in the following manner:

> The [water] line, a 2-inch [pipe], supplied the entire facility and it was laid on top of the ground.... the water when it arrived at our shower room was so hot you could have made tea with it.... it was so hot we couldn't take a shower after a day's work so we would just go and flake out on our sacks and go to sleep. Someone would always wake up about midnight and shout "Showers are ready" and we would all get up and go take a shower as the water had cooled off enough for human toleration. (120:—)

Ye Old Greasy Spoon, Asansol Cafeteria
The plastered brick and thatched-covered tile roof was characteristic of the abandoned British base. *Courtesy of 1ˢᵗ Air Commando Association*

Because of the conditions of the camp and of the group, Colonel Gaty allowed the men to take advantage of a liberal leave policy. Using the Indian railroad system or available Dakotas for transportation, some chose to recuperate by ranging into New Delhi, visiting Calcutta, or touring Agra, site of the Taj Mahal. The scenes were overpowering; however, Indian culture could also be disquieting. Private First Class William H. Morison never forgot the image of an unattended fly-infested corpse at the railway depot. No one paid attention to the dead man—he was an "untouchable."

Many commandos elected to travel north to Ranikhet, a rest camp in the rugged territory of ancient Kashmir. Not all the activities at this mountain resort were relaxing, though. On one trip, a couple B-25 Mitchell pilots, Captain Carl E. Ziegler, Jr. and First Lieutenant Frank B. Merchant, took off from Central India in a C-47 bound for a calming furlough in Kashmir. The day of the flight, the passengers could not see the majestic Himalayas below because of a solid layer of clouds. Nearing the destination, the aircraft suddenly developed engine trouble and in the rarefied air, the Dakota began to steadily lose altitude. Tension filled the air. The order was given to lighten the load, and as they had done so often before over Burma, the air commandos hurriedly began pushing bundles, suitcases, and equipment out the yawning side cargo door. Only a few personal belongings were safeguarded—primarily those belonging to the pilots. When the Dakota broke through the cloud deck and the countryside became visible, Captain Ziegler discovered the aircraft was directly over a rail line leading to a station. A field large enough to land was nearby. As repairs were made to the engine, the enterprising passengers borrowed a push cart and headed back up the tracks. By the time the Dakota was flight worthy, the air commandos recovered nearly 60 percent of the disgorged baggage.

Despite troubles such as these, the trips to India's capital, surrounding cultural centers, and the grandeur of Kashmir acted as a balm to the spirit of the group. On the manicured grounds of the Taj

Ranikhet Rest Camp
A view of Ranikhet, a rest camp in the rugged territory of ancient Kashmir. Personnel were quartered in a house boat; among the outdoor activities were horseback riding and water skiing. *Courtesy of 1ˢᵗ Air Commando Association*

Mahal, within the buttressed walls of the Red Fort, and in the countryside of the pristine Himalayan retreat, the men of the 1ˢᵗ Air Commando Group enjoyed the mystic surroundings, imposing architecture, scenic beauty, horseback riding, fishing, and boating of India. The terrors of war seemed more than just miles away.

Besides the strain on the men, the aircraft used by Cochran's old command required depot-level maintenance and restoration. In short order Colonel Gaty's men flew their ailing aircraft from Asansol to Bangalore, the major repair site located in Southern India. Often, after information gathered from crew chiefs and a thorough inspection by technical specialists, the aircraft were found in such war-weary condition, they had to be shelved. The Dakotas still operationally capable were put to use during Operation STAMINA.

To replace the current mixture of fighters, the air commandos requisitioned P-47D-23 Thunderbolts. The Republic-built aircraft featured a water injected turbo-supercharged Pratt & Whitney R-2800-59 power plant capable of producing 2,000 horsepower—crew chiefs cursed it. The Thunderbolt's engine had 18 cylinders and required 36 spark plugs. With eight .50-caliber machine guns and an ability to carry 2,500 pounds of ordnance, *Jugs* were formidable fighter-bombers. Most important for the CBI, the rugged Thunderbolt's range of 800 miles allowed deep forays into Central Burma.

Staying apace, the bomber section upgraded to a B-25H model that included a newly designed gun package. The 1,700-horsepower Mitchells embodied a new lighter version of the 75 mm cannon while increasing the total firepower to 14 Browning .50-caliber machine guns. Carrying more than 5,000 rounds of ammunition, the

Offbase Transportation
The jinrickisha taxi stand at the 1ˢᵗ Air Commando Group's rear gate. *Courtesy of 1ˢᵗ Air Commando Association*

in mid-September, the group could see clearly that events along the Indo-Burman border prior to and during the monsoons implied the next Allied step would be on Burmese soil.

A flurry of activities at all levels within the China-Burma-India Theater had occurred between the Battle of Imphal and the end of the monsoons. Admiral Lord Mountbatten began by replacing his pessimistic Chief of Staff, Lieutenant General Sir Henry Pownall, with Lieutenant General Frederick "Boy" Browning. Browning had not lost his luster despite the recent defeat of his parachute forces at Arnhem. He would provide the energy that was so often lacking in SEAC's strategic plans. Below SEAC Headquarters level, other personnel changes were needed. General George Giffard, his dislike for Mountbatten clearly evident, was sent home and his XI Army Group disbanded. In the place of XI Army, SEAC formed the Allied Land Forces Southeast Asia (ALFSE). To lead the newly formed integrated Anglo-American Headquarters, Admiral Lord Mountbatten welcomed Lieutenant General Oliver Leese who previously had commanded the VIII Army in Northern Africa. Britain's Prime Minister Churchill saw this move as an opportunity to "ginger-up...the slothful India Command." ALFSE would control XIV Army, NCAC, and the Logistics Command.

The new command structure freed General Slim's headquarters to plan the invasion of Central Burma. His first move was to find a man with instincts to lead the charge into the very belly of the Japanese dragon. When Lieutenant General Scoones, IV Corps commander, received a promotion to Commander-in-Chief, Central Command, India, General Slim replaced him with a leader who

was "not too calculating of odds," Lieutenant General Messervy. (44:322) The reorganization placed the Commoner General at the head of the single largest army of World War II. Lieutenant General Messervy's IV Corps joined Lieutenant General Stopford's Imphal-hardened XXXIII Corps, and Lieutenant General A. F. Philip Christison's XV Corps to make up General Slim's XIV Army. With the changes, General Slim believed he had a stable of spirited horses to make a sprint into Burma—if properly blended with an aggressive strategy.

The swirling events that triggered the Japanese recoil from the Imphal Plains influenced the minds of General Slim's strategists. Throughout the war, SEAC planners continually wrung their hands when confronted with dislodging Japanese forces from Burma. A constant impediment to an invasion into Burma from the north was logistics. The topography, meager roads, and torrential monsoons made offensive approaches from India seemingly impossible. The major Burmese port of Rangoon long served to feed Central Burma, but the infrastructure marked this a one-way street. Many on the SEAC staff feared troops pushing southward were too far from stockpiles to sustain firepower or maintain momentum. General Slim saw things differently and analysis showed the unhinged U-GO offensive created a vortex that magnetically pulled his XIV Army into Central Burma.

All along the mountainous defiles of the Chin Hills was evidence of the rout—in addition to thousands of enemy dead or dying, the Japanese left behind weapons, equipment, and means of transport. Only the monsoons saved the Emperor's retreating army

B-25H Mitchell Gunship
In addition to the four .50-caliber machine guns and 75 mm nose-mounted cannon, North American B-25H Mitchells included twin packs under each cockpit side window. The total compliment of Browning .50-caliber machine guns was 14. *Courtesy of William Quinn, 1ˢᵗ Air Commando Association*

7 Volunteers, Replacement UC-64 Norsemen Pilots
***Back Row* (L-R) Second Lieutenant Donald C. Limburg; Flight Officer Albert E. Hainey; Second Lieutenant Jack A. Schweier; Second Lieutenant Neal B. Saxon** *Front Row* **(L-R) Second Lieutenant Dexter J. Taylor; Flight Officer Henry "Hank" Simon; Flight Officer Donald K. Miller** *Courtesy of Donald K. Miller, 1ˢᵗ Air Commando Association*

Replacement Pilots
New Air Commandos stopover at Natal, Brazil, en route from Miami, Florida, to Karachi, India, August 1944. Identified on the front row is Second Lieutenant Edward W. Auman (dark wheel hat); Second Lieutenant Jean E. Freiwald (right of Auman); and Second Lieutenant Allen W. Abrahams (right of Freiwald) *Courtesy of Allen W. Abrahams, 1ˢᵗ Air Commando Association*

from further losses. Torrential rain transformed the fair-weather dirt track lines of communication into a quagmire of mud that became known as the Chocolate Staircase. Even though the rain-drenched ooze slowed General Slim's pursuit, the downpour could not dampen the enthusiasm of his strategic planners. Brian Bond, Professor of Military History at King's College, London, and President of the British Commission for Military History, pointed to General Mutaguchi's failed invasion of India as the reason.

> By a strange final quirk of fate, Mutaguchi's foolhardy incursion into India served to consolidate British planning, just as Wingate's first expedition had been instructive to Mutaguchi. It was a curious reversal of fortune for the British high command. They had never really wanted to re-conquer Burma overland...Just as Wingate's example had invited Mutaguchi into India, so Mutaguchi's attempt and its failure inexorably drew Slim back into Burma on the heels of the shattered 15th Army. (4:235-236)

By the end of the monsoon season, XIV Army staff believed they could pass to the offensive. Tasked to "exploit the development of a land route to China," XIV Army planners no longer saw reasons to procrastinate or restrain themselves to such a limited objective. The center of gravity within the theater, altered by the victory inside India's borders, inspired XIV Army strategists to write and rewrite many plans to take the fight into Northern Burma west of the Irrawaddy River.

General Slim was already concocting his offensive before the Japanese began to retreat from India. On the Plains of Manipur, General Slim overcame terrain by striking the enemy where tank warfare was favorable to SEAC forces. Beyond the Chindwin River, General Slim's staff observed the flat Central Plains of Burma offered the same topographical advantages. To maintain their lines of communication, visionaries looked to Colonel Cochran's support of the Chindit operation when Wingate cut his umbilical cord and relied on air power. Admiral Lord Mountbatten expressed such an idea earlier by observing, "After seeing the performance of Stilwell's forces and hearing of the wonderful show which Wingate and Cochran's No. 1 Air Commando have put up, I am becoming convinced that Allied forces could march all over Burma provided they have adequate air supply and air support." (83:104-105)

Operation THURSDAY demonstrated Dakotas could sustain a mobile division. During the Battles of Imphal and Kohima, the CBI honed aerial re-supply procedures to an even keener edge. Furthermore, because transports were able to supply troops during the monsoon season, General Slim believed air re-supply could replace

Modified L-5 Sentinel
Staff Sergeant John C. "Jack" Gallagher and Technical Sergeant Glen W. Snyder modified an L-5 to allow easier loading of stretcher patients. *Courtesy of 1ˢᵗ Air Commando Association*

Baksheesh Landing Ground
While checking out newly arrived planes and pilots, the liaison squadrons experienced so many forced landings they christened an emergency field the *Baksheesh Landing Ground*. Courtesy of 1ˢᵗ Air Commando Association

land lines of communication. He began to craft an all-out offensive based on sustaining IV Corps and XXXIII Corps in Central Burma. His hole card was the ability to air transport crews to shoulder an advancing army on their wings. The key issues were range and payload. In part, these would be answered by XV Corps operations in the Arakan.

One casualty of the XIV Army planning effort was General Arnold's proposed Air Task Force. In reality, the Air Task Force had never appeared anywhere other than on paper and in the heart of its designer. On 14 September 1944, Eastern Air Command organized the Combat Cargo Task Force (CCTF) in lieu of Arnold's prototype. The Combat Cargo Task Force controlled transport, glider, and liaison aircraft from the 1ˢᵗ Air Commando Group, the 1ˢᵗ Combat Cargo Group (consisting of the 1ˢᵗ, 2ⁿᵈ, 3ʳᵈ, and 4ᵗʰ Combat Cargo Squadrons), and RAF 177 Transport Wing. Although the combat aircraft of the 1ˢᵗ Air Commando Group officially belonged to the CCTF, control was delegated to the RAF's 221 Group. Brigadier General Frederick W. Evans was selected to head the new organization; Air Vice Marshal J. D. I. Hardman joined as Deputy Commander. When General Evans assumed command, the responsibilities of the Combat Cargo Task Force were threefold:

(1) Delivery by air of supplies to units of the Northern Combat Area Command, XIV Army and such other forces as required,
(2) Transport of ground and airborne troops by air, and
(3) Air evacuation of personnel.

The failure of General Arnold to gain acceptance of his Air Task Force idea led to the assimilation of the 1ˢᵗ Air Commando Group into the normal chain-of-command structure of the theater. It was almost inevitable. As early as 24 March 1944, British Air

Marshall Baldwin, Commander of the 3ʳᵈ Tactical Air Force, wrote General Stratemeyer, saying, "I do hope that you will be able to arrange to absorb [the 1ˢᵗ Air Commando Group] into the appropriate commands which already exist. The longer this remains an independent outfit working with the Special Force, the harder it is going to be to get it away from Wingate." (80:24 March 1944 Letter) As the fortunes of war in the Pacific turned to the side of the Allies, conventional American forces, such as 10ᵗʰ Air Force and Eastern Air Command, eagerly devoured General Arnold's special units. Given the parochialism of Air Marshall Baldwin's testimony, the desire to throw a rope over mavericks and bring them back to the herd was predictable. Realizing his dream had faded away, General Arnold agreed to send the 2ⁿᵈ Air Commando Group to the CBI; the 3ʳᵈ Air Commando Group was assigned to the Philippines.

Beginning in September 1944, elements of the 2ⁿᵈ Air Commando Group began to arrive in India. Earlier, General Arnold ordered existing reconnaissance fighter squadrons and observation squadrons to be consolidated with newly constituted airlift units to form the 2ⁿᵈ Air Commando Group. The group activated on 22 April 1944; Colonel Alison forged and trained the unit at Drew Field, Florida, and nearby Lakeland Army Air Field. The flying squadrons included the 1ˢᵗ Fighter Squadron (Commando) and the 2ⁿᵈ Fighter Squadron (Commando) equipped with P-51D Mustangs; the 317ᵗʰ Troop Carrier Squadron (Commando) made up of C-47 Dakotas and CG-4A Waco gliders; and the 127ᵗʰ Liaison Squadron (Commando), 155ᵗʰ Liaison Squadron (Commando), and 156ᵗʰ Liaison Squadron (Commando) which included UC-64 Norsemen and L-5 Sentinels. Between September and November personnel arrived and assembled in theater; the base at Kalaikunda, India, became home for Colonel A. R. Debolt's 2ⁿᵈ Air Commando Group.

TABLE 5
1944-45 1st Air Commando Group
Command Structure

Squadrons	Commander/First Sergeant	Primary Aircraft
5th Fighter Squadron (Commando)	Captain Roland R. Lynn MSgt Melvin Haug	P-47 Thunderbolts
6th Fighter Squadron (Commando)*	Captain Olin B. Carter TSgt James W. Moore	P-47 Thunderbolts
Bomber, Night Intruder Section	Captain Edward (Sam) Wagner	B-25 Mitchells
164th Liaison Squadron (Commando)	1Lt David C. (Buck) Beasley, Jr. MSgt Charles E. Bowden	L-5 Sentinels L-1 Vigilants# UC-64 Norsemen
165th Liaison Squadron (Commando)	Captain Vincent L. Ulery MSgt James C. Ferry	L-5 Sentinels L-1 Vigilants# UC-64 Norsemen
166th Liaison Squadron (Commando)	1Lt Fred H. Van Wagner MSgt Arnold C. Zahorsky	L-5 Sentinels L-1 Vigilants# UC-64 Norsemen
319th Troop Carrier Squadron (Commando)	Major Neil I. (Nipper) Holm MSgt Samuel L. May	C-47 Dakotas CG-4 Hadrians

* Formally constituted on 22 September 1944
#During first week of September 1944, the group's L-1 Vigilants were turned into 10th Air Force at Ledo.

Because Colonel Alison had organized the new commando groups to conform to the Air Task Force squadron structure, Eastern Air Command instructed Colonel Gaty to follow suit. On 9 August, he began reorganizing the 1st Air Commando Group to agree with normal unit designations. Special Order Number 151 was published on 1 September 1944 officially reforming the group's organizational structure. Colonel Gaty's original flying squadron commanders are shown in Table 5.

In addition to the aviation squadrons, the 1st Air Commando Group consisted of a Headquarters unit with Sergeant Silas H. Rhodes named as First Sergeant, the 1st Air Commando Engineering Group commanded by Major John H. Jennette, and the 285th Medical Dispensary (Aviation) Squadron led by Captain William S. Piper. Medical facilities were established in remodeled buildings complete with an operating room; four new flight surgeons were assigned to bring the 36-bed dispensary to strength. First Lieutenant Ben Solomon was the group dental officer.

At the time the 319th Troop Carrier Squadron (Commando) was founded, Dakota pilots and maintenance crews were still in the field; many did not know of the change in organizational structure. Transport personnel of the 1st Air Commando Group were engaged in flying passenger and cargo services between Calcutta, Chittagong, and the Imphal Plain. Admiral Lord Mountbatten's patchwork air transportation system, constructed to bring relief to Imphal, quietly had broken into separate pieces after the siege was lifted.

The 3rd Combat Cargo Group reverted to 10th Air Force and two British units, the 31 Squadron RAF and 62 (Transport) Squadron RAF, were withdrawn for a much needed rest. Left to deliver supplies, munitions, and medicine to IV Corps and XXXIII Corps were the fatigued 1st Air Commando Group's Dakotas and two RAF transport squadrons. Although less aircraft were available, the three squadrons ably met demands from Central India and from the Arakan as well.

By the middle of September, the strategic planning and operational tempo within the China-Burma-India Theater was heady. Between Imphal and the end of the monsoons, SEAC changed command structure, personnel, and strategic plans, but the level of activity was about to increase even more. Generalissimo Chiang and General Stilwell continued to recklessly clash throughout the monsoons of 1944. On 1 August 1944 with the capture of Myitkyina eminent, President Roosevelt promoted Stilwell to full general, but this subtle signal of approval was ignored. The rife continued. It reached crisis proportions during the Octagon Conference in Quebec. The *West Point Military History Series* recorded the account thusly:

… a setback in early September on the Burma Road made the Generalissimo threaten to withdraw his Y-force from the north Burma campaign. Ironically, the Japanese Salween counteroffensive was halted on September 14, its objective having been merely to relieve pressure on the 56th Division. Moreover, the monsoon was about to lift, and full-scale renewal of the Allied offensive in north Burma was scheduled to begin in a few weeks. The crisis point had come in Sino-American relations. When word of Chiang's decision to withdraw Y-force reached President Roosevelt at the Octagon Conference

Light Cargo Section Formation Flying Training
Leading the formation is Captain Edward "Sam" Wagner and Staff Sergeant Felix C. Lockman, Jr., in aircraft 35208; First Lieutenant Julius Goodman and Staff Sergeant George C. Gregson (35202) followed; while First Lieutenant Fred H. Van Wagner and Staff Sergeant Lawrence N. Poepping (35201) bring up the rear. Other than Operation THURSDAY, UC-64 pilots rarely flew formation. *Courtesy of 1ˢᵗ Air Commando Association*

in Quebec, he approved a reply which was sent to Stilwell for delivery. On September 19, 1944, Stilwell delivered the President's note to the Generalissimo. It read, "The only thing you can now do in an attempt to prevent the Jap[anese] from achieving his objectives in China is to reinforce your Salween armies immediately and press their offensive, while at once placing General Stilwell in unrestricted command of all your forces." It was an ultimatum. Believing that Stilwell had deliberately engineered this confrontation, Chiang publicly declined to appoint Stilwell as field commander of the Chinese forces and asked for Stilwell's recall on 2 October ... Stilwell had become Chiang's scapegoat. (20:225)

The irascible Infantry General, now almost blind, was unable to mount sufficient support to keep the President from making the move everyone expected. Always controversial, General Stilwell left amid mixed reviews. General Slim called him a "fighting soldier" who somehow made the Chinese advance when no one else could, but General Brooke admitted "he did a vast amount of harm..." (1:387) He had assured greater supplies to China via a lower altitude Hump routing, afforded air transport staging bases nearer to China, and established a petroleum site in Burma, but in the end, President Roosevelt's faith in Stilwell's leadership was undermined by the constant barrage of complaints. Named to replace him at Generalissimo Chiang's headquarters was Lieutenant General Wedemeyer, SEAC Deputy Chief of Staff, a man General Stilwell considered sometimes conceited and always ambitious. If there was a silver lining in the black cloud of his departure, it was the re-

moval of the unwieldy command structure that plagued operations in Northern Burma.

Since late summer of 1944, the War Department had contemplated restructuring the far-flung China-Burma-India Theater. Generalissimo Chiang's request made the timing right. Lieutenant General Daniel I. Sultan was named to command the newly initiated India-Burma Theater on 24 October 1944. He also took over Stilwell's Northern Combat Area Command. On the last day of the same month, General Wedemeyer assumed Stilwell's duties as Chief of Staff to Generalissimo Chiang as well as command of the separated China Theater. Mountbatten's Administrative Officer, Lieutenant General Raymond Wheeler, was elevated to Deputy Supreme Commander, SEAC, to fill the last of Stilwell's three hats. Showing his contempt, General Stilwell left China on 27 October 1944, 4 days prior to General Wedemeyer's arrival in Chungking.

At the same Octagon Conference that precipitated General Stilwell's downfall, SEAC Headquarters proposed two alternative operations to secure Burma. Operation CAPITAL constituted an overland approach into Northern Burma; the second plan, named DRACULA, was a joint amphibious drive on Rangoon. Operation CAPITAL called for General Slim's XIV Army to cross the Chindwin, join with Chinese Forces approaching from Northern Burma, and secure operations north of Mandalay. Prior to the 1945 monsoon season, XIV Army would secure Northern Burma and hold.. More aggressive but much more resource intensive, DRACULA was a fallback to amphibious plans of previous years. Admiral Lord Mountbatten reviewed the plans and plainly preferred the joint seaborne and airborne operation to capture Burma's major

Glider Training
To maintain glider pilot proficiency, UC-64 pilots towed TG-5 gliders. Double tow was attempted but Colonel Gaty ordered it discontinued. The practice was too great a strain on the Norseman's engine. *Courtesy of 1ˢᵗ Air Commando Association*

1ˢᵗ Air Commando Group Reorganization
Major General George C. Stratemeyer congratulates Colonel Clinton B. Gaty on the reorganization of the 1ˢᵗ Air Commando Group in September 1944. *Courtesy of 1ˢᵗ Air Commando Association*

port of Rangoon. Nevertheless, he personally delivered both plans to Prime Minister Churchill at the Octagon Conference in Quebec. Although DRACULA was accepted by the British Military Staff, it was turned down by Washington. Once again, the landing craft needed from Europe could not be spared. Operation CAPITAL was on.

"I was heartily in favour of [CAPITAL]," wrote General Slim some years later. (44:312) In addition to assigning the major role to XIV Army, he thought it offered as much potential to achieve the military, political, and strategic imperatives of Great Britain as Operation DRACULA. To transition from defense to offense, a radical departure from the normal makeup of warfighting units was required to advance into the heartland of Northern Burma. As preparation for the post-monsoon campaign continued, General Slim ordered XIV Army's land forces be fashioned in a completely new mold. Looking across the Chindwin toward the post monsoon offensive, General Slim presumed General Katamura's 15ᵗʰ Army would engage in an area known as the Shwebo Plain. Part of the Dry Belt of Central Burma, the area was a triangular loop of land contained between the country's two great rivers, the Chindwin and Irrawaddy. General Slim believed the Japanese would dig in and wait for the British to attempt a crossing of the Chindwin River. Once XIV Army forces were on the east side with the Chindwin blocking retreat, Slim believed the Japanese 15ᵗʰ Army would attack before armor and air could influence.

The coming contest presented a challenge for XIV Army. For 2 years the British had fought in rugged hills and wild jungles, but once they crossed the Chindwin, there would be open country and room for tanks to maneuver. For the coming offensive, XIV Army redefined formations, trained tactics that emphasized movement, derived alternate targeting procedures, established close air support policies, and emphasized air re-supply methods. Gone from the corps' organizations were logistics and quartermaster elements; General Slim also eliminated the normal mixture of animals and mechanized transport. In their place, he fully relied on air rather than ground lines of communication to support his redesigned mechanized divisions. A reserve brigade was made totally air transportable—only jeeps and narrow-axled artillery were allowed. Leaving behind the defensive crouch of 1943, General Slim recast his army for speed and depended on air transportation for logistics.

Weighing the potential of a synchronized land-air conflict, General Slim quietly debated the strategic objective assigned to XIV Army by SEAC headquarters. If able to catch General Katamura before his battered forces could fully recover from the defeat on the Imphal Plain and the bar fights that ensued, General Slim considered Mandalay, not merely Northern Burma, within reach before the May monsoon season. On 6 November, IV Corps detailed a brigade to reconnoiter routes east of the Chindwin. The re-conquest of Burma is marked from that date. In hindsight, it mattered little that General Slim had incorrectly anticipated the location for the impending battle against the Japanese on Burmese soil. As events would prove, the degree of Japanese opposition and speed of XIV Army's advance into Northern Burma would define an opportunity to extend operational objectives. His ability to push across the Irrawaddy and capture the ancient Burmese capital of Mandalay before the next wave of monsoon rains was borne by the flexibility and determination of his air lines of communication.

9

Operation CAPITAL

In broad terms, SEAC divided Burma into three sectors: Northern Burma, Central Burma, and Arakan. General Sultan's Northern Combat Area Command had responsibility for British and Chinese operations in Northern Burma; General Slim's XIV Army, composed of IV Corps and XXXIII Corps, was assigned the Central Region; and detached from XIV Army, General Slim's XV Corps was to control the Arakan coastal area. Special Force was held in a reserve status as it re-equipped and trained replacements. Activities in all sectors and use of reserve units were coordinated by General Leese's Allied Land Forces South East Asia. Organized against The British Army were ten Japanese divisions and two mixed brigades. Facing NCAC between the Burma Road terminus at Bhamo and the Salween River was Nippon's 33rd Army made up of the 56th Division, 18th Division, and, on temporary loan, 2nd Divi-

Liaison Squadron Headquarters, Palel, India, October 1944
Captain Vincent L. Ulery established Liaison Squadron Headquarters in a derelict C-47 carcass at Palel, India *Courtesy of 1st Air Commando Association*

sion. Deployed against XIV Army was General Slim's nemesis, the Japanese 15th Army. Composed of the vestiges of 15th Division, 31st Division, and 33rd Division, General Katamura's forces were strung out roughly along the Railway Corridor between the Chindwin and Irrawaddy Rivers. Rounding out the Japanese defenses were two divisions of 28th Army in the south. The 54th Division held territory north of Akyab along the Burmese coast while 55th Division linked up to form a defensive perimeter extending to an area east of the Irrawaddy Delta.

The outcome of the battle on the Imphal Plateau put the two great powers in Southeast Asia on a collision course. Wheels were set in motion when advance parties of the 19th Indian Division infiltrated Japanese-held territory and reported the feasibility of establishing a number of bridgeheads across the Chindwin River. General Slim's strategic plan for the invasion of Burma had begun. Operation CAPITAL discarded the comfort and security of visible supply lines—truck routes, railroad tracks, barge traffic, or storage sites. In particular, roadways were nonexistent. Combat Engineers would have been required to do the impossible—pave roads while advancing under fire. Instead, General Slim replaced lines of communication with abstractions regarding controlled airspace, air bridges, and predetermined schedules. Only an occasional runway carved out of rice paddies would be tangible evidence of logistics support. The plan's air re-supply concept involved a risk borne of necessity and hazarded from the success of the Wingate-Cochran partnership. Never before had an entire army's advance been so completely reliant on air movement of men, supplies, and materiel.

Despite normal concerns that accompany any new idea, Admiral Lord Mountbatten was convinced the logistics theory was sound thinking. He had been impressed with the praise of airlift given by the commander of the British 36th Division. When asked if air supply was unpredictable, Major General Francis W. Festing replied, "In 8 months of fighting through the monsoon there has been only one day that our supplies did not arrive." These words strengthened arguments for the planned dry season offensive. Admiral Lord Mountbatten and General Slim put their trust in the airmen of the India-Burma Theater.

As the monsoon rains gave way to the dry season, IV and XXXIII Corps maintained contact with General Katamura's retreating 15th Army. While XIV Army was clearing pockets of stubborn Japanese resistors from India, a flight of light planes from the 165th Liaison Squadron, led by Captain Ulery, moved forward from Asansol. Navigating around thunderstorms and braving 500 miles of adverse weather, eight Sentinels arrived at the Palel airfield on 6 October 1944 where they reunited with fellow air commando pilots of the 319th Troop Carrier Squadron. Captain Ulery established the liaison squadron headquarters in the wingless hulk of an abandoned C-47 fuselage. Without a pause, the 165th Liaison Squadron began evacuating casualties and an extremely high number of troops felled by typhus in the Kabaw Valley. Billeted in native huts near the airfield and served British rations of canned Argentinean beef,

Light Plane Pilot
General Slim's XIV Army relied on pilots such as Sergeant William D. Chapple to evacuate the wounded, injured, and medically unfit from the front lines. Note the Vargas girl on the door. *Courtesy of Bill Chapple, 1st Air Commando Association*

the air commandos worked with General Slim's army as it positioned for Operation CAPITAL.

By 14 October, British troops advanced to the Indo-Burman border and swept the Japanese from the old RAF runway at Tamu—an airstrip promptly made long enough for fighters, bombers, and transports. Within days, a second flight of liaison planes flew from Asansol over 8,000-foot peaks to the vital strip in the Kabaw Valley. Protected by 20 mm cannons and Gurkha soldiers, the camp began to take shape. Drinking water, brought in small tanks pulled behind a jeep, was treated with halazone tablets to make it drinkable. Air commandos dug foxholes, staked out tents on high ground, and brought in cots and mosquito netting. Engineers installed a generator, strung electrical lines, built a mess tent, and established telephone communications with radar stations on the frontier. With improvements yet underway, Captain Ulery pronounced the light plane unit operational.

A narrow stream near the camp provided a tranquil contrast to the danger evidenced by deep bomb craters, scarred trees, and gutted enemy aircraft inside the perimeter of the lodging. Irregular enemy harassing attacks kept the front line airfield on the alert. On one occasion, a British RAF Spitfire, returning from an interdiction sortie, was followed to Tamu. The lone Oscar pilot riddled the ramp with machine guns; he left a B-25 blazing and a few Sentinels damaged.

Ahead of the small air strips the British were engaged in fierce ground fighting. Quickly, XIV Army learned to rely on the light planes of Tamu augmented by UC-64 Norsemen. As the British pried the unyielding Japanese from dugouts, caves, and trees, light planes were nearby to evacuate casualties—wounded, injured, and medically unfit. On return legs, the Sentinels and Norsemen carried replacements, light cargo, mail, whole blood, or other medical supplies to forward units. For the month, the 165th Liaison Squadron evacuated 1,048 wounded, transported 259 other passengers, and moved 140,000 pounds of miscellaneous cargo.

Rations, heavier equipment, and major muscle movements flowed through Palel in air commando transports. A detachment of Dakotas also operated from Dum Dum Air Field near Calcutta. Almost 1,300,000 pounds of fresh meat from the East Indian port city was transported to various Northeastern Indian bases by the *Mutton Marauders* of the 319th Troop Carrier Squadron. Additionally, missions into inaccessible areas were accomplished by Dakota and

Hadrian pilots of the 1ˢᵗ Air Commando Group. On 9 October, glider operations began in the Khampat sector. Code named Kate, the location was only 15 minutes south of Tamu but had been cut off by impassable flooded roads. Swampy conditions in the Chocolate Staircase area sometimes precluded even L-5 operations.

In response, Captain John K. "Buddy" Lewis, who before the war was a superb third baseman and outfielder for the Washington Senators, towed First Lieutenant Fred P. "Plaster of" Paris in a CG-4A to overhead Kate. Lieutenant Paris released, landed in the mire, loaded nine wounded, and set up snatch gear while Lewis' Dakota, *The Gray Fox,* circled nearby. By nightfall, the snatched Hadrian had returned the men to Indian-based hospitals. Air Commodore S. F. Vincent, commander of 221 RAF Group, sent congratulations with the following observation: "It is obviously so important that this first attempt should be successful, and thereby break down any prejudice there may be - somewhat naturally - in the minds of the wounded against being 'snatched up' into the air with what would appear some terrific jolt." (135:14 October 1944 Letter) The process proved highly successful; by the end of the month, two Dakotas and four Hadrians worked continuously with troops assigned to the Khampat area. In all, the gliders airlanded 30,100 pounds of materiel and carried out 123 casualties in 25 snatches before operations at Kate ceased.

Throughout invasion preparations there were nagging concerns expressed about protection of ground forces. Surface transportation became increasingly more difficult as General Slim's troops advanced. Consequently the British Army had less artillery support than normal, yet as they pressed eastward, the need for self-defense increased. This deficiency could be overcome, in part, if Allied fight-

Kamphat Operations
In stretcher configured CG-4A Hadrian gliders like this one, the 1ˢᵗ Air Commando Group snatched wounded and typhus cases from the Kamphat area. Hadrians flew two-way missions, carrying supplies in and casualties out. *Courtesy of 1ˢᵗ Air Commando Association*

Rangoon Fighter Raid
Before their Thunderbolts could be painted with theater markings, Colonel Gaty's composite fighter squadron moved up to Cox's Bazar to conduct raids on airfields in Central Burma. The Air Commandos outperformed all others accounting for almost 70 percent of the enemy destroyed. *Courtesy of 1ˢᵗ Air Commando Association*

5th Fighter Squadron Leaders
(L-R) Captain Hamer R. Davidson, Captain Roland R. Lynn, First Lieutenant Malcolm J. Wilkins *Courtesy of 1st Air Commando Association*

The group's new Thunderbolts joined other 10th Air Force and RAF Third Tactical Air Force fighter units to prepare the way for General Slim's operation. In October, SEAC Intelligence reported enemy strength of 64 combat aircraft predominately located in Burma's interior. On 17 and 20 October, SEAC's impromptu fighter task force flew two massive sweeps to Nippon airfields in the vicinity of Rangoon—a round trip of more than 850 miles. The missions were the largest of their kind in Southeast Asia and proved highly successful. Eastern Air Command reported 16 enemy aircraft destroyed, 15 more damaged, and 2 probables at Mingladon, Zayatkwin, and Hmawoi airfields. Colonel Gaty's pilots showed they lost none of their skills and trained new arrivals well.

Even though he was still unfamiliar with the location of all Thunderbolt switches, Captain Carter was high scorer, and the 6th Fighter Squadron accounted for the majority of the destroyed aircraft. Second Lieutenant Marion C. Ball achieved his first air-to-air kill and First Lieutenant Everett L. Kelly downed another aircraft over Mingladon. Kelly's report was confirmed by seeing the pilot's chute open after he fired a long burst at close range. Table 6 shows 11 of the enemy aircraft destroyed, 1 of the probables, and 3 of the damaged airplanes were bagged by air commandos. There were no losses, but one very close call. Second Lieutenant Lee F. "Moon" Mullins took a round through the canopy into the armor glass in front of his face. The shell rattled and ricocheted around the cockpit, finally falling harmlessly at Mullins' feet. Despite flak and opposition from Japanese Oscars, Captains Lynn and Carter reported only two Thunderbolts damaged during the October operation at Cox's Bazar. These missions established a friendly rivalry between the two squadrons.

ers and bombers were free from the threat of the Japanese air force. To completely dominate Burmese skies, General Stratemeyer urged a vigorous air offensive when the monsoons allowed. Although not all pilots were fully trained, Colonel Gaty volunteered the 1st Air Commando Group's newly designated fighter squadrons for the renewed air campaign. When accepted by SEAC, the group scrambled to constitute a combat ready force.

On 15 October 1944, Colonel Gaty offered a combined fighter unit of air commando pilots and planes. Four flights emerged by mixing 13 officers and 22 enlisted personnel from Captain Lynn's 5th Fighter Squadron with 14 officers and 27 enlisted men of Captain Carter's 6th Fighter Squadron. In addition to Lynn and Carter, the flight leaders were Captain Younger A. "Sonny" Pitts, Jr., and First Lieutenant John E. "Jack" Meyer. Among the pilots, only 12 previously had seen combat duty during Operation THURSDAY and the follow-on support to Wingate's Chindits. Once formed, the composite squadron departed Asansol for Cox's Bazar, India—a small beach front British airfield in Arakan near the Burmese border.

Close Call
During the raid on Rangoon, Second Lieutenant Lee F. "Moon" Mullins took a shell through the canopy. Staff Sergeant George W. Beers was Mullins' crew chief. *Courtesy of 1st Air Commando Association*

TABLE 6
First Combat Missions from Cox's Bazar, India
17 October 1944 and 20 October 1944

		Destroyed		Damaged		Probables	
		Air	Ground	Air	Ground	Air	Ground
5ᵗʰ Fighter Squadron (Commando)							
Captain	Lynn, Roland R.			2		1	
1ˢᵗ Lieutenant	Wilkins, Malcolm J.		1				
2ⁿᵈ Lieutenant	Ball, Marion C.	1					
2ⁿᵈ Lieutenant	Weesner, Hilton D.		1				
2ⁿᵈ Lieutenant	Mullins, Lee R.			1			
6ᵗʰ Fighter Squadron (Commando)							
Captain	Carter, Olin B.		3				
1ˢᵗ Lieutenant	Kelly, Everett L.	1					
1ˢᵗ Lieutenant	Klarr, Jack U.		1				
1ˢᵗ Lieutenant	Setnor, Joe		1				
2ⁿᵈ Lieutenant	Bayne, Edward D.		1				
2ⁿᵈ Lieutenant	Vanderyerk, Allen H.		1				

Before the end of October, the composite squadron flew back to Asansol. Maintenance personnel immediately readied the Thunderbolts for more fighting by painting them with theater markings and the 1ˢᵗ Air Commando Group's distinctive five diagonal stripes. In less than 2 weeks, the unit was declared combat ready; normally this transition from activation to combat status required 4 to 6 months. Discordantly, there appeared to be little reason to rush. Due to the large number of raw recruits in XIV Army ranks, General Slim was forced to push back the invasion timetable to conduct training. Formally, Operation CAPITAL was rescheduled to begin 15 November 1944.

At Lalitpur, India, 3 officers and 33 enlisted men of Lieutenant Beasley's 164ᵗʰ Liaison Squadron, 3 Thunderbolt pilots, and 1

Fiery Accident at Yazagyo, Burma
The burned frame of Second Lieutenant Winfield C. S. Eng, Jr.'s UC-64 Norseman. *Courtesy of 1ˢᵗ Air Commando Association*

Mitchell crew participated in training activities leading up to General Slim's planned invasion. After time at reception camps for convalescence, the Chindits were reformed. General Lentaigne maintained command, but General Slim held the unit in reserve. A few personnel with Operation THURSDAY experience were mixed with an overwhelming number of replacements to form the new Special Force. As the organization rounded into shape, air commando UC-64, L-5, P-47, and B-25 pilots joined the Chindits in a series of intensive ground-air exercises. Light plane crews displayed precise cross-country navigation over a 500-mile course and demonstrated photo reconnaissance, supply airdrop, message pickup, and medical evacuation capability. The fighters and bomber completed close air support and interdiction exhibitions by dive-bombing and strafing targets with live ammunition. The exercises began early November and, with some reductions in participation, extended into early February. For the first time, the British Army, other than the Chindits themselves, realized the 1ˢᵗ Air Commando Group's full potential to support ground operations.

Meanwhile, SEAC used General Slim's reprieve to continue its attack on Japan's air arm. As Colonel Gaty's composite squadron prepared to head back to the Burmese border area, Captain Carter, an original member of General Arnold's Project 9, received orders to the United States. He had flown more than 80 combat missions over Burma. As he departed Asansol, Captain Carter yielded the 6ᵗʰ Fighter Squadron reigns to his Operations Officer, Captain Pitts. Returning to Cox's Bazar, Colonel Gaty's composite squadron immediately flew two more missions; again, the targets were in the Rangoon area. On 3 and 4 November 1944, the air commandos continued pummeling the Japanese Air Force by damaging two Nippon aircraft in air-to-air combat. Second Lieutenant Joe

Memorial for a Fallen Air Commando
The two markers indicate the burial site of Private First Class Louis Simon. He died in Lieutenant Eng's UC-64 at Yazagyo in October 1944. *Courtesy of 1ˢᵗ Air Commando Association*

Setnor destroyed a Sally on the ground at Hmawoi, and air commando pilots damaged two other aircraft during the raids. These missions prior to XIV Army's advance effectively dismembered the Japanese Air Force in Burma. As a result, conservation of the Emperor's combat aircraft became so acute that enemy bombers could no longer mount a coordinated offensive, resorting to harrying hit-and-run missions. With a notable exception in November when a Japanese assault force shot down five transport aircraft, fighters were withheld for defense of only the most important targets; when threatened, Nippon pilots practiced extreme avoidance. The anemic response to air attacks confirmed speculation the Japanese would be unable to withstand a robust offensive campaign. General Stratemeyer had achieved his goal of unchallenged air superiority.

After the successful Cox's Bazar missions, the men of the composite squadron returned to Asansol and broke up into their respective units. From this home base, the two air commando fighter squadrons operated as finely calibrated pistons. When one was forward deployed flying cover or interdiction missions for General Slim's army, the other was in the rear area performing maintenance, conducting tactics training, and otherwise preparing for succeeding air combat operations. Every month, the squadrons traded places, sometimes overlapping each other for a short time. The two squadrons continued to challenge one another's performance. The similar tactics and harmony between the air commando fighter units gave the British continuity throughout the impending dry season campaign.

As XIV Army punished the Japanese in the Kabaw Valley, the light planes of the 1ˢᵗ Air Commando Group followed. On 6 November, Captain Ulery's 165ᵗʰ Liaison Squadron left Tamu and flew to a forward evacuation strip named Yazagyo nestled against the bank of a river. Located near Mawlaik 60 miles south of Tamu and given the code name Yell, the small strip was prepared for light

planes by Major General C. C. Fowkes' 11ᵗʰ East African Division—spearhead division of General Stopford's XXXIII Corps. The British were engaged by a strong Nippon force and desperately needed heavy artillery. Several light planes were loaded with 37 mm cannons; lashed to the engine cowling, the piece extended from the rear cockpit out through the side window. Air commandos flew the gauntlet of fire and the fieldpieces were in action a few minutes after delivery. Unfortunately, the action interrupted the installation of runway lighting.

Later that night, a UC-64 Norseman, bringing the last seven air commandos to Yell, attempted an approach in the fading light. On rollout after landing, Second Lieutenant Winfield C. S. Eng, Jr.'s right wing tip clipped a parked aircraft and instantly burst into flames. Private First Class Louis Simon died immediately; later he was buried at the field in the shadow of the skeletal remains of the Norseman. After Major Edwin S. White, flight surgeon for the group, administered first aid and plasma to the injured, Private First Class Emil J. Eastwood was transported 6 miles overland to the nearby Belgian Congo Hospital. He succumbed before morning. The other two burn victims were air evacuated to Army General Hospital at Ledo. General Fowkes expressed his sorrow, "Will you please accept the sincere sympathy of myself and all the men of my Division. We have come to regard you as part of the Division and con-

Casualty Staging Area
Gurkhas transfer a wounded comrade into a UC-64 Norseman. Light plane pilots brought casualties from the front line to staging airfields where UC-64 pilots collected the wounded and transported them to rear hospitals. *Courtesy of 1ˢᵗ Air Commando Association*

sequently feel your loss as you do yourselves." (135:6 November 1944 Letter) After attending funeral services, the somber air commandos began setting up tents and preparing the camp. Captain Ulery ordered supplies and POL; when the gasoline was delivered and strained for rust and water, operations began.

The Yazagyo airfield was frequently badgered by Japanese fighter attacks and enemy ground patrols were often reported nearby. Exposed to enemy air and ground attacks, the RAF commander at Yell requested a self protection package shortly after operations began. With top cover provided by 10 Thunderbolts from the 5ᵗʰ Fighter Squadron, transports and gliders of the 319ᵗʰ Troop Carrier Squadron moved a complete antiaircraft battery to the strip. To protect against ground assaults, Gurkha Rifles established interior security; land mines kept intruders at a distance. Captain Ulery's daily air support missions enabled Allied forces to inch closer to the Chindwin River; anticipation began to build. When a prowling hyena mistakenly set off a land mine in the middle of the night, the camp remained on tenterhooks.

Light plane activity at Yell was fatiguing as the Flying Sergeants evacuated casualties and medical patients to Palel for transfer to area hospitals. On 13 November, members of Lieutenant Van Wagner's 166ᵗʰ Liaison Squadron arrived to relieve Captain Ulery's men. The transition was completed in a week. The squadron's UC-64 pilots immediately began working closely with an ongoing Waco glider operation. In late Fall 1944, typhus cases remained abnormally high in the Kabaw Valley—totaling nearly 600 soldiers. Many initially were extracted by CG-4A Hadrians. Lieutenants McKaig, and Turner, and two other glider pilots flew exhausting hours to evacuate typhus cases for transfer to ambulance-configured UC-64 Norsemen. The UC-64 could haul four litter cases plus three to

Air Commando Light Cargo Pilot
First Lieutenant Fred H. Van Wagner, Commander of 166ᵗʰ Liaison Squadron, wears the survival gear of an Air Commando—.45 caliber pistol, canteen, and webbed survival belt. He is standing in front of his UC-64 Norseman. The ship had two names: "Jessie Ann," the name of his wife, is visible under the door and "Slow Freight" is displayed behind the engine cowl. *Courtesy of 1ˢᵗ Air Commando*

Night Intruder Insignia
The midnight blue background was encircled by a white border. Silhouetted against a yellow full moon located in the upper right of the field, a black bat with fully extended wings carried a white bomb. Five red stripes in the form of a chevron appeared near the bomb's nose. *Courtesy of Scott Merchant, 1ˢᵗ Air Commando Association*

Night Intruder Section Commander
Captain Edward "Sam" Wagner flew UC-64 Norsemen during Operation THURSDAY. By the 1944-45 Campaign, Colonel Gaty named him Commander of the Night Intruder Section of B-25H Mitchells. The Night Intruders were known as locomotive specialists. *Courtesy of 1ˢᵗ Air Commando Association*

four more wounded sitting on the floor. Specially designed stretchers on the Noorduyn bush plane locked into the cargo section to prevent shifting in flight. To fit in the airplane, the stretchers were narrower than standard; consequently, patients had to be shifted from the larger British litter before transfer to the Norseman. If stretchers were not required, another arrangement was used. Depending on the severity of wounds, seven or more sick sat on the floor; however, the crew had to be careful to ensure ailing soldiers were not loaded in a tail heavy configuration.

The 166ᵗʰ Liaison Squadron continued to use Yell as its primary base, but British engineers hacked out Spartan runways as General Stopford advanced. As each strip was built, it was given a code name. This was as much to simplify the unpronounceable Burmese names as for security reasons. Yeshin became Yes, Nazelyn was known as Nazi, Nanbon was shortened to Nan, Hpangash was simply Ha, and Ontha was christened Ona. Brigadier D. F. "Haffy" Wilson-Haffenden, Deputy Adjutant and Quartermaster General of XXXIII Corps Logistics, used a simple rule of construction: "350 yards long, 12 yards wide, and open country on one end." (135:) Lieutenant Van Wagner flew approaches into each to determine suitability. Often more work was required before the field passed

muster. By the close of November, the two liaison squadrons had completed 4,998 combat missions. Captain Ulery and Lieutenant Van Wagner's men evacuated 2,388 casualties, transported 10 prisoners, and flew in 460 reinforcements. Additionally, the air commandos moved 112,671 pounds of cargo, dropped 13 messages, and flew 104 visual and 14 photo reconnaissance sorties.

As the date of the invasion neared, recently promoted Major Lynn took the 5ᵗʰ Fighter Squadron southeast to Fenny, India. East of the Bengal delta near Calcutta, the airstrip was ideally located to help General Slim's push onto the plains of Central Burma. Dakota and Hadrian pilots from the air commando's 319ᵗʰ Troop Carrier Squadron helped move the squadron's officers, men, and equipment to their temporary home. Accommodations were adequate, but the quarters were 5 miles from the flight line and transportation back and forth was ever a source of problems. All sections were still getting settled—no telephones, lights, nor furniture—while operations began on 10 November. Initially, the 23 Thunderbolts flew escort missions for B-25 Mitchells of the 12ᵗʰ Bombardment Group. Japanese opposition to the bomber flights proved scarce and the fighter's attention soon widened to other targets of opportunity—mechanized road and railroad traffic, sampans, bullock-drawn carts, airfields, antiaircraft artillery positions, and troop encampments. Burma was a target-rich environment.

To unsettle Japanese logistics support, air commando pilots targeted trains and major bridges. At first, results were mediocre yet sometimes spectacular. Second Lieutenant Benton W. "Benny" Hall vividly described how a short burst from .50-caliber machine guns could knock a boxcar completely off the tracks. Others recalled the effect of tracer rounds piercing locomotive boilers—dark gray columns of steam belched violently skyward 50 to 100 feet high while the train suddenly decelerated to a stop. As the month wore on, accuracy improved. River crossings at Saye, Myingatha, Shwebo, Madaunghla, and Myitnge were severed, and the Mu River bypass became a recurring objective. On 17 November pilots of

Night Intruder Target
Although the Japanese attempted to hide locomotives in the jungles during the day and operate after dark, Night Intruder raids destroyed Burma's interior transportation system. *Courtesy of 1ˢᵗ Air Commando Association*

5th Fighter Squadron scored a direct hit on the vital supply railway bridge spanning the Mu River, a tributary of the Irrawaddy. Less than 4 days later, it was back in operation. On 22 November the air commandos damaged supports and destroyed tracks near the bridge, but Japanese repair crews soon made it serviceable again. Eight days later, the 5th Fighter Squadron targeted the Mu River bridge one more time before heading back to Asansol. Leading a 2-ship attack loaded with 1,000-pounders, Captain Lynn dive bombed the target and scored two direct hits knocking it out of commission. The bridge had a 25-foot breach in the center section of the span. The flow of materiel from Japan's primary Central Burma supplyhouses and stockpiles from Meiktila via the Railway Corridor again was curtailed.

Continuously flying through the end of the month, unit pilots flew 51 missions against the Japanese in Central Burma. In just 21 days, 355 sorties were flown while the squadron accumulated 1,335 combat hours. Often assigning inexperienced newcomers as his wingman, Captain Lynn flew 25 combat missions. His operations officer, First Lieutenant Malcolm J. Wilkins, flew two less during the period. Their primary target remained aircraft of the Rising Sun. Two enemy aircraft were destroyed on the ground, one each at Nawnghkio on 11 November and at Laihka on 12 November. Later in the month, P-47 pilots damaged another Japanese plane at Hmawoi. On the other side of the ledger, three air commando Thunderbolts were lost. Second Lieutenant Franklin J. Misfeldt crashed during takeoff, escaping with minor injuries. Second Lieutenant Hilton D. Weesner was hit by ground fire while strafing Meiktila airfield; he survived but was captured and interned as a prisoner of war at Rangoon. Second Lieutenant Walter C. Lair crashed after taking a burst of antiaircraft artillery over Monywa and managed to make his way back to Fenny after evading the Japanese for 39 days in Burma.

In addition to strikes on Japan's combat arms and interior logistics system, the 5th Fighter Squadron gathered intelligence data that shed light on Japanese troop movements. Air commando pilots reported enemy airfield activities, placement of dummy aircraft, construction work, gun positions, camouflaged carts thought to be loaded with gasoline, and tank locations. All information was passed to XIV Army intelligence centers as General Slim moved eastward.

Allied airmen put such reports to immediate use. Less and less enemy activity was noted as the month progressed because the Allied air campaign made Nippon movements during daylight hours hazardous. In response, Japanese motor convoys, using blacked out light and traveling under cover of jungle trees, sought shelter in darkness. Enemy rail traffic practically stopped during the day. The Japanese hid locomotives in camouflaged shelters at the end of tracks extending deep into the jungle. To keep 15th Army in a weakened condition, SEAC initiated counter measures. Near the end of November, the first night bomber missions were assigned to air commando B-25 Mitchells. Departing Asansol, four bombers of Captain Wagner's Night Intruder Section flew to Chittagong where they began combat operations. On 23 November, the first night intruder sorties were flown. Colonel Gaty and copilot Captain Daniel A. Sinskie led the raid; Captain Merchant and Lieutenant Archie L. McKay flew on Gaty's wing. Section Commander Captain Wagner and his copilot Captain Zeigler climbed out and joined them in the number three position. Used between the first and last quarter moon of each month, the Night Intruder Section tormented Japanese night operations. Moonlight was the major source of target illumination, but Mitchell crews also employed M-8 flares. Dropped at 1,500 feet, the flares normally allowed B-25 crews to make two passes before burning out. The accuracy of the Mitchell's 75 mm cannon made passes on locomotives particularly lethal. During the month of November, the Night Intruder Section of the 1st Air Commando Group destroyed four locomotives and large quantities of rolling stock, mechanized transports, and river traffic in only nine sorties. Valuable information gathered during these night sorties was passed to the fighter units during morning debriefing sessions.

Fighting deeper into Burma, XIV Army reconnoitered several bridgeheads across the Chindwin River and was prepared to enter the Shwebo Plains. General Slim anticipated the Japanese would attempt to hold a line from Kalewa to Mandalay. On 3 December, a brigade of XXXIII Corps started across the Chindwin River at Mawlaik followed the next day by IV Corps units at Sittaung. Pouring onto the Shwebo Plains, the British were uninformed about current enemy movements; light plane pilots' 134 visual reports and 39 photo reconnaissance sorties during the month provided much needed operational intelligence data. As the British relent-

Light Plane Reconnaissance
Moving swiftly, the British overran their intelligence capability. In addition to emergency air evacuation missions, light plane pilots provided real-time visual and photographic reports of enemy movements and positions. *Courtesy of 1ˢᵗ Air Commando Association*

Air-to-Air Combat over Central Burma
First Lieutenant Jack U. Klarr scored a possible kill over the Rangoon area. He is wearing the 1ˢᵗ Air Commando's distinctive Fighter Squadron patch. *Courtesy of Elwood Jamison, 1ˢᵗ Air Commando Association*

teered to fly Sentinels into the clearing although it was known to be swarming with enemy troops. The two L-5 pilots flew low over the tree tops, pinpointed the strip, and executed a demanding approach to the site. Without any wasted motion, the air commandos loaded the casualties and were rapidly airborne again. All the time the planes were in the area, a small cadre of British soldiers held the Japanese at bay.

Missions such as these made light plane pilots an integral part of XIV Army's mobility; air commandos never declined when tasked to support British troops engaged in battle. Staff Sergeant Stamford N. Robertson described precautions and tactics required when flying into or over enemy-held territory:

> Safe flying in a combat area required flying as low as possible. As time went on, we would raise a wing to clear [a] tree instead of jumping over it. I spent hours trying to figure out what would give me the best odds to stay alive. I had installed a shoulder harness that came out of a Flying Tiger P-40 and soon after, all the planes had them. When one of our planes was hit while climbing a hill, I figured a way to get over...while still being a silhouette. I would fly directly at the hill and at the last moment turn and go up it diagonally, across the top and then down it in the opposite direction. This kept me pretty much on course and seemed to work for me. I tried to use up the gas in the tank over the exit door so I would have less gas to get through if I was shot down. I avoided if possible all open fields. We wore chutes, but since we seldom were high enough to use them I would just fasten the straps so they would stay clear of the flap handle. (73:11)

On 19 December, the 165ᵗʰ Liaison Squadron returned to Burma to support General Stopford's exhausted men. Almost at once, Captain Ulery moved operations to Kawlin, a captured Nippon-constructed airfield. When the Japanese pulled out, they attempted to destroy the runway by implanting explosives and detonating them. Their method was simple, crude, and mostly unsuccessful. A brick was tied to a tripod over the fused end of the bomb protruding from the ground. The rope was set afire and when the rope burned through, the brick fell, setting off the bomb. Few cratered the runway. After removing the remainder, operations went on unabatedly. Although records are somewhat fragmentary, for December, the number of casualties flown to medical encampments increased to 2,439 but recorded movement of materiel decreased to 88,996 pounds.

After a month of intense air activity, Captain Lynn's men headed west for Asansol leaving Fenny to the 6ᵗʰ Fighter Squadron. Accompanying Captain Pitts was the newly-arrived 326ᵗʰ Airdrome Squadron. Three airdrome squadrons, the last pieces of General Arnold's dream organization, had arrived in the India-Burma Theater near the end of November. The units came from separate locations in the United States:

lessly pushed across the banks of the Chindwin, the 166ᵗʰ Liaison Squadron increasingly operated into a newly spaded runway at Kalemyo, code name Ky, located west of Kalewa. Constantly on the move, XXXIII Corps requested the light plane pilots add-on support missions of food, medical supplies, and POL. As always, casualties were the priority. To maximize loads and improve responsiveness, freshly promoted Captain Van Wagner directed the 166ᵗʰ Liaison Squadron to In, a new forward strip at Inbaung on 6 December. Shortly thereafter, Lieutenant Beasley's squadron joined the effort. From Inbaung, a profusion of jungle runways, mere coordinates on maps, sprouted with only code names—Saw, Pan, Kad, Ram, and one noted as merely in the vicinity of Katha.

Light plane pilots were ready to respond whenever called. In early December, a British vanguard force working in the Railway Corridor area was jumped by the Japanese. After a fire fight, the unit notified Inbaung radio operators of an urgent need to evacuate two badly wounded soldiers. The pickup point was only rough coordinates to a makeshift 600-foot strip near Katha on the Irrawaddy River. Master Sergeant Edward W. Schnatzmeyer and Technical Sergeant Charles S. Fessler of the 164ᵗʰ Liaison Squadron volun-

TABLE 7
Airdrome Squadrons

Squadron	Type Services	Origination
72ⁿᵈ Airdrome Squadron	Transports	Casper Army Air Field, Wyoming
309ᵗʰ Airdrome Squadron	Light Planes	Smoky Hill Army Air Field, Salina, Kansas
326ᵗʰ Airdrome Squadron	Fighters	Hunter Field, Georgia

Arriving on the *USS General H. W. Butner*, the logistics squadrons disembarked at Bombay on 23 November. From the West India coastal city, they traveled to Asansol by train. Upon reaching their new home, the men learned for the first time they were part of the 1ˢᵗ Air Commando Group. After a year of maintaining their own airplanes, air commando units welcomed the new arrivals with open arms. During in-processing, Major Moist instructed the 326ᵗʰ Airdrome Squadron to marshal at nearby Ningha Air Base, organize for deployment, and await further instructions. Colonel Gaty selected the 326ᵗʰ Airdrome Squadron to initiate front line maintenance operations for the group.

The maintenance and munitions men were greeted warmly by members of the 6ᵗʰ Fighter Squadron at their beddown location of Fenny and immediately the unit made its presence felt. The number of missions flown during December skyrocketed. For the month, the 6ᵗʰ Fighter Squadron averaged 22.36 sorties a day with 23 available planes. Major Pitts reported over 20 aircraft were in commission each day for an average availability of 87.133 percent. Sortie reliability also improved; the squadron flew 440 sorties for the month with only 15 planes failing to complete their mission—a 96.51 percent success rate.

Primary mission of the fighter squadron remained bomber escort and the air commandos conducted sweeps of the airfields at Heho, Meiktila, and Kangaung while accompanying 12ᵗʰ Bomb Group. Meager enemy opposition persisted. In a combined mission on 12 December, 19 aircraft from the 6ᵗʰ Fighter Squadron, 19 more Thunderbolts of the 5ᵗʰ Fighter Squadron, and aircraft from two RAF squadrons flew escort duty for 12 Liberators of the 99ᵗʰ Squadron. The armada's targets were the airfields of Myaikto and Hninpale in the Rangoon area. Twelve Oscars intercepted the flight, briefly engaged, but carefully avoided prolonged air-to-air combat. Air commando pilots pursued, managing only a single gun pass. Captain Jack U. Klarr claimed a possible kill while Lieutenant Hauert reported damaging another aircraft of the Rising Sun.

The air commandos' dive bombing attacks also had a sobering impact on Japanese ground defenses. Using enemy tracers to direct them to targets, Captain Pitts' men bombed and strafed gun emplacements, runways, and hangars at Nyaungbinywa and Magwe inflicting significant damage. In time, the Japanese discontinued the use of tracer rounds in self-defense. Interspersed between escort missions, the 6ᵗʰ Fighter Squadron returned to operations against bridges, rail lines, locomotives, rolling stock, trucks, river barges, and Nippon command and control radar sites. Unfortunately,

Captain Pitts lost Second Lieutenant Brents M. Lowrey during a strafing run on box cars northwest of Yonsingyi when an explosion occurred. It was Lowrey's first combat mission.

The men of the 6ᵗʰ Fighter Squadron repeatedly struck the Mu River bridge—four scheduled missions and one serendipitous excursion. In the target rich central Burma river countryside, the air commandos' dive bombing attacks left gaping holes in sections of track and roadways at Wetlet, Myotha, Saye, Ketka, Taungtha, Myitnge, Sinthegon, and Minbu. Rail and bridge repair became a constant job for the Japanese resulting in the invention of a diesel powered locomotive with two sets of wheels—one was for operating on tracks, the other was a set of tires for gaps in the rail line. The vehicle was known as a *loco-truck* and became a trophy sought by every pilot. Despite such reactions to air attacks, Japanese lines of communication were tangled and disemboweled by the incessant attacks from Captain Pitts' Thunderbolts aided by Captain Wagner's B-25 Mitchell crews.

Major Wagner's Night Intruder Section continued to operate during the 13-day moon period between 23 December 1944 and 3 January 1945. Results were impressive. Engineering modified the Mitchells with internal fuel tanks to extend range; the crews added supply dumps to the increasing list of targets. When POL products or munitions came under the crosshairs of B-25 crewmen, night became day. Moonlight-aided B-25 strafing runs devastated locomotive traffic throughout Central Burma; the Night Intruder Section claimed 14 destroyed and 14 more damaged during the month. Likewise, motor transports also fell prey to the night intruders—58 were destroyed and more than 138 were reported damaged. Although the missions were highly successful, the cloak of darkness did not always ensure B-25 night intruder sorties were completely unseen by the Japanese.

Captain Merchant and Lieutenant McKaig (a glider pilot flying as a B-25 copilot) had been flying a night intruder mission; as they made their last pass before heading home, Japanese tracer rounds hit the bomb bay and left wing. Initially engine readings were normal, but Technical Sergeant Ralph E. Duddeck, the crew chief, reported visible signs of fluid streaming from the number one engine nacelle. Merchant climbed to 6,000 feet and turned west toward Chittagong; within 5 minutes, the oil pressure dropped to zero. Increases in tachometer readings and propeller noise confirmed the worst. Depressing the feathering button, Captain Merchant ordered the crew to lighten the load, but the Mitchell began a gradual descent. Making matters worse, the fuel transfer line had also been severed, the radio was unresponsive, and ground fog covered the landscape. Low on fuel, the crew could not get back to base but were sure the aircraft was over friendly territory. Holding wings level, Merchant ordered the crew to bailout. Fortunately, all members were recovered safely. Apart from this mission, the rhubarb raids on Japanese night activities proved so successful, Captain Wagner was allocated three more B-25 aircraft. The new Mitchells brought the section's authorized compliment to seven.

While the air commandos pounded Nippon targets, the remainder of General Stopford's units crossed the Chindwin at Kalewa. Unexpectedly, after an initial strong showing, Japanese resistance crumbled. Similarly, Major General T. W. "Pete" Rees led the 19th Division across the Zibyu Taungdan Range virtually unchecked. Well ahead of the forecast timetable, he joined up with General Festing's 36th Division at Wuntho on 16 December. The Burmese villages where only days before Japanese units massed were now empty. General Leese acknowledged air commando efforts as part of the reason for this unexpected change in Japanese tactics, "Not only was [Burma Area Army's General Kimura] short of transport, but lacking air supremacy, his movements by day were restricted, and his lines of communication [were] damaged by bombing." (109:1892) In short, the Japanese had little capacity to fight; there were few other choices than to stall.

Expecting a fierce fight as soon as his army crossed the Chindwin, General Slim braced to engage the enemy. He anticipated the need to aggressively fight his way to the banks of the Irrawaddy River before the tropical rains of May and secure Northern Burma. Yet when operations began, reports from unit commanders indicated Operation CAPITAL was based on the wrong assumption. General Kimura was not spoiling for a conflict; instead, he patiently waited and prepared. Time was profitable to the Japanese; it would allow the Emperor's army to reorganize and heal. General

Slim's foe intended to permit the Allies to reach Central Burma where his logistics would become increasingly difficult. At the same time, Japanese supply difficulties would be simplified because of the proximity to their bases. Given the circumstances, General Kimura was confident his 10 divisions could overcome the Allies. Therefore, he issued orders to harass and delay any advance, but avoid a finishing fight until the British were drawn across the Irrawaddy.

If General Slim became ambitious, the Japanese openly invited XIV Army further east, intent on opposing the Irrawaddy River crossing with strength when Allied supply lines were overextended. Win or lose, General Kimura anticipated battle on the Central Plains of Burma would be a climactic finish to operations in Southwest Asia. His plan was orthodox and sound except that it failed to appreciate Allied air capabilities. On the other hand, XIV Army's fate rested on air superiority that must never be relinquished even for a moment. The risks were obvious to General Slim and his staff, but so were the opportunities—Mandalay was achievable before the monsoons.

The change in situation was not easily adjusted. General Slim needed a new plan. To ensure men, supplies, weapons, and equipment were available, normal red tape channels required him to seek consent from each level of command. British Army planners in India and the SEAC Headquarters staff in Ceylon would have to approve; his plan then would require the concurrence of the British Chiefs-of-Staff in London. If it passed all others, the last hurdle would be an agreement in Washington from the Combined Chiefs-of-Staff. Additionally complicating was the prospect that Generalissimo Chiang might balk. For an army engaged in the field, any delays in the approval process could be fatal. General Slim decided to sidestep the administrative millstone. Straightway, he formulated Operation EXTENDED CAPITAL and initiated the revised operation without formally obtaining approval.

Captain Merchant's B-25H Mitchell Crew
Front Row* (L-R) Technical Sergeant Ralph E. Duddeck, Crew Chief and Top Turret Gunner; Staff Sergeant Harland P. Smith, Radio Operator; Second Lieutenant Harry L. McKaig, Copilot *Back Row* (L-R) Captain Frank B. Merchant, Pilot; Staff Sergeant Leroy H. Baker, Tail Gunner; unidentified individual who asked for an orientation flight *Courtesy of 1ˢᵗ Air Commando Association

10

The Irawaddy River

In brief, EXTENDED CAPITAL was based on surprise, deception, and overwhelming force—a feint toward Mandalay while the primary thrust targeted the trimodal supply hub at Meiktila to the south. The seeds of the plan were planted during the early successes of Operation THURSDAY. Typical of his indirect approach, General Wingate had suggested the way to further weaken the Japanese ability to fight was to attack the dragon's underbelly in Meiktila. The site was the nexus of Nippon rail, road, and air logistics. Through this crossroad city all supplies for Northern Burma passed. General Leese, ALFSEA commander, described Meiktila's importance to Japanese operations:

> ... all the Japanese communications radiated from Meiktila and Thazi; north to Mandalay and Lashio, south to Rangoon, north-west to Myingyan, west to Kyaukpadaung and thence to the oil fields at Chauk and Yenangyaung, and east, *via* Kalaw, to Siam. Meiktila was the advanced supply base for all the Japanese forces in Burma, with the exception of those in Arakan. At Meiktila, too, were located the principal Japanese airfields, the capture of which would be of inestimable value to us. If we could seize Meiktila, and hold it, the whole structure of the Japanese defense in Central Burma was bound to collapse. (109:1901)

While the British Army in the India-Burma Theater planned EXTENDED CAPITAL, circumstances in China worsened. The impact would be felt by General Slim. During the Burmese monsoons, the Japanese armies in China initiated an offensive, Operation ICHI-GO, targeting Allied airfields. In the wake of the Nippon assault, Chinese ground forces were bowled over from Yochow to Liuchow. General Chennault's 14th Air Force bases in east China systematically fell to the more experienced forces of the Emperor—Ling-ling, Kweilin, Liuchow, and Nan-ning submitted. By November, the communication center at Kweiyang, the airfields of Kunming, and China's wartime capital of Chungking appeared threatened. Their loss meant Hump operations were in jeopardy.

Downplaying General Slim's situation, General Wedemeyer argued for the return of Chinese divisions currently under General Sultan's NCAC.

Specifically, Generalissimo Chiang insisted on the recall of the Chinese 14th and 22nd Divisions. Several other smaller units were also demanded—the Chinese 6th Army Headquarters, a heavy mortar regiment, two mobile hospitals, and a signal company. The drain from the campaign in Burma would total more than 25,000 Chinese soldiers; between 250 and 400 Americans; 1,596 horses and mules; four dozen each howitzers, heavy mortars, and antitank weapons; and 42 jeeps. Over Admiral Lord Mountbatten's protest, the Combined Chiefs-of-Staff decided in favor of the Generalissimo and authorized the airlift.

Operation GRUBWORM
When Japan's Operation ICHI-GO threatened Chinese airfields, Generalissimo Chiang Kai-shek demanded the return of two divisions. In December 1944, Colonel S. D. Grubbs assigned the 319th Troop Carrier Squadron and 317th Troop Carrier Squadron the responsibility of moving the divisions' mules and horses across the Himalayas. The 1st and 2nd Air Commandos operated from Warazup, Burma, and flew 488 missions over the Hump. *Courtesy of 1st Air Commando Association*

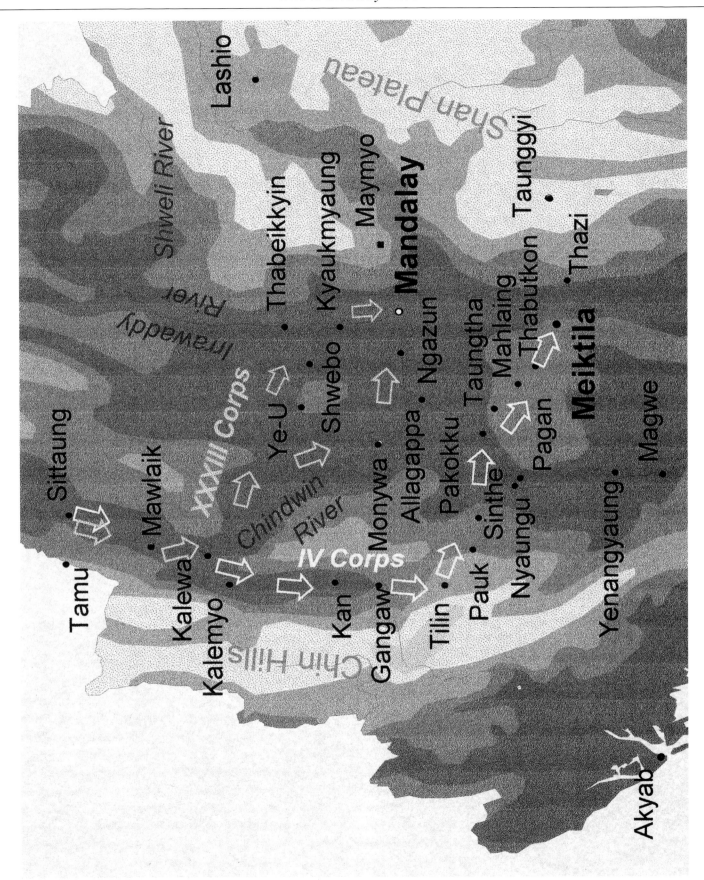

Map 9- North Central Burma 1944-45: Operation EXTENDED CAPITAL

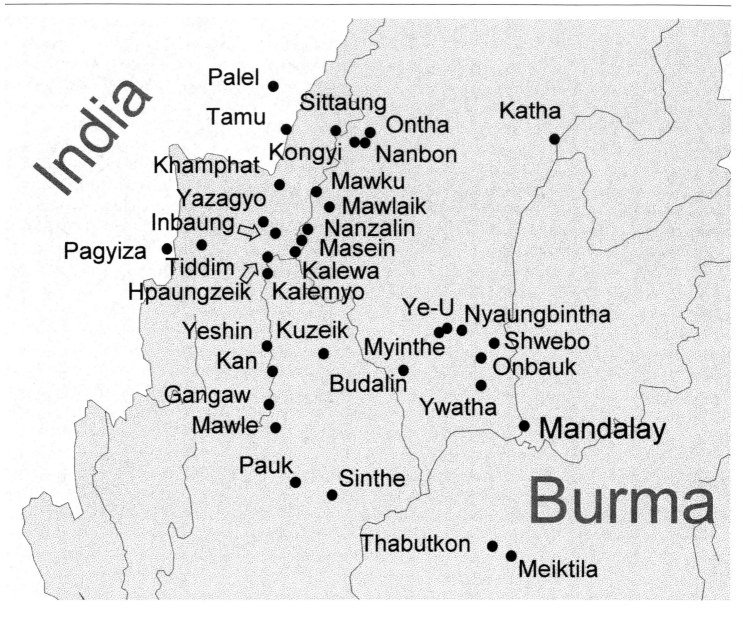

Map 10- North Central Burma 1945: Light Plane Operating Airfields

Reluctantly, SEAC released Dakotas from both the 1ˢᵗ Air Commando Group and 2ⁿᵈ Air Commando Group along with C-46 Commandos of Air Transport Command. Originally labeled Operation GLOWWORM, the transfer from Burma was renamed Operation GRUBWORM when Colonel S. D. Grubbs, Deputy Chief of Staff, 10ᵗʰ Air Force, assumed responsibility. Operations began 5 December from five separate airfields in Northern Burma— Myitkyina North, Myitkyina South, Sahmaw, Warazup, and the newly completed Nansin. Myitkyina South was the hub of the transfer due to its 24-hour capability and fuel storage facilities.

Members of the 319ᵗʰ Troop Carrier Squadron were inexperienced in Hump flying but up to the task. Private Robert J. Byrne, radio operator, recalled losing an engine at 10,000 feet on the first flight. As the aircraft slowly drifted toward the mountains below,

the crew frantically tried to airstart the engine. When it finally relit, the crew was past halfway; they elected to continue. Repeatedly, Dakota crews had to use all their skills. The flights were tedious and aircraft were subject to swirling winds and sudden downdrafts. Marking the accomplishment upon landing in China were the following words on the control tower at Kunming: *Congratulations. You made it again.* Initially, the air commandos were not accustomed to the rigors of the route over the Himalayas. After an unusually high number of headaches were reported on the first day of the operation, the men were issued and instructed to use oxygen masks.

On 10 November, Colonel Grubbs decided to reserve the C-46 Commandos for troop transportation, so he tasked the 319ᵗʰ Troop Carrier Squadron and the 2ⁿᵈ Air Commando Group's 317ᵗʰ Troop

Carrier Squadron to move the animals. Working along side Chinese laborers, air commandos reconfigured their airplanes by removing seats, covering control cables with tarpaulins, placing cocoa mats on the floor to prevent slipping, spreading hay over the matting, and constructing bamboo stalls. Each sortie transported a team of four to seven handlers along with the primary load of four to five animals. Originally using ramps to load the beasts, the air commandos discovered direct transfer from trucks was easier and faster than shoving or dragging truculent animals. As a result, Chinese laborers were instructed to dig an excavation ditch to match the height of the truck bed to the Dakota's cargo floor.

Once loaded and airborne, air commando crews left the access door opened for ventilation—five guard ropes were clipped to lugs mounted on the door frame for restraint and safety. Drugs were considered to keep the horses and mules sedated during flight, but it was unnecessary—the high altitude made the animals lethargic. Only one horse was lost; it broke a leg when deplaning without a ramp in China. Unfortunately two C-47 Dakotas from the 317th Troop Carrier Squadron crashed into the mountains on the first day of GRUBWORM. After that, Major Holm insisted a ground-to-air radio station be established to maintain constant contact with each aircraft from takeoff to recovery at the end of the mission. Beyond command and control, the radio helped maintenance personnel to cycle flightworthy aircraft into the flow while they performed repairs and services on others.

Generalissimo Chaing's troops were known to be ruthless and rowdy. Because many did not want to return to China, some flights required military police escorts. Corporal Robert J. Schieferstein, a C-47 aviation mechanic normally assigned to Major Holm's crew, noted his flight departed Burma with six bullock and six handlers.

Dakota Leaders
Dakota pilots of 1st Air Commando Group (L-R) Captain Edgar L. "Snakebite" Barham; Captain Thomas R. Baker; Captain Neil I. "Nipper" Holm. *Courtesy of 1st Air Commando Association*

On arrival in Kunming, only five handlers were aboard. When questioned, a handler, in gestures and hand signals, indicated the man had either jumped or was thrown out the open access panel over the Himalayas. None of the Chinese soldiers seemed overly concerned. The remaining flights were without serious incidents. When the movement of Chinese units ended on 5 January 1945, 1,328 sorties had been flown—488 by the two air commando squadrons.

Operation GRUBWORM's disruption to XIV Army plans was significant. At the moment, General Slim suffered the loss of aircraft more than the 25,000 Chinese soldiers. He described the circumstances in later years:

> At dawn on December 10 I was awakened in my headquarters at Imphal by the roar of engines as a large number of aircraft took off in succession and passed low overhead. I knew loaded aircraft were due to leave … but I was surprised at this early start…. To my consternation, I learned that, without warning, three squadrons of American Dakotas [sic](seventy-five aircraft), allotted to Fourteenth Army maintenance, had been suddenly ordered to China…. The supplies in the aircraft, already loaded for Fourteenth Army, were dumped on the Imphal strip and the machines took off. The noise of their engines was the first intimation anyone in Fourteenth Army had of the ad-

Animal Transport
C-47 ground crews removed seats, covered control cables with tarps, placed cocoa mats on the floor, spread hay over the matting, and constructed bamboo stalls. Leaving a door panel open for ventilation, the air commandos discovered the animals were docile in the rarefied air. *Courtesy of 1st Air Commando Association*

ministrative crisis now bursting upon us…. It meant that the second foundation—a firm allotment of air lift—on which all our plans had been based, was swept away…. Thanks to great efforts by ALFSEA and SEAC and by drastic reductions in XV Corps' air lift the lost tonnage was gradually replaced, but our plans were delayed by a fortnight or three weeks. (44:329-330)

The interruption affected General Slim's efforts to overcome the mistaken first foundation of XIV Army's plan—a fight on the Shwebo Plains. In the original plan, Operation CAPITAL, the British were arrayed against the Japanese in an arc with Mandalay as the focal point. When XIV Army crossed the Chindwin, General Messervy's IV Corps advanced southeastward flanked by General Sultan's NCAC on the north and General Stopford's XXXIII Corps from the west. That alignment shifted when XIV Army met token opposition on the eastern side of the Chindwin. Still without full approval of Operation EXTENDED CAPITAL, General Slim subtly modified each corps' direction of march as XIV Army neared the west bank of the wide Irrawaddy River. Assigning General Stopford's XXXIII Corps a distinctly straight and visible approach on Mandalay via Ye-U and Monywa, General Slim wanted to affix General Katamura's 15th Army on the defense of Mandalay. With XXXIII Corps maintaining Japanese attention, General Slim directed IV Corps to slip behind Stopford's advance and march secretly due south to Pakokku. To cover the missing corps, XIV Army transferred 19th Division to General Stopford, established a fake IV Corps headquarters, and originated bogus message traffic to show General Messervy was still advancing along his earlier course.

Heavy Fighter
First Lieutenant Jack U. Klarr's P-47D Thunderbolt, *Miss Lillian II*, loaded with three 1,000-pound bombs. In a similarly configured P-47D, Major Younger A. "Sonny" Pitts, Jr.; Major Roland R. Lynn; and First Lieutenant Malcolm J. Wilkins demonstrated the Thunderbolt's deep interdiction capability. *Courtesy of Elwood Jamison, 1ˢᵗ Air Commando Association*

Success of Operation EXTENDED CAPITAL was dependent on the invisibility of IV Corps. General Stopford crossed the Chindwin River on a 1,154-foot Bailey bridge at Kalewa and began a deliberate advance on Mandalay encouraging the Japanese to mass defenses around the Burmese capital. After allowing XXXIII Corps center stage, IV Corps began marching 150 miles down the Gangaw Valley to swing around the Japanese flank. Movement of XXXIII Corps was synchronized with the pace set by General Messervy. If at any time, a lone Japanese soldier, detached unit, or observant pilot reported IV Corps' location, the element of surprise would be lost and the entire operation could be compromised. A cover plan was released of another Chindit-style LRP operation in case IV Corps was detected, but the bulk of the plan's security rested on the wings of India-Burma Theater airmen. Their crucial mission was to shield IV Corps movements from the eyes of all Japan.

As General Slim prepared Allied troops for Operation EXTENDED CAPITAL, the capacity of airlift within the India-Burma Theater defined the campaign—even the size of XIV Army's commitment of forces. Before the decision to cross the Irrawaddy River, General Slim summed up the operational constraints in the following manner:

> The problem, as almost all in Burma were, was one of supply and transport. I had available for the battle six and two-thirds divisions and two tank brigades, and I could, if I could use them, get another division, perhaps two, from India. But we should be four hundred miles from railhead; two hundred and fifty miles of that distance only fair weather road, unless we could rebuild it before the monsoon. After much discussion I had been given a firm allotment of supply aircraft on which to plan, but our airlift would come mainly from Comilla and Chittagong, at the extreme limit of practical range; even Imphal was two hundred miles away and not served by rail. Scheme as we might, take risks to the limit of reason, we could not maintain trans-Chindwin [operations with] more than four and two-thirds divisions and the two tank brigades. (44:316-317)

The prospect of ranging across Burma's most celebrated river set in motion adjustments to Allied timetables and assignments for the Dry Season Offensive of 1944-45. Two primary issues placed increased emphasis on securing forward air bases: logistics support and force protection. When XIV Army crossed the Irrawaddy River, the added distance between Indian supply sites and General Slim's army resulted in higher fuel consumption for transport aircraft. Forced to include additional fuel, load planners decreased cargo tonnage proportionately. Hilary St. George Saunders wrote of the added strain on flight crews, "By the time the plains of Burma were reached, the crews of Dakotas flying from Chittagong, Comilla, and Tulihal had to take off at first light and if they had orders to make three trips, did not complete their work until long after dark."

To overcome concerns about long-range fighter missions, Colonel Gaty's men conducted a demonstration of the Thunderbolt's deep interdiction capability. On New Year's Eve at Asansol, Major Pitts, 6th Fighter Squadron commander, proved the feasibility of carrying heavy bomb loads by taking off in a P-47 laden with three 1,000-pound general purpose bombs. The following day, the deployed 5th Fighter Squadron incorporated the capability into a mission. After arming a pair of aircraft with three 1,000-pound bombs, munitions specialists watched Major Lynn and Lieutenant Wilkins depart Fenny for Central Burma. During the sortie, the two air commandos cleared a 10,000-foot mountain range, attacked an important railroad bridge 3 miles northwest of Taungdwingyi, released all six bombs resulting in a direct hit on the span, and returned to Fenny. Fellow 5th Fighter Squadron air commando, Second Lieutenant William S. Burghardt reported, "When they landed, they had nothing showing on their gas gauges." (120:—) The record breaking round trip covered over 700 miles but came too late to dissuade General Slim.

By 12 December 1944, General Christison's XV Corps was already responding to orders to renew an advance in the Arakan to capture the vital airfield on Akyab Island. Spearheading the campaign southward in the Kaladan Valley was the 81st West African Division and giving flank protection astride the Mayu Range was the 82nd West African Division. The two units, supported by a detachment of four L-5 Sentinels of the 166th Liaison Squadron, moved in parallel across the estuary-etched dagger of land toward Foul Point, the tip of the Arakan peninsula. Working their way down the chaungs and jungle-clad coast, the African divisions encountered soft resistance. Fate had smiled on XV Corps.

At approximately the same time as General Christison received his operational orders, General Kimura was reacting to XXXIII Corps' conspicuous march on Mandalay. Lieutenant General Shozo

Southern Belle
Second Lieutenant William S. Burghardt and Staff Sergeant Robert Cebrelli stand before P-47D Thunderbolt No. 10, *Southern Belle.* **Courtesy of 1ˢᵗ Air Commando Association**

(43:348) Each mile east of the Chindwin River meant Assam bases were of less value as supply sites.

Similarly, greater distance adversely affected escort and close air support coverage. While sustaining XIV Army beyond the Irrawaddy, Dakotas would be entering enemy-held air space and subject to constant harassment by Japanese fighters. General Kirby described the situation in this way: "Though fighter cover and standing patrols were to be provided in the forward areas as and when possible, there would be times when, as the Allied armies progressed deeper into Burma, transport aircraft might have to operate in front of any warning system and without protection." (26:402) General Slim's ground troops also required air power to provide airborne artillery deep on Burmese soil to sustain offensive operations. Therefore, Admiral Lord Mountbatten believed it necessary to capture and develop airfields along the coast of Burma. In this way, SEAC could shorten lines of communication, maximize cargo loads, and broaden fighter and bomber protection.

Fongutongu Bombing Missions
Shown on the fuselage of the B-25H Mitchell are two markings. The upper symbol, similar to the Night Intruder Section insignia, denoted 14 night missions. The lower bombs signified 6 day missions. Night Intruder crews got credit for one and a half missions for each night mission flown. *Courtesy of 1ˢᵗ Air Commando Association*

Light Airfield Recognition Photos
Operating out of various dirt strips in Burma, light plane pilots used aids such as this to review visual airfield recognition features prior to flight. *Courtesy of 1ˢᵗ Air Commando Association*

Flying Pay Officer and Jack of All Trades
Major Robert E. Moist scheduled, cajoled, or bribed his way around India, Burma, and China to ensure 1ˢᵗ Air Commando personnel were paid. He later saved much of the unit's history from destruction. *Courtesy of 1ˢᵗ Air Commando Association*

Sakurai, 28th Army commander, involuntarily allowed 15th Army to siphon off Arakan units to shore up Mandalay's defenses. Able to advance swiftly, XV Corps marshaled its forces for an attack on the airfield at Akyab. Converging on the spit of land across the Mayu River from Akyab was an overwhelming force. Joining the 81st and 82nd West African Divisions were the 25th Indian Division, 3rd Commando Brigade, a squadron of medium tanks, a medium artillery regiment, a naval bombardment force of three cruisers, and 200 planes of the 224 Group RAF.

General Christison established D-Day as 3 January 1945. As the new year began, the men of XV Corps momentarily hesitated in anticipation of a decisive battle. Unexpectedly, the dramatic pause lingered. Instead of a blood bath, the capture of Akyab proved anticlimactic as recorded in the following account:

> On 2nd January, 1945, the pilots in two Hurricanes, flying low over Akyab, saw a number of its inhabitants waving their arms to signify that the Japanese had left the island. A few hours later the former Judge of the island, Wing Com-

mander J. B. G. Bradley, of the Royal New Zealand Air Force, landed in a light aircraft, to be greeted by the local doctor. Akyab [the prize of so many strategic plans] was occupied without opposition... (43:349)

Unprepared for the news, XV Corps' commander proceeded with the invasion as planned. After all areas were reported clear of Emperor Hirohito's troops, General Christison personally verified the Japanese had decamped. Once confirmed, 224 Group RAF commander, Vice-Marshal the Earl of Bandon, ordered RAF Spitfires to begin using the airfield the following day. These strategic airfields were vital to SEAC plans. From Akyab, Nippon forces at Toungoo were within reach and the twin airfield in the Bay of Bengal were highly vulnerable. Staff Sergeant Woodrow W. "Woody" Cheek was assigned to fly an Airborne Engineer from Calcutta to survey the Akyab airfield for possible improvements. En route, Sergeant Cheek maneuvered around barrage balloons at 1,500 feet only to be jumped by two Japanese Oscars. Caught between the Rising Sun and Allied antiaircraft artillery, he headed for the tree tops. As the Oscars slowed to near stall speed and began descending, a Mark 6 Spitfire suddenly appeared from off the deck and entered a climbing turn to intercept. Freed from the Japanese air attack, Sergeant Cheek landed quickly and the British engineering officer began the process of making the airfield all weather capable. By early February, the forward bases of Ramree and Cheduba were in British hands; from that time on, Rangoon was within the outstretched wing of Allied fighters and bombers.

On the Northern front, fighting between Japanese and Chinese troops continued in the upper Salween Valley. Chinese General Wei Li-huang's Y-Force, under the operational control of General Sultan's NCAC, steadily drove the last stubborn Japanese units from the Burma Road. The Chinese advanced from the mountainous defiles along the Sino-Burman border toward the occupied city of Wanting while General Sultan attempted to linkup with General Wei's troops. Dug in Japanese units attempted to stand between NCAC and the primary goal of American strategy, the reopening of the Burma Road. As British and Chinese forces converged near Mong-Yu, General Sultan's men mistook Y-Force for Nippon soldiers. Only the valor and leadership of Brigadier General George W. Sliney avoided fratricide and allowed the two armies to combine and expel the last Japanese from the road. On 27 January 1945, Admiral Lord Mountbatten sent a signal to British and American staffs announcing the first Burma Road convoy in nearly 3 years was scheduled to leave Namhkam, Burma. At last the overland route from Indian supply bases to China was open. To further aid Generalissimo Chiang, a POL pipeline from Ledo to Kunming was also underway. As the air commandos completed Operation GRUBWORM missions, Dakota crews quickly were put on detached service at Tingkawk Sakan to haul pipe.

Meanwhile in the Central Region, General Stopford's XXXIII Corps continued to advance southward on Mandalay. His men occupied Shwebo on 10 January. Three days later, Major General T. W. "Pete" Rees, commander of the 19th Indian Division, initiated a crossing of the Irrawaddy River 50 miles north of Mandalay at the town of Thebeikkyin. Unlike previous probes into the underbelly of the Japanese dragon that met weak return fire, this time General Kimura's reaction was swift and ferocious. The Japanese threw the 15th Division and 53rd Division against the bridgehead in what General Slim described as "the heaviest artillery concentration our troops had yet endured on so small a front..." (44:345) For a brief moment, they carried the battle, but in time, the undermanned Japanese units were unable to hold the British. After being temporarily thrown back, General Rees expanded his bridgehead. After securing Thebeikkyin, 19th Division reconstituted a few miles downstream and General Rees' men successfully completed the Irrawaddy crossing at Kyaukmyaung on 17 January. In short order, General Stopford had established a 3-pronged attack on Mandalay and riveted Japanese attention on the defense of the Burmese capital.

Aiding XXXIII Corps' advance and IV Corps' swing outside General Stopford's right flank were light plane pilots of the 1st Air Commando Group. Captain Beasley's 164th Liaison Squadron began 1945 flying missions from Inbaung, Burma. The squadron, equipped with 26 Sentinels and 4 Norsemen, supported General Messervy's IV Corps ground operations in the Kabaw and Myittha River Valleys. To the northeast, the 165th Liaison Squadron, operating from Kawlin, directly supported 19th Division's spearhead advance of XXXIII Corps toward Mandalay along the Railway Corridor. As General Messervy pressed south and General Stopford southeastward around XXXIII Corps' right flank, L-pilots responded by hop scotching across Burma toward Pakokku and the key rail center at Shwebo.

In their wake, the air commandos established several temporary dirt strips in the untamed countryside. The 164th Liaison Squadron operated from new dirt strips at Kan, Kuzeik, Gangaw, and Mawle while Captain Ulery's men opened Budalin, Myinthe, Nyaungbintha, Shwebo, and Ywatha. Dust was a constant problem primarily because of water shortages in the immediate area. The largest runway, Budalin, was 6,000 by 225 feet; Mawle, only 900 by 40 feet, was the smallest. During the month-long migration, the two liaison squadrons overlapped operations often using the same

Logging Light Plane Missions
Master Sergeant Charles E. Bowden completes his dispatch log for Staff Sergeant Jospeh P. Eagan. The Air Commandos tracked each flight to ensure pilots were accounted for during a mission. *Courtesy of 1st Air Commando Association*

Washed Out
Flight Officer Donald K. Miller's UC-64 *Grin and Bear It* after accident at Ye-U in January 1945. Also injured in the accident was Second Lieutenant John R. Tuck. *Courtesy of Donald K. Miller, 1ˢᵗ Air Commando Association*

airstrip to support both corps. Makeshift runways and clearings had the unlikely code names of Bak, Ben, Kal, Kon, Leg, Mun, Paul, Sal, Tab, Tuck, and Zee. At each airstrip, the Flying Sergeants found surgical and ambulatory cases staged for return to Indian hospitals.

Dutifully, each month, jack-of-all-trades administrative officer, Major Moist, searched the landscape for each segment of the 1ˢᵗ Air Commando Group. Known affectionately to the men in the field as the Flying Pay Officer, Moist scheduled, cajoled, or bribed his way around India, Burma, and China to ensure Colonel Gaty's men were paid and official orders were delivered. Although not a certified pilot, Moist learned to fly while working as an assistant maintenance officer at the Spartan School of Aeronautics during a stint in civilian life. Over time, he convinced others he could conduct his business more efficiently if a Sentinel were left at his disposal—with or without a pilot. His only safety-related incident was a forced landing over the Ganges River, but that did not deter him. No matter how far flung the group, Major Moist always found the men.

On 9 January, Major Ulery (DOR: 5 January 1945) led his men to Kangyi where British heavy artillery was pounding Japanese bunkers along the railroad tracks. Quickly responding to the fighting, 165ᵗʰ Liaison Squadron pilots initiated a hub-and-spoke operation out of Ye-U, temporary home of XXXIII Corps Headquarters, and began picking up sick and wounded from surrounding airstrips. General Woodburn, British World War II historian, made the following observation concerning the contribution of Colonel Gaty's air commando liaison squadrons:

The only alternative to air evacuation meant a difficult journey lasting for several days, with many changes by road,

river, and rail, and the spread of the available medical facilities over great distances. The use of air transport made it possible to evacuate casualties who could not possibly have been moved safely by any other means. Not only did this save many lives and eliminate long painful journeys over bad roads, but the knowledge that the seriously sick and wounded could be in well-equipped base hospitals within a few hours was a potent factor in maintaining the high morale of the army. (26:413)

British soldiers fully appreciated the impact of the air commando medical evacuation flights. Often, General Stopford and members of the XXXIII Corps personally wrote letters commending the light plane pilots. The following extracts from a few of those letters show the close relationship and respect established between XIV Army and the air commandos:

You and your men [of the 164ᵗʰ Liaison Squadron] are doing a magnificent job, getting the casualties back; without you, our men would suffer a lot. I was only today [1 January 1945] praising your show to General Oliver Leese, and he fully appreciates the work you are doing for us, and only wishes he had more planes. I will soon be leaving these parts, and when I do, I will carry along with me a picture of America helping us with considerable success out of our difficulties. *Major General Richardson, War Office, London* (120:—)

I know that everyone in the [165ᵗʰ Liaison] Squadron has worked flat out in flying out casualties and thereby you have undoubtedly saved many lives and much pain. In addition to this primary task I would like you to know how greatly I have appreciated all that you have done to help me, personally, and members of my Staff in getting round the KABAW VALLEY to see the fighting troops. I have been greatly impressed by the unfailing cheerfulness and courtesy of your pilots who are always on top of their form however long hours they have been working and however short the notice to carry out a job. With best wishes to you and all ranks and I hope that we may operate together again one day. *Major General Stopford, Commander, XXXIII Corps* (131:November-December 1989:4)

Once more I am happy to be able to write and express my gratitude for the excellent work which has been done by Captain F. H. Van Wagner and 166 Liaison [Squadron] (Commando). I know that all the pilots have had to work very long hours in evacuating casualties, but as in the case of Captain Ulery's squadron, they have always remained cheerful and most helpful. It is a great pleasure to me and my staff to work with these most efficient liaison squadrons and I can assure you that what they have done is very thoroughly appreciated. *Major General Stopford, Commander, XXXIII Corps* (136:—)

I am sorry to hear that your [Major Ulery's] squadron is leaving...I particularly regret that you yourself are going, as there had grown up a very happy liaison between you and my staff, founded in the less restricted days when your squadron first came down and you did so many useful if unorthodox missions for us. Please thank your pilots and ground staff on my behalf for the valuable assistance they have given to my Division in the time they have worked with us. *Major General Fowkes, Commander, 11ᵗʰ East African Division* (135:—)

Despite the pace, not all events during the month concerned British casualties. As the air commandos moved further east, weather and more urgent missions periodically interrupted the sustaining flow of supplies and food. Flight Officer Kenneth Georgeson and Staff Sergeant Thomas J. Crosby, Jr., growing tired of a steady diet of corned beef, set out on their own to correct the problem. They decided to fly to Zing to trade silk parachute material, chocolates, salt, sugar, tobacco, and cloth for food stocks. After much haggling, the pair triumphantly secured 35 chickens from the local tribal chieftain. Transporting the precious cargo proved more difficult than the negotiations themselves. Staff Sergeant John E. Whitaker described the flight home:

> After loading the bamboo coops [in the L-5], no room was left for [both pilots]. Because of Jap[anese] patrols in the area, it was dangerous to leave an unguarded man on the strip, so after a few grunts and groans both men squeezed into the single front cockpit and took off for home. A few minutes out rough air broke open a coop, chickens flew everywhere. Holding on for dear life as the ship landed, [Lieutenant Georgeson] was unable to brush off the roosters perched on his head and shoulders. (133:15-16)

164ᵗʰ Liaison Squadron Pilots
Standing **(L-R): Staff Sergeant Rodney E. Petty, Jr.; Technical Sergeant Glen Abell; Staff Sergeant Thomas H. Denlea; Staff Sergeant Alexander Podlecki; Staff Sergeant Russell L. Parrott, Jr.** *Kneeling* **(L-R): Staff Sergeant John A. Nicholson; Staff Sergeant Raymond J. Ruksas; Staff Sergeant Julian Chiml** *Courtesy of 1ˢᵗ Air Commando Association*

For all the hazards of flying hens and roosters, the mission was pronounced a success. In a rare moment at the front lines of Burma, Captain Ulery's men and their British compatriots had all the chicken and dumplings they could eat.

Operations kicked into high gear in January indirectly causing a UC-64 Norseman to be lost unnecessarily at Ye-U. Second Lieutenant Don Miller and Second Lieutenant John R. Tuck, returning from the rear area, were forced into a prolonged holding pattern while larger transports outprioritized their approach. Lieutenant Miller remembered the incident differently from the official records. Elbowing their way into the L-5 pattern, the two pilots decided to land on the smaller strip parallel to the main runway. Unfamiliar with the approach, Lieutenant Miller unsuccessfully attempted to leap frog a lone tall standing tree. The Norseman, named *Grin and Bear It*, dropped like a rock, struck a mound of dirt, and flipped over. Lieutenant Miller remembered the incident as pilot error, but in written reports, the records stated the Norseman ran out of gas. Both pilots survived the wreckage, but Lieutenant Miller suffered a broken ankle and Lieutenant Tuck sustained a slight head injury. The UC-64 did not fair as well; maintenance declared the aircraft "washed-out."

By 12 January, the two liaison squadrons had advanced nearer the Irrawaddy. At Onbauk, where L-pilots shared runway operations with UC-64 Norsemen and C-47 Dakotas, the proximity of Allied forces posed a threat to Japanese security and spawned a grave retaliation. Although enemy aircraft activity essentially had been dormant since the monsoon season ended, a flight of 16 dark gray Oscars mounted a midmorning surprise attack on the front line airfield at Onbauk. In low, strafing passes, Japanese fighter pilots shot down two Dakotas and damaged another C-47 on the ground. Additionally, a Norseman carrying evacuation soldiers was attacked as it began its takeoff run. With Oscars passing over the field, the UC-64 pilot, Flight Officer Simon, braked sharply, deplaned, and angrily emptied his pistol at the receding enemy. All three Dakotas were lost; despite numerous holes, the durable Norseman, christened *Sympathizer*, was repairable.

The rapid advances of XXXIII Corps left pockets of Japanese around the newly constructed runways. Within the confines of air commando operating bases, ominous intelligence reports kept airborne antiaircraft batteries vigilant and Gurkha sentries on constant perimeter watch. Within sight of Nippon troops, light plane pilots conducted their primary aeromedical evacuation mission as well as transferred six Japanese POWs and a Burmese spy to rear headquarters for interrogation. While air commandos transported mail, medical supplies, and essential cargo to advancing troops, the proximity of the two great armies placed added emphasis on responsive search and rescue, air reconnaissance, and movement of senior XXXIII Corps personnel. Increased liaison operations were noted in all categories. By the close of January, 2,716 casualties and 228,974 tons of supplies were transported by the combined efforts of the 164ᵗʰ and 165ᵗʰ Liaison Squadrons.

As XXXIII Corps advanced in early January, 1ˢᵗ Air Commando fighter pilots shifted emphasis from enemy lines of communication to include attacks on Japanese troop positions. Marking targets along the intended path of XXXIII Corps and IV Crops, Colonel Gaty's Thunderbolts raided the Irrawaddy River towns of Myingyan, Pakokku, Pingyaung, Singu, Kangan, and Kawbet. Japanese units concentrated near the key airfields at Toungoo, Meiktila, Heho, and Nawnghkio fell under the air commando sights regularly. It was on one of these missions that First Lieutenant Richard T. Gilmore was jumped by two Japanese Oscars while strafing the airfield at Heho on 18 January. He attempted to use water injection to outrun them but his engine quit. Able to bail out and land safely, Lieutenant Gilmore was believed to be in friendly hands. Major Lynn radioed arrangements to drop supplies to him. Unexpectedly before Lieutenant Gilmore could be extracted, he was captured by a band of searching Nippon troops. An original member of the Cochran-Alison Group, Lieutenant Gilmore remained in the Rangoon POW Camp under the cruelest and most inhumane conditions for the remainder of the war. Although he survived the ordeal, his health was never the same.

Even though the Allies owned South-East Asian skies, the primary task of the 5ᵗʰ Fighter Squadron remained B-25 escort missions. Late in January, Major Lynn led his men to Sagaing near the renowned breast-shaped pagoda to soften up the rail yard defenses prior to the arrival of a B-25 Mitchell formation. The air commandos did such a good job, intelligence reports stated antiaircraft artillery effectiveness was cut in half by the time the bombers made their run. No airplanes were damaged during the Sagaing mission, but the 5ᵗʰ Fighter Squadron lost three airplanes during the month. In addition to Lieutenant Gilmore, Second Lieutenant Price was forced to bail out over the Chin Hills; he returned safely in February. A third aircraft crashed at Fenny on 19 January after takeoff roll. The pilot, Second Lieutenant James A. Knight, Jr., was uninjured but his P-47D was destroyed completely.

Back in Asansol, air commando fighter, bomber, transport, and liaison crews conducted training exercises as the SEAC staff rehearsed options for the Central Burma offensive. Captain Van Wagner's 166ᵗʰ Liaison Squadron worked extensively with British ground troops and Major Holm's Dakota pilots practiced force insertion procedures at Lalitpur during January. Although air commando tug pilots were highly experienced, night glider demonstrations were not without incident. After circling the field and flying the prescribed route, Dakota pilots were to locate the objective area and release their Wacos. Once free of gliders, transport crews discarded their tow lines in a designated field away from the exercise area. Due to miscommunication inside the aircraft, one C-47 inadvertently disconnected the suspended cable before reaching the clearing. At the morning debriefing, the crew discovered they had been right over the 1ˢᵗ Air Commando Group headquarters building when the line was released. The freefalling line plummeted through the thatched roof, finally coiling in a heap in Colonel Gaty's office.

Narrow Escape
Second Lieutenant James A. Knight, Jr., was uninjured when his aircraft crashed at Fenny after takeoff roll. *Courtesy of 1ˢᵗ Air Commando Association*

Fortunately no one was injured. In a magnanimous move, Colonel Gaty declined to investigate the identity of the crew.

Except occasional escort missions to Hninpale, Ondal, Meiktila, Kangaing, and Hedan, the Thunderbolts of the 6ᵗʰ Fighter Squadron operated out of Asansol during January. Ground crews concentrated on improving air-to-ground and air-to-air capability. Noting an unacceptable number of bomb release malfunctions, the Armament Section decided the mechanical devices needed to be modified. Immediately, they began scrounging the India-Burma Theater for available electric bomb release parts. Due to the irregular supply system, much of the month was devoted to installing and wiring the newly secured bombing mechanisms. Ground crews completed all conversions by the end of January and trials proved the system improved dive bombing accuracy. Second Lieutenant William S. Terranova, 6ᵗʰ Fighter Squadron Armament Officer, also obtained drawings of a new gun film assessor from the United States that showed target range, off angle, and lead angle when analyzing film. With help from the Group Utilities Section, the armament section constructed an exact duplicate of the film assessor. The device tested operationally ready when Lieutenant Ball's shoot down of an Oscar was studied using the new film equipment. The true test would come the following month during General Slim's assault on Meiktila and Mandalay.

Throughout the month, 1ˢᵗ Air Commando raids strangled Japanese rear communications. Thunderbolt pilots hit oil installations and gun emplacements at Yenangyaung to strip the Japanese of their vital sustainment petroleum supply. Miscellaneous attacks destroyed rail supplies, barges, road and railroad bridges, and a munitions plant. The Night Intruder Section intensified activities during the last 10 days of January by bombing Japanese concentrations in IV Corps' sector. After Colonel Gaty eliminated stationary motor transports and locomotives from target lists, silver Mitchells with five blue diagonal stripes specialized in antiaircraft and machine gun positions near bridges. To overcome the accuracy of 75 mm cannon fire, Japanese emplacements quit using tracers so air commando crews could not hunt down their prey. The tactic had some success with six aircraft taking hits, but only one was significant. Carrying an assortment of ordnance, Captain Wagner's men countered the Japanese tactic. Lieutenant Merchant described 1st Air Commando targeting methods:

> The most lucrative targets were the locomotives. We would normally fly 300 to 500 feet above the terrain and to one side of the tracks. It seemed that [the Japanese] would spot or hear us about the same time we saw them, because the sparks would start flying from their braking efforts to stop the train. I always carried a load of incendiary bombs, and would drop two or three clusters on my first pass as close to the locomotive as possible, not so much to do damage, but as a very visible identification to guide me on subsequent passes. My next several passes would be cross-track at the locomotive—and all crew members got into the action. With the eight forward firing 50's, and using the incendiaries to guide me, I would "walk" in to the locomotive. Once I passed over the target, I would pull up steeply, and the top-turret and tail gunners would open fire with twin 50's. Then I would go into a steep turn and let the waist gunner get in his licks. Usually not more than three passes were needed to make sure that the locomotive was out of commission, and again, the incendiaries would help in the verification process. I would maneuver to get the locomotive between me and the incendiaries and see steam coming out of hundreds of bullet holes in the engine. Then we would work on the boxcars for maximum damage. (120:—)

Flying 36 sorties during the 10-day period, Mitchell crews destroyed or damaged 15 locomotives, 255 motor transports, 128 pieces of rolling stock, and 1 small boat. Fighter and bomber operations were part of a general air campaign designed to incrementally destroy the Emperor's combat power in Burma by isolating truck and train traffic, depleting enemy stores, withering Japanese resolve, and keeping 15th Army off balance.

In doing all these things, the air commandos helped mask General Messervy's movements. The redirection of IV Corps auspiciously was given the code name CLOAK. General Slim's chief engineer, Major General W. F. "Bill" Hasted, assumed the formidable task of putting down a road while IV Corps followed behind. The combat engineer stated the road would take 42 days if bithess, a bitumen-treated runway material, was used. He estimated General Messervy would be in position for an Irrawaddy crossing by mid-February. Laying the road as they marched, IV Corps steadily tramped southward toward the river town of Pakokku. Lieutenant Colonel J. H. "Elephant Bill" Williams and 10 conscripted elephants helped pave the way by clearing fallen trees and other debris from the access pathway. General Leese described the road construction effort as follows:

> There was an unmetalled track of sorts from Kalemyo to Pakokku, but it required widening throughout its length and much bridging. The only difficult sections were some rocky hill stretches amounting in all to about 40 miles. The main problems were, first, to work on a narrow road without impeding the continuous stream of traffic which flowed throughout the 24 hours and, secondly, the movement of engineer units and equipment forward in the limited amount of transport that was available, and their maintenance. In general the plan adopted was that the divisional engineers worked forward bringing the track up to a standard to carry three-tonners and Corps engineers followed making it passable for heavy lorries and transporters, including construction of the water crossings. (109:1895)

Deception plans, natural concealment of the Pondaung Range, and the impenetrable shield afforded by Allied airmen shrouded IV Corps' trek. Because they were unaware, the Japanese fully believed 19th Indian Division's crossing was the advanced guard of XIV Army's thrust to Mandalay. Only one sighting of General Messervy's route was known to have occurred. On a rare aerial reconnaissance flight into Allied-held territory, a lone Nippon pilot observed a long line of mechanized transports west of the Irrawaddy between Tilin and Pauk. The pilot estimated almost 2,000 vehicles were involved. Due to either encoding or decoding errors, by the time the account was forwarded to division headquarters, the number of motor transports was vastly understated. Lieutenant General Tanaka, 33rd Division commander, assigned no particular importance to a singular account of only 200 vehicles and elected to disregard the pilot's report. It was a fatal error in judgment.

Night Stalkers at Chittagong, India
Like the P-47D Thunderbolts, Captain Wagner's Night Intruders flew silver aircraft with five blue stripes banding the fuselage. Due to their lethality, Japanese gunners quit using tracers. *Courtesy of 1ˢᵗ Air Commando Association*

11

The Devil's Noose

Early February was spent preparing and synchronizing XXXIII Corps and IV Corps river crossing schedules. With a front of nearly 200 miles along Burma's main waterway, General Slim wanted to created as much uncertainty in the mind of General Kimura's staff as possible. Major General Rees' crossings at Thabeikkyin and Kyaukmyaung were accepted by senior Japanese officers as Allied intent to attack Mandalay; hence, 15th Army troop concentrations were postured to the north. Keeping his options open and employing Allied air superiority as a shield, General Slim hid his army's progress well. Japanese Intelligence could not locate the 5th and 17th Indian Divisions and believed they suffered such severe casualties at Kohima that XIV Army decided to withhold them from the campaign. By late January, these unseen units were inching toward Irrawaddy River crossing sites. Eager to enter Japanese-held Burma, XIV Army's generals began stockpiling supplies. Before proceeding though, General Slim had to wrestle with a nagging shortfall.

Support to XIV Army forces beyond the Irrawaddy hinged almost entirely on air supply. As XXXIII Corps and IV Corps approached the main crossing sites, General Slim's plans still suffered the effect of losing three transport squadrons to Operation GRUBWORM in December. Ground crews of the 72nd Airdrome Squadron and other maintenance teams kept transport aircraft flying, but the work was backbreaking. Flying hours consistently exceeded maximum aircraft utilization rates. General Slim tipped his hat to the unsung crew chiefs of the theater; in later years, he highlighted the reason they continued to work agonizingly long hours:

> I really believe that the heroes of this time were the men who kept ... the wings flying—-the Air Force mechanics, stripped to the waist, who laboured in the sun by day and the glare of headlights by night to service the planes. All of them were magnificent to watch. They identified themselves utterly with the troops ahead; they were and felt themselves to be a part, and a vital part, of the team. They had the pride and bearing of fighting men, for they were one with them. (44:343)

As General Slim analyzed his sustainment requirements across the Irrawaddy, he firmly believed air support was insufficient and reported it as such to SEAC Headquarters. To meet XIV Army's anticipated supply tonnage per day, Admiral Lord Mountbatten sent his Chief of Staff, General Browning, as a personal courier to Whitehall. SEAC requested the return of the transferred troop carrier squadrons by 1 March. In a surprise move, General Wedemeyer announced he was prepared to return two air commando Dakota squadrons to India-Burma Theater on 1 February if China Theater was allowed to retain the third combat cargo unit indefinitely. Admiral Lord Mountbatten accepted. To make up for the remaining airlift shortage, the British Chiefs of Staff diverted a transport squadron from the Middle East to the India-Burma Theater. The RAF squadron was ordered to arrive in Karachi by 15 February. Having secured sufficient airlift, Admiral Lord Mountbatten convened a meeting to discuss execution of Operation EXTENDED CAPITAL.

> Representatives from XIV Army, IV Corps, 17th Division, 221 Group R.A.F., the C.C.T.F., and Nos. 1 and 2 Air Commandos [sic] attended a conference on the 26th January at which IV Corps' plan was further developed. It was decided that the two air commandos would provide support for the corps with fifty Mustangs and seven Mitchell bombers, augmented from mid-February by fifty Thunderbolts; 221 Group R.A.F. was thus freed to use its whole strength for tasks in support of XIV Army and XXXIII Corps. The 8th February was fixed as the target date for IV Corps' crossing of the Irrawaddy and the 20th February for the advance on Meiktila by way of Welaung and Mahlaing by 17th Division...As soon as a suitable airfield was available in the Meiktila area, 99th Brigade was to be flown in; gliders were to be used, if necessary, to bring forward airfield engineers, petrol and ammunition. (26:181-182)

Almost immediately, the scheduled crossings were delayed. While awaiting the return of transport aircraft from China, General Slim gave airlift preference to IV Corps which consistently caused

General Stopford's XXXIII Corps to outrun its supply lines. Shortages of ammunition and fuel proved unacceptable. Contributing to the situation were poor roads, lack of motor transports, under estimated supply requirements, and reliance on airdrop of supplies during a period of bad weather. The permutations prevented a build up of reserve stockage and left troops strung out west of the Irrawaddy. In late January, General Stopford's staff estimated a 2-week delay might be required before they could cross the Irrawaddy. The news was relayed to IV Corps to ensure proper coordination and the invasion date ultimately was established as the night of 12 February.

The IV Corps ground plan was given a thoroughly British name—Operation MULTIVITE. In a whimsical way that defined the optimism of the campaign, British planners wrote a prescription of four distinct doses of medicine for success.

(1)   Vitamin A:Concentration of IV Corps, less non-motorized elements, in the vicinity of Pauk.

(2)   Vitamin B:Securing a bridgehead in the vicinity of Nyaungu.

(3)   Vitamin C:Concentration of motorized elements of IV Corps across the Irrawaddy in the bridgehead [area].

(4)   Vitamin D:Advancing rapidly to Meiktila and seizing or constructing an airfield in that area for the fly-in of a Brigade Group of 17th Division.

Air commando light plane support for Operation MULTIVITE was already in place. On 30 January, Captain Van Wagner's 166th Liaison Squadron returned to action at Kan and began replacing some of Major Ulery's war weary men. The first week in February, the squadron moved 80 miles south to Sinthe to be close to the Irrawaddy. On the Mandalay front, Captain Beasley's men began

Field Maintenance
Light Transport Section Maintainers overhaul UC-64 Norseman. General Slim wrote, "…the Air Force mechanics stripped to the waist, who laboured in the sun by day and the glare of headlights by night to service the planes. All of them were magnificent to watch."*Courtesy of 1ˢᵗ Air Commando Association*

arriving Shwebo on 12 February. For a time, members of all three squadrons operated side by side. As General Messervy's IV Corps began its final deceptive strokes, liaison pilots were asked to transport civilians hurt in fighting near Pakokku. Sergeant Gourley recorded on 8 February he evacuated a Burmese baby and mother; the woman had lost a leg during a fire fight at her village. A little while later, he transported a Burmese father and young son to Indian hospitals. Both had received phosphorus burns from bombs.

While last minute preparations were underway, members from Headquarters, Combat Cargo Task Force; the 1ˢᵗ Air Commando Group; the 2ⁿᵈ Air Commando Group; and the 931ˢᵗ Signal Battalion flew to IV Corps Headquarters near Pauk, Burma, on 8 February. Their purpose was to review General Messervy's support requirements. With IV Corps positioning to cross the Irrawaddy and spar with the Japanese en route to Meiktila, Colonel Charles H. Anderson, commander of ADVON CCTF, worked out responsibilities for coordinating and controlling all air re-supply and close air support during the advance. To direct air commando operations, Colonel Anderson tasked CCTF teams to accompany IV Corps across the Irrawaddy.

An important outcome of the 26 January meeting were recommendations to remix squadrons of the two air commando groups into three provisional organizations. A suggestion to consolidate the six liaison squadrons under Major Ulery was not accepted, but General Stratemeyer approved other proposals. As a result, Dakotas, Norsemen, Sentinels, and Wacos of the 319th Troop Carrier Squadron and 317th Troop Carrier Squadron united with other aircraft of the 1ˢᵗ Air Combat Cargo Group early in February. The amalgamation was designated the 1ˢᵗ Provisional Troop Carrier Group. Major Holm was named Commander and Major Orlo L. Austin took over the 319th Troop Carrier Squadron. Former 1ˢᵗ Air Commando Major Taylor, posted to Eastern Air Command, was asked to supervise the glider phase. The troop carrier group established operations at Palel; for command and control purposes, Major Holm's unit fell under the Combat Cargo Task Force. Captured Japanese airfields were an integral part of IV Corps' recipe for success. Therefore, in one of its first missions, the 1ˢᵗ Provisional Troop Carrier Group delivered two bulldozers to British troop columns so airfield repairs would not be delayed.

At the same time, the 1ˢᵗ Provisional Fighter Group was formed by combining 1ˢᵗ Air Commando units—B-25 Mitchells of the Night Intruder Section and P-47 Thunderbolts of the 5th and 6th Fighter Squadrons—with P-51 Mustang squadrons from the 2ⁿᵈ Air Commando Group. General Evans placed Colonel Robert D. Gapen, a member of Combat Cargo Task Force, on the 224 Fighter Group RAF Headquarters' staff to exercise operational control over the provisional group. In actual practice, the RAF directed the 1ˢᵗ Provisional Fighter Group's activities—a clear violation of General Arnold's original edict. Colonel Levi R. Chase of the 2ⁿᵈ Air Commando Group was named commander of the provisional assault group. Directed to move up to Indian airfields at Hay and Cox's

Munitions Specialists
Ordnance specialist load bombs on P-47D Thunderbolt, *Yankee Witch*. General Slim added, "...they were and felt themselves to be a part, and a vital part, of the team. They had the pride and bearing of fighting men, for they were one with them." *Courtesy of 1st Air Commando Association*

Bazar, the 1st Provisional Fighter Group was operational by 11 February.

The first week of February, 5th and 6th Fighter Squadrons prepared and completed last-minute aircraft modifications. Earlier in January, air commando armament technicians recalibrated gunsights and communication specialists began to refit aircraft with SCR-522 Very High Frequency (VHF) radios. After adding VHF capability to the fleet, seven P-47 Thunderbolts were selected to retain the reliable SCR-274-N High Frequency (HF) radios. New radios were expected to allow British ground units to contact air commando aircraft directly, but almost immediately, the provisional group encountered communication problems. Battery life was short and VHF reception was only fair. The Mustangs of the 2nd Air Commando Group, equipped with only VHF radios, were hamstrung; their close air support mission suffered markedly.

In response, former RAF officers of Wingate's Special Force, who previously trained with Colonel Gaty's men at Lalitpur, were attached to British columns. Relying on HF radios, ex-Chindit Wing Commander Thompson established several Visual Control Posts to maintain the close contact required. Recognizing that only Colonel Gaty's P-47 pilots were on the HF net, Colonel Chase resolved the problem by having 1st Air Commando Thunderbolts fly overlapping patrols to relay instructions. Normal practice required at least one 1st Air Commando P-47 accompany each 4-aircraft flight of Mustangs from the 2nd Air Commando Group.

By 11 February both 1st Air Commando fighter squadrons and the Night Intruder Section completed the move to Hay Airfield in Eastern India. The 1st Air Commando's new home, a 6,000-foot by 200-foot grass strip near the Bay of Bengal, was only 8 miles from the 2nd Air Commando's forward base at Cox's Bazar. Members of the newly-formed 1st Provisional Troop Carrier Group moved light

equipment and squadron ground personnel; heavy equipment was railed to forward bases. Basha huts about a mile west of the strip became home for the air commandos. Arrangements were made for food to be flown in from Tezgaon, water purification and shortage problems were solved, and laundry services were set up with Asansol before the first missions launched.

While the Hay Airfield beddown took place in India, air commando transports and gliders swung into action to preposition radar equipment intended for Meiktila. On the morning of 12 February, a Waco with snatch equipment was released over Mawlaik on the west bank of the Chindwin. Ground crews immediately loaded equipment and personnel, configured snatch poles, and secured nylon tow ropes to the attaching point on the Waco's nose. Four more gliders arrived to assist the move. Once loads were ready, Dakota pilots swooped low snatching each glider and proceeded southwest to the fair-weather airfield at Yazagyo. Disconnecting from their tow over the forward base, the Waco pilots delivered 19,500 pounds of radar equipment, 2,000 pounds of fuel, a jeep, trailer, tow ropes, and 30 men. One glider was damaged on landing, but the others were towed back to Palel.

Beginning 12 February, the 1st Provisional Troop Carrier Group operated daily supply missions from Palel in support of XIV Army. During the unfolding of Operation EXTENDED CAPITAL, the 319th and 317th Troop Carrier Squadrons responded to the dynamic actions in the Irrawaddy area. As air crews expended ordnance, provisional transport units responded by moving more than 360,000 pounds of rockets, 500-pound bombs, fragmentation-cluster bombs, and .50-caliber ammunition to air commando fighter bases. They also transported 814 passengers and 2,792,780 pounds of critically needed cargo to support 356,000 front line troops during the first 4 days of the invasion.

Night Intruder Pilots
(L-R) Captain Carl E. Zeigler, Jr.; Captain Archie L. McKay; Captain Daniel A. Sinskie; Captain Edward "Sam" Wagner; and McKay's dog, Jasper. *Courtesy of 1st Air Commando Association*

Glider Approach
CG-4A Hadrians were used extensively during Operation EXTENDED CAPITAL. After XIV Army overran the enemy, Civil Engineers would land in gliders to repair craters and prepare Japanese airfields for Allied use. *Courtesy of 1ˢᵗ Air Commando Association*

General Kimura knew XIV Army would cross the Irrawaddy, but he did not know where or when. He believed both XXXIII and IV Corps were in the Mandalay area and the remainder of IV Corps would follow 19th Division into Burma via Thabeikkyin and Kyaukmyaung. Attempting to dislodge General Rees, General Kimura launched successive attacks, but Japanese soldiers defensively fell back after suffering high casualties. Subsequently, he concentrated troops and artillery near the most likely crossing sites coiled to strike. General Slim wrote, "My hope was to persuade [General Kimura] to believe that all serious crossings would be north and immediately west of Mandalay; then, when he was committed in desperate fighting there, to catch him off balance with the decisive blow at Meiktila." (44:342)

To further draw the Japanese north, General Slim decided to lead with XXXIII Corps' crossing at the village of Allagappa. The river was 1,500 yards wide (almost four times as wide as the Rhine River in Germany) and exposed at the bend selected. However, the site also was the crease between the Japanese 31st Division and 33rd Division. Using makeshift boats built by General Hasted from native teakwood trees and what few boat motors were available, the crossing began at 0400 on 13 February. Despite problems with submerged sand bars, underpowered boats, and strong currents, landings on the eastern bank were completed by 0800. Predictably, Japanese reactions were confused and slow to develop. By evening twilight on 13 February, XXXIII Corps had established a beachhead on the east bank of the Irrawaddy.

The Japanese expected XXXIII Corps' crossing, but General Messervy's whereabouts and objective remained veiled. General Slim forade the use of wireless radio by divisional units. Concur-

rently, IV Corps Headquarters purposely emitted phony transmissions. Earlier, General Slim authorized widespread deception measures to indicate a Chindit-size raid was in progress in the Gangaw Valley. Bogus signals indicated the oil fields at Yenangyaung were

Munitions
Ordnance specialists attach the fin to a 500-pound bomb at Hay Field, India, February 1945. *Courtesy of 1ˢᵗ Air Commando Association*

Unarmed UC-64 Norseman
Over the bridgehead at Pakokku, Norsemen pilots set propellers at high pitch and dove through clouds at a concentration of Japanese troops. The diversion kept Nippon heads down until B-25H Mitchells arrived on the scene. *Courtesy of 1st Air Commando Association*

its objective. To strengthen the misdirection toward Pakokku, the 1st Provisional Fighter Group launched a coordinated 22-ship package involving both 1st Air Commando fighter squadrons prior to IV Corps' crossing. Flight lead reported demolishing four buildings and igniting numerous small fires along the river bank. The following day, on 12 February, eight aircraft mopped up to help move tank and mechanized transports to the intended beachhead. To further obscure his intentions, the morning of XXXIII Corps' crossing, General Messervy sent one of his divisions on a feint to the river port of Chauk to trigger a Nippon reaction. His movements were supported by air commando Thunderbolts. When he received an indication the subterfuge worked, General Messervy turned XXXIII Corps south to Nyaungu. Admiral Lord Mountbatten's report stated:

A fortnight beforehand, we discovered that we had again chosen an area which lay exactly on a Japanese inter-formation boundary; this time, between his 15th and 28th Armies. Nyaungu was, topographically, an unlikely crossing-place, and was therefore covered by only a weak enemy force; we made two local feints (at Pakokku and at Chauk)—the enemy swallowed the bait and concentrated strong forces opposite both these places. The operation had been well planned and came as a complete surprise to the enemy. (A captured Intelligence of-

ficer of 28th Japanese Army H.Q. later revealed that the enemy assumed—as Lieutenant General Slim had intended—that only one division had been advancing down the Gangaw Valley; and that it would remain on the west bank of the Irrawaddy, and continue to exploit southward towards Yenangyaung.) (81:129)

The IV Corps crossings were not without difficulties though. Three waves of British troops were scheduled to negotiate the Irrawaddy at separate locations on the night and following morning of 13 February. Soon after sundown, equipment and boats began moving silently across the Irrawaddy River; darkness enveloped the South Lancashire Company in the moonless night. No power boats were used on the first assault and the lead company gained a lodgement without firing a shot. For the second and third wave, IV Corps waited until all troops and pontoon sections were in place before silently pushing off. Plans to use outboard motors to propel pontoon bridge sections once underway were thwarted. Several motors failed and other boats leaked badly. The irregular start coupled with strong winds and treacherous river currents reshuffled the crossing sequence. As the sun began to light the eastern sky, the main body was caught in midstream.

When enemy guns opened fire, the situation appeared desperate. Responding to the crisis, Captain Van Wagner, First Lieutenant

Show Stopper
1ˢᵗ Air Commando P-47D Thunderbolt pilots were deadly accurate. Intelligence reported, "The display of air power was so impressive, in fact, it might be argued that it actually delayed ground operations, since a tendency was noted to watch the exhibition rather than to go on with the attack." *Courtesy of 1ˢᵗ Air Commando Association*

Frank N. Davis, Lieutenant Saxon, and Second Lieutenant Robert J. Quigley departed Sinthe in two UC-64 Norsemen heading for the bridgehead. They arrived just before dawn at 0505 on 14 February. Setting propellers at high pitch, they dove through a cloud layer at the concentration of Japanese troops on the eastern bank. Sounding like a formation of fighters, the two unarmed Norsemen remained over the crossing for more than an hour. The cacophonous distrac-tion kept heads down, muffled the drone of British tanks advancing the west bank, and overpowered the sound of outboard motors on the Irrawaddy.

The Norsemen were replaced by three Mitchells of the Night Intruder Section at 0635. Using smoke and fragmentation cluster bombs, the B-25 pilots attacked targets in the Pagan-Nyaungu area. Bomber pilots reported six to eight flashes from inaccurate artil-lery before the guns were silenced. Roaming the river front, the Mitchells made repeated cannon passes. At 0745, five P-47 Thun-derbolts from Hay joined the air assault. Just before arriving over the bridgehead, Colonel Gaty detached from the flight to bomb a smoke-designated target on the northwest end of Nyaungu. The re-maining 4-ship was unable to establish VHF radio contact, so the air commando fighter pilots each dropped two 500-pound bombs on smoke and worked the radios. At 0920 the flight established contact with Visual Control Posts and were directed to an enemy position south of the British troops. Strafing attacks started a large fire and suppressed Japanese operations. An iron roofed building with a high chimney housed Nippon resistance and became the fo-cus of repeated air strikes. Heavy showers began building to the west as another formation of P-47 aircraft arrived over the smoke-stack to relieve the first flight of Thunderbolts. Before leaving the area at 1730, the 1ˢᵗ Provisional Fighter Group left fires raging at Nyaungu and on the islands near Pakokku.

Colonel Chase provided continuous daylight coverage over the beachhead by tag teaming 4-ship formations of Thunderbolts and

Thabutkon Operations
The 1ˢᵗ Provisional Troop Carrier Group completed 665 sorties, airlifted 586,600 pounds of equipment and supplies, transported 3,847 troops, and evacuated 66 casualties in 5 days. *Courtesy of 1ˢᵗ Air Commando Association*

Mustangs the entire day. The airfields at Hay and Cox Bazar were too distant to provide immediate support to IV Corps if normal operating procedures were followed. Therefore, the 1ˢᵗ Provisional Fighter Group established aircraft on strip alert for quick responsiveness and *cab rank* missions for flexibility over the objective area. Flights of Thunderbolts or Mustangs departed Indian airfields at regular intervals without identified targets; nearing IV Corps' front, the pilots set up orbits to await instructions. When air commando fighters and bombers established contact, Visual Control Post personnel, traveling with British columns, provided vectors to bunkers, trenches, gun emplacements, and troop concentrations. Concerning air support to Vitamin B operations, Major Leon S. Dure of the Joint Intelligence Collection Agency wrote:

> Both demolition and fire bombs were used—the P-47s carrying 2 x 500 of the former, the P-51s employing napalm fire bombs. All close support was directed by a "heavy [HF]" [Visual Control Post] at brigade headquarters overlooking the position. Mortar smoke was laid on all targets in range of fire, and the aircraft followed up with such a demonstration of accuracy as to evoke enthusiastic comment. The display of air power was so impressive, in fact, it might be argued that it actually delayed ground operations, since a tendency was noted to watch the exhibition rather than to get on with the attack. (103:7)

Although cab rank patrols were an inefficient use of airframes when tactical targets were not readily available, these sorties added tremendous and timely firepower to advancing columns. Major Pitts noted the value of on-demand air attacks: "An indirect beneficial result of the cab rank was as a counter battery keeping enemy artillery fire down. The [Japanese] developed a distaste for using their guns even their machine guns to some extent with bomb carrying planes ready to blast their positions once they were disclosed." (115:February Report:1) Intermittent VHF communication was a constant problem; however, only once was a ground recognition signal used to differential between British and Japanese troops. The Visual Control Post RAF officer merely hoisted a yellow umbrella to establish his position. Working around the radio difficulties, British troops and air commandos developed smoke patterns described below to identify enemy positions. When the Japanese tried to confuse target acquisition with smoke of their own, Allied forces responded with a variety of pre-coordinated white, yellow, yellow-green, or red smoke.

(1)   Pattern 1 Pinpoint smoke on target
(2)   Pattern 2 Line with target on end fartherest [sic] from own troops
(3)   Pattern 3 Triangle with target at the center
(4)   Pattern 4 Square with target at the center

Air patrols continued as IV Corps solidified its bridgehead, moved east to capture Pagan, and continued an advance toward Meiktila. Attacks widened outward from the immediate vicinity of bridgeheads. Air commando Mitchell and Thunderbolt pilots found prey south of the Irrawaddy near the Japanese-held Toungoo airfields. To the north, the villages of Myingyan and Wetlu were raided. In addition to cab rank missions, specified interdiction targets ahead or to the flanks of columns included enemy headquarters, troop concentrations, tanks, stores, fuel dumps, motor transport, locomotives, and ox carts.

Typically, Colonel Gaty's men flew a line abreast formation from Hay. They transitioned to an echelon right and then flight lead initiated a left-hand circle over the objective to allow pilots to pin point targets. The procedure was highly effective and "contributed to the harassment, confusion, and losses of enemy rearward elements and installations." (103:14)

Air commando P-47 Thunderbolts flew 885 sorties during the 23-day period from 11 February, the beginning of Operation MULTIVITE, through its conclusion at the height of Meiktila operations on 5 March. The Night Intruder Section recorded 52 sorties during the same period. In the midst of the operation, Major Pitts was injured in a takeoff accident and Captain William J. Hemphill assumed the duties of commander of the 6ᵗʰ Fighter Squadron.

Missing in Action
On 26 February, Colonel Clinton B. Gaty flew south toward Meiktila. He was never heard from again. *Courtesy of 1ˢᵗ Air Commando Association*

Flight Leader
First Lieutenant Charles M. Poston, Jr., recorded his first air-to-air kill the same day Colonel Gaty's airplane was lost. *Courtesy of 1ˢᵗ Air Commando Association*

General Kimura still thought the crossing at Nyaungu was minor compared to the threat on Mandalay. Despite the display of air power around Nyaungu, the Japanese 15ᵗʰ Army brought reinforcements from all over Burma to northern defensive positions when General Stopford introduced another crossing midway between Mandalay and Allagappa on 24 February. Applying pressure against XXXIII Corps bridgeheads, General Kimura virtually ignored IV Corps as it nipped at his heals. Pakokku and nearby river islands easily yielded under the onslaught of British armor and infantry. As General Slim expected, Japanese opposition against the Nyaungu-Pakokku bridgehead was halfhearted and lethargic.

In contrast, with the help of their air armada, IV Corps' operations developed at lightning speed. By 22 February, IV Corps completed establishing infantry and tank units on the eastern shore. Poised to strike out for Meiktila, General Messervy's tank brigade barely slowed despite difficult country and deep chaungs. During IV Corps' advance, Major Holm placed 25 gliders on strip alert at Palel to fly supplies and other heavy equipment as needed to ensure airfield operations were not hindered. To avoid the turbulence problems previously experienced over the Chin Hills during Operation THURSDAY, glider pilots took precautions to anticipate the assault on the airfield at Meiktila. When IV Corps rushed eastward past Pagan, eight gliders loaded with 22,097 pounds of runway construction equipment were towed from Tilagaon to Sinthe. The following day, eight more loads of heavy engineering materials and machines flew to the air commandos' base to position as far forward as possible.

The movement was prudent but not necessary as IV Corps surged toward Meiktila. On 24 February, Japan's primary Central Burmese maintenance center at Taungtha was overrun and General

Kimura lost storehouses for all types of supplies, equipment, and ammunition. On successive days, Mahlaing and Thabutkon fell. Capture of the key airstrip at Thabutkon, 15 miles northwest of Meiktila, triggered an immediate fly-in of the air transportable brigade from Palel. When IV Corps overran the airfield at Thabutkon on 26 February, former Broadway engineer First Lieutenant Brackett reported the runway was cratered but repairable. He directed engineers to use a rubber-tired tractor, a grader, and the two bulldozers moving with units of IV Corps to fill more than 40 broad cavities and slit trenches obstructing the 4,800-foot fair-weather airfield. By nightfall, the runway was back in operational condition and Palel was alerted to prepare for the deployment of the British 99ᵗʰ Brigade.

The following day, a C-47 Dakota towed a glider to Thabutkon under the protective pinion of two 2ⁿᵈ Air Commando P-51 Mustangs. Onboard the Waco were Major Frank O. Hay, ADVON CCTF transportation officer; a British engineering officer; and 2,995 pounds of radio and runway lighting equipment. The arrival was greeted by 166ᵗʰ Liaison Squadron pilots and Colonel Anderson who had landed 10 minutes before. Major Hay rapidly accomplished an inspection of the runway and signaled the airfield was serviceable. He included a request for receiving and load handling personnel from Sinthe.

The first full day, air commando transport pilots completed 63 sorties—the initial four gliders included cargo handlers, public relations officers, and news correspondents. Nearing sunset, an aircraft overshot the airfield and was destroyed, but there were no injuries. In the days that followed, the airfield was subject to intermittent mortar and sniper fire, but Dakotas continued flying. The 1ˢᵗ Provisional Troop Carrier Group completed 665 sorties, airlifted 586,600 pounds of equipment and supplies, transported 3,847 troops, and evacuated 66 casualties during the 99ᵗʰ Brigade lift. British Dakotas added seven more supply sorties during the 5-day employment. Before terminating Thabutkon operations, the air commandos added 1,288,720 pounds of POL, rations, ammunition, medical supplies, and signal equipment along with 359 reinforcement troops. Flown out during the same time were 16 enemy prisoners, 25 wounded Japanese, and 80 Indian National Army casualties. Major Hay ordered the airfield closed at sundown on 3 March. During the tactical movement, air crews logged more than 12 hours of flying per day. Minimum ground time averaged only 15 minutes between landing, unloading, loading, and takeoff.

Captain Van Wagner's 166ᵗʰ Liaison Squadron transported numerous staff officers between IV Corps Headquarters and Thabutkon, tended to their air evacuation mission, and used *Yankee ingenuity* to further XIV Army's advance. Major Dure observed, "The importance of these aircraft—L-5s and UC-64s—has been demonstrated over and over again on all three of the Burma fronts, and they are now an indispensable part of any ground campaign." (103:14) His report illustrated the lengths the men of the liaison squadrons were willing to go to accomplish the mission:

The spirit of the light plane pilots, flying literally all day into small and tricky fields, is particularly notable.... During the period 12-28 February, 166 Squadron flew in 1333 reinforcements and 253,445 pounds of rations and supplies. A total of 1549 casualties were evacuated.... The pilots of the squadron generally adapted their aircraft to the needs of the moment, in a number of instances going beyond what is expected of such planes. (One officer was grounded by the squadron commander for jeopardizing his aircraft when he indulged in throwing hand grenades from it at Japanese light antiaircraft positions). (103:12, 14)

With grave suddenness in the midst of the Thabutkon operation, a dark cloud cast a shadow on the 1ˢᵗ Air Commando Group. Shortly after noon on 26 February, Lieutenant Klarr led a flight of eight P-47 Thunderbolts on a cab rank patrol in the area of Mahlaing, 20 miles northwest of Meiktila. The flight leader reported the day was sunny and crystal clear; he estimated visibility was between 10 and 15 miles. Settling into an orbit at 1305, Lieutenant Klarr received a radio call from Colonel Gaty saying he would rendezvous with the flight over the target area. Corporal Rader, unit munitions

Last Commander of 1ˢᵗ Air Commando Group
Colonel Robert W. Hall took command of the 1ˢᵗ Air Commando Group after Colonel Gaty was officially declared missing in action. *Courtesy of 1ˢᵗ Air Commando Association*

expert, recalled arming Gaty's plane at Fenny—he flew an older model olive drab P-47. En route, the leader of the 1ˢᵗ Air Commando Group passed Second Lieutenant Allen W. Abrahams' 4-ship flight circling an area near Wetlu. Colonel Gaty made contact and reported he was heading south. Meanwhile, Lieutenant Klarr maintained his formation over Mahlaing and loitered. Later, he recalled the incident, "I held as long as I could. As we were getting low on gas, we completed our run and headed back. I called him several times but received no answer. I figured he had aborted, but on return to the base he was not there." The air commandos reluctantly filed a missing aircraft report at 2030.

The information immediately was classified. Hoping to find their commander and Second Lieutenant William E. Davison who also was shot down on 26 February, the air commandos launched an extensive rescue effort. On 27 February, four Thunderbolts and two Mitchells blanketed the area along the rail line connecting Taungtha, Mahlaing, and Meiktila, then they broadened the hunt toward the Irrawaddy to include Natogyi, Wetlu, and Zi. Captain Klarr reported seeing a mirror flash, but it could not be located again. Captain Van Wagner led a party of light planes from Sinthe. Staff Sergeant Duane Fudge admitted probing the area around Meiktila several days for evidence of the colonel's plane. During the search, air commandos sighted and photographed a partially destroyed silver aircraft. Only the tail section and part of the wing were intact, but otherwise, the aircraft was unidentifiable. Leading to the airplane were deep motor transport tracks. Colonel Gaty never was found and officially was listed as missing in action; he remains so today.

No one knows what happened to the group commander. There were isolated reports Colonel Gaty was held at Rangoon or perhaps the Bangkok Prisoner of War Camp, but they were unconfirmed. Hours before Colonel Gaty was last seen, a flight of Air Commando Thunderbolts encountered four Oscars over Mahlaing. Lieutenant Charles M. Poston, Jr., and Second Lieutenant Glen R. Feickert salvoed bombs and belly tanks and pursued. Each downed an Oscar, but two Japanese aircraft broke clear and fled the dog fight. Many air commandos believed Colonel Gaty's lone P-47 was jumped by these lurking aircraft.

Captain Zeigler noted in his diary following the unsuccessful search, "This has been a great loss to our group. He was one of the squarest men and best commanding officer I've yet met." (120:5 March 1945 entry) At times a complex man, Colonel Clinton B. Gaty demanded the best from his men; to him there was no compromise. After the incident, all missed his crusty personality, lantern jaw, and piercing eyes. Every single person knew him as a man of his word. The men respected him for his courage, straight forward manner, and leadership. Lieutenant Klarr summed up the feelings of the organization by saying, "I loved that man and I hated for us to lose him." (131:November-December 1988:10) For a time, the organization could not bring itself to replace Colonel Gaty, but finally on 7 April, almost 45 days later, Colonel Robert W. Hall was named to take command of the 1st Air Commando Group. Meanwhile, the organization continued its mission.

There was no time to pause or mourn. The British and Japanese troops were locked in a life-or-death struggle as IV Corps approached Meiktila. The success of air commando operations allowed the British to advance ahead of expectations. By 27 February, lead units of British armored cavalry were merely 8 miles west of Meiktila when they encountered opposition in strength. After attempting a frontal attack, the British withdrew under withering machine gun fire. Visual Control Post RAF officers called on overhead 1st Air Commando fighters for an air strike; due to mechanical problems, only three Thunderbolts were flying cab rank at the time.

Coming off the perch, the fighter pilots began strafing the identified position; on the third diving pass, each aircraft took a direct hit. Two Jugs managed to recover at Thabutkon. The third, piloted by Lieutenant Feickert, shuddered and broke into small pieces. Witnesses were certain the pilot could not have survived. It was just 1 day after Lieutenant Feickert's first and only air-to-air victory. When the strikes were completed, Sherman tanks were in position to move. After a skirmish the British tallied the dead; 56 Japanese were found at the machine gun emplacement. Louis Allen recounted a gruesome scene on the same day at the same time that is eerie in detail. Major Alasdair Tuck of the 255 Independent Tank Brigade described the following event to the former intelligence officer:

255 Brigade had a very pleasant American liaison officer with whom Tuck was friendly, and he could not forbear asking him some time later why his jeep stank so much. The American told him he had watched a Thunderbolt pilot pull out too late after dive-bombing the Japanese, and his tail had hit the ground. The liaison officer had collected the pilot's remains in a sandbag and put them in his jeep tool bin as he knew the boy's parents in America would want them. Tuck begged him to bury them and send back the dog tags with a map reference so the bones could be collected later. At first the American demurred, but after another 24 hours of Central Burma heat, he did it. (1:435)

As February closed, all three liaison squadrons registered significant increases in evacuations, tonnage, and troop reinforcements. Major James R. "Green Hornet" Woods, 1st Air Commando Group Intelligence Officer, recorded 3,908 Indian, African, and British casualties; 468,275 pounds of miscellaneous cargo; and 2,104 replacements were transported to and from front line airstrips. Sunday, 18 February was illustrative of the scramble of activity during the drive across the Irrawaddy River. Sergeant Gourley logged 6:05 flight hours, evacuated seven casualties, flew one senior officer forward, transferred two replacements, and carried medical supplies and blood plasma into battle areas. While significant, these numbers would pale in comparison to the work accomplished by liaison squadron pilots the following month.

By the beginning of March, IV Corps soldiers had worked their way to the outskirts of Meiktila. Facing General Messervy's men were a garrison of 3,500 soldiers and a collection of 1,000 to 2,000 administrative soldiers and discharged hospital patients. Drawing from well-stock armories, Major General Kasuya, commander of the Meiktila area, armed able-bodied soldiers with machine guns and ordered them to defend to the last man. The Japanese also recast their antiaircraft artillery batteries to provide antitank defense. Admiral Lord Mountbatten's report to the Combined Chiefs of Staff briefly described the battle:

The assault on Meiktila began at dawn on the 28th February from four directions; and by nightfall after very heavy fighting, the town was entirely surrounded. Three days and nights of savage hand-to-hand fighting followed; in which small units of our infantry, supported by tanks, fought their way into the centre of the town—killing and blasting the enemy: bunker by bunker, and house by house. Almost every Japanese was armed with an automatic weapon, with which he fought to the death. By early morning on the 4th March the greater part of Meiktila, including the principle airfield (Meiktila Main) and the railway station, was in our hands. (81:131)

Commander Reviews Air Commando Operations
Colonel Robert W. Hall met with members of his new command (L-R) Colonel Hall, Lieutenant Colonel Samson Smith, Captain Donald C. Tulloch, Major James R. "Green Hornet" Woods, and Captain David C. "Buck" Beasley, Jr. *Courtesy of 1st Air Commando Association*

General Kimura realized Burma Area Army's peril; his position was virtually hopeless. To support Mandalay's defense, he had to receive supplies through Meiktila. Yet his only source of Meiktila reinforcements was from Mandalay defenses. Forced to scrap a planned Japanese counteroffensive, General Kimura ordered a 2-prong approach to relieve Meiktila. He directed General Tsunoru Yamamoto's 72nd Independent Mixed Brigade to move from the Yenangyaung area to sever the Allied supply line passing through Nyaungu. Simultaneously borrowing from Peter to pay Paul, General Kimura threw the equivalent of six brigades plus artillery and tank units from Mandalay at the deteriorating situation. The influx of approximately 9,000 Imperial troops under Lieutenant General Masaki Honda gave the Japanese a numerical advantage over the equivalent of four British infantry brigades and one tank brigade. General Leese noted the dilemma for the Allies was not so much in numbers of soldiers but in the vulnerability of Allied supply lines. When British lines of communications across the Irrawaddy were disrupted, the airfield at Meiktila Main became even more important.

Faced with increasing opposition, IV Corps radioed Combat Cargo Task Force to initiate Operation BETTY—airlift of the British 9th Brigade from Palel to Meiktila. Twenty crews of the 319th and 317th Troop Carrier Squadrons took off on 15 March at 0715 to relieve Nippon pressure. At the same time, Japanese Imperial troops mounted a ferocious but uncoordinated attack on the northwest corner of the airfield. When Major Holm arrived overhead Meiktila, the leader of the Dakota flight learned the airfield was under enemy fire. On board the Dakotas were critically needed British Airborne troops, equipment, ammunition, and fuel. Without delay, Major Holm landed amid the melee and began directing ground operations. Fierce fighting ensued as Japanese guns dominated the airstrip; one Dakota was damaged. The second flight of Dakotas departed Palel at 1330 but diverted to Naungu until the airfield was secured. Interspersing arrivals between fire fights, the air commandos completed 53 sorties on the first day. The following day was a continuation. First Lieutenant Chester A. Amedia recounted Major "Nipper" Holm's actions during the first fateful days of Operation BETTY.

I ... remembered him as a "Lean," "Cool" leader, directing us in our C-47s while under mortar fire at Meiktila in [March 1945]. The [Japanese] had control of half of the field. (It had parallel grass runways) As we landed we would pull off perpendicular and Nipper was standing there on the grass in the middle of the field ... telling (signaling) us to just cut the left engine only while soldiers unloaded mostly ammunition.... Things got worse and on our second day, third sortie, the [Japanese] captured the tower (bamboo) and we circled (about 20 airplanes) the field for about 30 minutes. Major John C. Sanichas led us off to another strip [Naungu] which really was only a stretch of sandy road near the junction of the Chindwin

Meiktila Operations
The Japanese sensed the loss of the major supply hub at Meiktila would spell defeat. They fought ferociously for 2 weeks but by the end of the month, lost the battle of attrition. *Courtesy of 1st Air Commando Association*

and Irrawaddy Rivers. We landed there and waited while our fighters strafed and dropped bombs on the [Japanese].... This went on for 3 days and during that time a [Japanese] mortar shell landed on a C-47 of the 2nd Air Commandos and it burned completely. Nipper was only about 100 feet distance away.... we all thought [Major Holm] would get the Silver Star for his action at Meiktila. (131:May-June 1985:5)

In the afternoon of 16 March, a flight of Dakotas landed among enemy shelling and mortar fire. An aircraft of the 317th Troop Carrier Squadron took two direct hits that set the load of two jeeps ablaze. The airplane was destroyed. Later, another C-47 was damaged after being loaded with medical patients. A shell burst in the radio compartment causing six of the soldiers to be rewounded. After transferring the casualties, the Dakota became a source of cannibalized parts. The fighting was very severe; the Japanese launched one attack on another. During the fighting, a 75 mm shell passed completely through the fuselage of another stretcher-configured C-47 and destroyed a British C-45 parked alongside. The ebb and flow of the battle for the airfield caused operations to be suspended from time to time while each army wrestled for control.

Admiral Lord Mountbatten noted in his report to the Combined Chiefs of Staff, "On several occasions, ... the enemy had succeeded in penetrating to the airfield itself—indeed, part of the second air-transpotable brigade had had to land under direct fire." (81:141) Braving the hail of bullets and shells, the two air commando units averaged 52.5 sorties during Operation BETTY sometimes unloading their own cargo of explosives and ammunition when ground crews waited in trenches. Private Byrne recalled a harrowing experience as his crew delivered 9th Brigade to the front line airfield:

One day we landed and the [Japanese] opened up and we scurried for some foxholes. The left engine took one indirect hit and damaged our feathering control. [Corporal Floyd B.] Kyea, our crew chief, and I tried to fix it and couldn't so the decision had to be made to hold over or try taking off. [The pilot] opted for the latter. As we were getting ready for takeoff, we took a second hit near the tail. Fortunately, I had gotten the tail locks out earlier and was holding the door open for Floyd who was getting the wheel locks out. I did however, get hit in the neck and shoulder. The tail had over a hundred holes though! We locked the brakes, revved the engines up to get somewhat of a jet effect, and managed to avoid a lot of shell holes in the strip to a successful takeoff. It was only a short hop to one of our light plane bases [Sinthe] to get me in a British field hospital. (131:Spring Edition 1994:11)

While Dakota crews braved the hail of bullets and shell, cab rank missions continued to support IV Corps' rush until 11 March. Fighting at close quarters between the streets and buildings of Meiktila made Thunderbolt fire suppression missions difficult thereafter. To isolate the city from reinforcements, the 1st Provisional Fighter Group began striking the road and rail network feeding the Japanese supply hub. Enemy lines of communication were broken repeatedly at Thawatti, Swa, and Toungoo. Flying long range interdiction missions, the air commandos kept up the relentless attack

by dropping demolition and incendiary bombs on Rangoon, Henzada, and other transportation hubs. The Japanese Air Force was not to be found, but ground-to-air defense batteries fought back. Two pilots from each Thunderbolt squadron were killed during the month. The 6th Fighter Squadron lost Second Lieutenant John J. Akston when he spun into the ground on approach. Second Lieutenant Ralph A. Selkirk died; his Thunderbolt exploded after a strafing pass at Myolila. Lieutenant Edward W. Auman was killed in action over the Toungoo railroad bridge and fellow 5th Fighter Squadron pilot Second Lieutenant Charles H. Hess, Jr., crash-landed north of Meiktila. Numerous air and ground attempts to rescue the young pilot were frustrated by heavy fighting.

While the organization experienced the heaviest fighting of the campaign, oddly timed personnel changes began to alter the composition of the group. On 24 March, Major Lynn was released from his command to return to the United States. The following day Captain Wilkins moved up from Operations Officer to take the vacated position. Earlier in the month, Captain Van Wagner transferred command of the 166th Liaison Squadron to Captain Julius "Goody" Goodman after receiving orders to head home to Detroit, Michigan. Under Captain Goodman, light plane pilots continued to extract casualties and fly artillery adjustment sorties until the squadron was ordered back to Asansol on 14 March. Replacing Goodman's overworked men at Sinthe was the 165th Liaison Squadron. Table 8 summarizes light plane operations under the leadership of the original liaison squadron commanders.

TABLE 8
Light Plane Activities
6 October 1944 - 16 March 1945

Month	Hours Flown	Sorties	Tonnage Cargo	Rein- force	Casualty Evac	PAX	Empty Trips	POW	Recce	Msg D&P	Artillery Adjust
Oct	1,342	2,096	121,567	264	576	216	540	2	46	7	0
Nov	2,224	4,998	112,671	460	2,388	386	2,311	10	113	13	0
Dec	2,825	5,681	88,966	249	2,439	290	1,258	7	134	4	0
Jan	4,513	7,631	228,974	363	2,674	1,088	3,422	10	194	14	0
Feb	5,483	10,946	468,275	2,104	3,902	1,183	1,926	11	195	19	9
Mar	3,633	8,508	267,805	1,507	3,804	889	1,470	30	98	85	46
Total	**20,020**	**39,860**	**1,288,258**	**4,947**	**15,783**	**4,052**	**10,927**	**70**	**780**	**142**	**55**

On 21 March the enemy finally coordinated an assault on Meiktila and the airstrip fell into Nippon hands. Landings at the main airfield were suspended from 22 March until 1 April. Dakotas reverted to airdrop resupply methods as British troops counterattacked. Air commando Flying Sergeants supplemented Dakota shipments with mail, consumables, medical supplies, and ammunition. Using a small strip within the British perimeter, L-pilots transferred wounded at the highest rate of the Burma campaigns. When March

drew to a close, Major Ulery was recalled to the United States; his replacement was Captain Elbert E. Davis, former Operations Officer of the 164th Liaison Squadron. As Major Ulery departed Sinthe, IV Corps was re-establishing the Nyaungu lines of communication and struggling to retake Meiktila Main.

To the north, XXXIII Corps advanced spectacularly and was inside Mandalay's perimeter by the first week of March. Captain Beasley was the only element of the 1st Air Commando Group par-

The Walls of Fort Dufferin
Encircled by a moat and encased in 20-foot walls, the fortress withstood Allied artillery and aerial rocket attacks. *Courtesy of 1ˢᵗ Air Commando Association*

shadow of Nippon guns. He totaled 8:30 hours during that day and amassed 140:10 flying hours for the month. As casualties mounted and reinforcements were required, he continued the pace averaging almost 12 sorties per day. Later, General Slim dispatched a letter of commendation to Captain Beasley because of the magnitude and criticality of the liaison pilots' effort. Table 9 recounts the breakdown of light plane activities during the Mandalay campaign.

TABLE 9
Mandalay Offensive: XXXIII Corps Light Plane Support
164ᵗʰ Liaison Squadron (Commando)
20 February - 31 March 1945

Operational Hours Flown	6,145
Operation Missions	14,759
Casualties Evacuated	6,137
Pounds of Cargo and Supplies	408,109
Passengers and Replacements	4,338
Reconnaissance Missions	106

ticipating regularly with XXXIII Corps during the Mandalay offensive. Operational tempo surged. The ceaseless operation began to show the need for serious repairs to the L-5 Sentinels, but the men flew hard day after day as casualties mounted. Facilitating XXXIII Corps' dash to Mandalay, the 164ᵗʰ Liaison Squadron relocated to Ondaw on 12 March to be closer to the fighting. While operating from the Mandalay race track, the squadron established new standards for casualty evacuations. Technical Sergeant Wilbur S. Mitsdarffer's flight records serve as an example of the marked increase in activity. On 5 March 1945, Sergeant Mitsdarffer extracted 27 British, Indian, and African casualties from under the

On 9 March, British, Indian, and African troops surged into the Burmese capital city and swept up the pagoda-covered Mandalay Hill. During the assault, Japanese resistance crumbled. After 24 hours of hand-to-hand combat, Britain's 98ᵗʰ Brigade held claim to the highest ground within Mandalay proper. Two days later, Maymyo yielded to an onrush of the 62ⁿᵈ Brigade. The Emperor's last holdout was Fort Dufferin. Encircled by an 80-yard moat and encased in 20-foot walls with earthen embankments more than 70 feet thick, the fortress presented a formidable goal of political importance. Attempts to storm the bulwark were beaten back and casualties were

Mandalay Operations
Members of the 164ᵗʰ Liaison Squadron *Back Row* **(L-R) Staff Sergeant Charles S. Fessler; Technical Sergeant Howard L. Smith; Sergeant Walter Kunda; Sergeant Van Natta** *Front Row* **(L-R) Powers; Corporal John Gallo; unidentified; Staff Sergeant Edward J. Brennan** *Courtesy of 1ˢᵗ Air Commando Association*

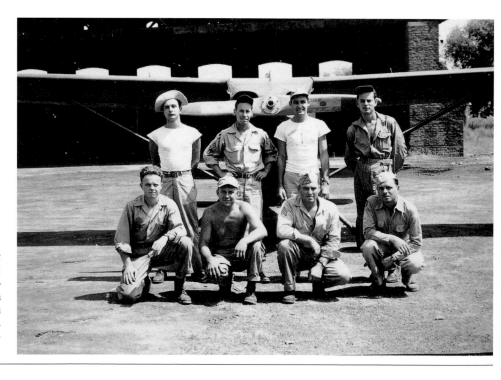

high. When artillery blasts from 500 yards and aerial rockets failed to topple the walls, siege warfare was adopted. In an experimental attack, three RAF B-25 Mitchells skipped 2,000-pound bombs across the moat and successfully breached the wall.

In anticipation of the pending British assault, Sergeant Mitsdarffer recalled flying his L-5 as far forward as possible. He landed inside the tree-rimmed polo field that rested only yards from the confines of the fortress. There he waited for XXXIII Corps to attack. The preparation was not necessary; the Japanese read the handwriting on Fort Dufferin's walls. When the British penetrated the fort the following day, they discovered the enemy had slipped out under cover of darkness abandoning caches of ordnance and a 30-day supply of rice. Also left behind were more than 6,000 Nippon dead.

Suffering incessant air attacks and the crucible of Britain's XXXIII Corps and IV Corps, Imperial troops maniacally tried to hold ground—often fighting to the last man. News of the British victory at Mandalay and General Messervy's successful reopening of Allied supply lines to Meiktila undermined Japanese resolve. Unable to win a war of attrition and festered with poor morale, the

Emperor's 15th Army fled southeastward from the onslaught of Allied soldiers. An army in flight, General Kimura's mauled command no longer resembled a disciplined fighting force.

The battle for Meiktila was decided the night of 28 March when the Japanese conceded defeat in the decisive struggle for central Burma…. General Tanaka … on his own authority ordered the 33rd Army to pass to a holding role so that the 15th Army might withdraw from the Mandalay area…. The victory in central Burma was Slim's, though there was still hard fighting ahead along the Irrawaddy. Henceforth, though Japanese regiments and some divisions could keep a fair amount of cohesion, the Japanese command in Burma slowly began to disintegrate on the retreat south and west. Army headquarters troops found themselves fighting as infantry. Confusion and disorganization began to spread through the Japanese rear areas as Slim's armored columns, moving ever faster, knifed through them. Thereafter, whether or not SEAC would take Rangoon depended primarily on the logistical support that could be allotted. (42:223)

Although XIV Army also was exhausted, General Slim sought to maintain the pace. He instructed his Corps Commanders to pursue without delay. Riding the crest of a wave, General Slim turned his attentions to the wharfs of Rangoon. Air assault and air resupply barely broke stride as they redirected airplanes southward to support XIV Army. Yet under the best of circumstances, there would be little time to establish an Allied port of supply in Rangoon before the dry season's abrupt end. It was clear to British generals the Nippon Army in Burma had shot its bolt. The Japanese could not hold Burma much longer; they could merely delay, hoping to retain the Burmese strategic port until the monsoons began. As General Slim set himself to again race the elements, he discovered another factor more foreboding than stubborn Japanese and pending rains. It appeared the Allies themselves were an obstacle to victory.

Mandalay Airman
Replacement liaison pilot Technical Sergeant Wilbur S. Mitsdarffer smiles from the cockpit of his L-5 Sentinel. He waited at the racetrack near Fort Dufferin but was not needed. The Japanese left before dawn.
Courtesy of 1st Air Commando Association

12

The Setting Sun

Early in 1945, SEAC planners cautioned that a victory at Mandalay would be inconsequential if XIV Army could not continue to Burma's major seaport of Rangoon. Simply stated, the Mandalay-Meiktila area represented no man's land to the British.

Second Lieutenant Charles B. Turner
Waco pilots bore the brunt of the overland preparation from Palel to Meiktila. Many, like Lieutenant Turner, had already distinguished themselves during Operation THURSDAY and in the Kabal Valley. *Courtesy of 1ˢᵗ Air Commando Association*

With Dimapur, the nearest railhead in Northeastern India, more than 500 miles from Mandalay, planners believed operations in Central Burma could not be sustained. Insufficient road, rail, and river-based transportation placed an enormous burden on airlift. Before the Allies crossed the Irrawaddy, aircrews delivered nearly 2,000 tons daily to General Slim's forward deployed soldiers. This required Dakotas and Commandos to operate two-thirds above normal utilization rates. With the advance to Rangoon, XIV Army commanders needed more airlift. If any transport aircraft were withheld during General Slim's march, SEAC would be forced to withdraw as many as two divisions from beyond Burma's main waterway. Fearing an unforecasted requirement for aircraft similar to Operation GRUBWORM, London formally raised the issue to Washington on 31 January 1945. Whitehall asked that the Combined Chiefs of Staff be the approving authority for any requests to transfer ground or air assets between India-Burma Theater and China Theater. Although the petition was ratified, the administrative victory did not allay British apprehensions. World War II historians Romanus and Sunderland recorded the arrangement in this manner:

> ...the Joint Chiefs gave an assent so highly qualified as to disturb Mountbatten, for they agreed only that the [Combined Chiefs of Staff] should "discuss" transfer, whereas the British had wanted the [Combined Chiefs of Staff] to control. The Joint Chiefs of Staff based their stand on the ground that: "The primary military objective of the United States in the China and India-Burma Theaters is the continuance of aid to China on a scale that will permit the fullest utilization of the area and resources of China for operations against the Japanese. United States resources are deployed in India-Burma to provide direct or indirect support for China." Mountbatten was concerned that his resources in transport aircraft might be lost to him. (42:225)

The SEAC Commander had reason to worry. In the midst of General Slim's decisive battles in Central Burma, developments in

Snatching Downed Aircrews (1)

Mr. William Burkhart, Technical Representative for All American Aviation, demonstrates his concept for rescuing downed aircrew members. In principal, the system was similar to that devised for snatching gliders. Poles and nylon cable are assembled. *Courtesy of 1ˢᵗ Air Commando Association*

Snatching Downed Aircrews (2)

After dropping equipment to the downed individual, the tug loitered. The aircrew member dons a harness assembly and attaches the nylon cable. *Courtesy of 1ˢᵗ Air Commando Association*

China threatened to chip away at the logistics foundation of his dash for Rangoon. General Wedemeyer's assessment of the war with Japan led him to conclude the center of strategic gravity should move east into China rather than south to Rangoon. Notwithstanding the United States' moral obligation to the British offensive in Burma, General Wedemeyer met with Admiral Lord Mountbatten on 16 February to discuss the recall and transportation of all Chinese troops fighting in Northern Burma. Alarmed by the prospect of losing men and machines, SEAC planners reacted decisively. Admiral Lord Mountbatten appealed to the Combined Chiefs of Staff: "May I have your firm and early assurance that all transport aircraft will be retained in support of my operations? We can then get on with the job to the best of our ability and with all possible speed." When asked how long, he assured them Rangoon could be captured by 1 June, but further documented aircraft would be needed 2 months after to establish continuous operations. The issue was viewed quite seriously by the British leadership.

Snatching Downed Aircrews (3)

The aircrew member prepares for the snatch. The concept first was tested on animals in a UC-64 Norseman; later, C-47 Dakotas snatched live personnel. However, there is no evidence the system was used in combat. *Courtesy of 1ˢᵗ Air Commando Association*

...on the 30th March, the Prime Minister asked Field-Marshal Sir Henry Maitland Wilson to convey his personal views orally and unofficially to General Marshall. The Prime Minister pointed out that at [the September 1944] Octagon [Conference] he had expressed his dislike of undertaking a large-scale campaign in the jungles of Burma but, as the Americans had attached the greatest importance to it as a means of opening the Burma Road, he had agreed. Despite the fact that Mountbatten had not received the forces he wanted from Europe, the campaign had been conducted with the utmost vigour, the Burma Road had been opened, and Mandalay captured. The battle now being fought at the end of a very difficult line of communication was important not only for Burma but for the general wearing down of the Japanese military and air power. Once Rangoon had been occupied, the powerful forces would be set free for further operations in combination with the general American offensive. He reminded Marshall that he had agreed to the retention in Italy of the three British/Indian divisions which Mountbatten had wanted for DRACULA, and that this had made it possible for five British and Canadian divisions to be withdrawn from Italy to increase the strength of General D. Eisenhower's forces for the Second Front campaign. "I feel therefore entitled," Mr. Churchill continued, "to appeal to General Marshall's sense of what is fair and right between us, in which I have the highest confidence, that he will do all in his power to let Mountbatten have the comparatively small additional support which his air force now requires to enable the decisive battle raging in Burma to be won." (26:319)

Flying Sergeant
Staff Sergeant John B. Craighead's 164th Liaison Squadron followed the Irrawaddy track and XXXIII Corps south to Rangoon. *Courtesy of 1st Air Commando Association*

Prime Minister Churchill's unprecedented appeal turned the tide. On 3 April, the American Chiefs of Staff conditionally agreed to continue General Slim's momentum. In a message, General

Glider Markings
Rare example of Waco CG-4A Hadrian glider with the five diagonal stripes of the 1st Air Commando Group. The marking indicates the photograph was taken during later operations such as Pyawbwe or Lewe. *Courtesy of 1st Air Commando Association*

Marshall promised United States transport aircraft would not be withdrawn until after the capture of Rangoon, or until 1 June, whichever date was earlier. Less than 2 weeks later, before the SEAC staff could respond fully, General Sultan introduced another plan for the withdrawal of all American and Chinese forces from Burma. In a final stroke, General Wedemeyer requested Admiral Lord Mountbatten release one transport squadron by 25 April to combat a Japanese drive on Chih-chiang. General Slim's plans were in jeopardy.

With a blunt exchange of radio signals, Admiral Lord Mountbatten detached the squadron from Northern Burma area and directed SEAC to push forward and be prepared to execute Operation DRACULA—an amphibious assault on Rangoon. Initially, General Slim's two Central Burma corps were to advance in a parallel axis toward Mandalay. General Stopford's XXXIII Corps began moving along the western approach down the Irrawaddy Valley while General Messervy's IV Corps traced the more direct railway corridor route. SEAC plans would be dictated by the speed of their progress. The race to Rangoon was on.

Provisioning of units and formations had to be brought up to strength before XIV Army could begin. Transport aircraft throughout the India-Burma Theater were busy during the early days of

Attempted Sabotage
At Toungoo in April 1945, a Nippon infiltrator attempted to blow up an Air Commando L-5 by holding the bomb next to the engine. He failed. The airplane flew the next day. *Courtesy of Bill Chapple, 1ˢᵗ Air Commando Association*

April ferrying reinforcements, replacements, artillery, motor vehicles, blankets, and rations to Mandalay and Meiktila. An integral part of the XIV Army plan to seize Rangoon included the use of glider-borne engineers to build air transport strips. Trying to beat pre-monsoon weather, on 10 April, crews of the 319ᵗʰ and the 317ᵗʰ Troop Carrier Squadrons began moving stockpiles of gasoline to Meiktila. The air commando Dakotas also towed CG-4A gliders forward from Lalaghat to Palel. Wacos bore the brunt of the overland preparation when the two air commando transport squadrons were diverted to prepare for an airborne assault on Rangoon. Prior to reporting for training at Kalaikunda, 319ᵗʰ and 317ᵗʰ Troop Carrier Squadron pilots towed 40 gliders from Palel to Meiktila. Inside the cargo compartment of the Wacos were 43.8 tons of cargo and aviation fuel. Waco pilots released at 600 feet to reduce the effect of 30 to 50 mile-per-hour winds on final. All cargo was delivered, but one mishap occurred. A glider departed the runway at Meiktila and crashed into an RAF Hurricane. The British fighter lost a propeller and the glider's tail was damaged.

Assisting IV Corps' movements from Meiktila through Toungoo, Nyaunglebin, and Pegu were elements of the Combat Cargo Task Force. On 16 April, Lieutenant Colonel Taylor again linked with the 1ˢᵗ Air Commando Group when he joined IV Corps

acting as the Combat Cargo Task Force liaison officer. Groundwork for the march to Rangoon was completed on 18 April when 15 more gliders departed Sinthe with 33.75 tons of jeeps, bulldozers, tractors, trailers, mess equipment, and various other items.

The British IV Corps' advance down the railway corridor was divided into four sections listed below in chronological order.

(1) Operation FIRST GUMPTION: Capture Pyawbwe by 17ᵗʰ Division
(2) Operation SECOND GUMPTION: Capture Lewe by 5ᵗʰ Division
(3) Operation FREEBORN: Cut off Japanese easterly escape routes at Pegu
(4) Operation LAST GUMPTION: Capture Pegu

General Slim intended to evacuate casualties by light planes from forward areas to three medical evacuation points. Meiktila was the main medical facility while XXXIII Corps planned a substation at Magwe and IV Corps envisioned another medical site at Toungoo. Glider pilots from the 1ˢᵗ and 2ⁿᵈ Air Commando Groups were involved in all phases of the advance except Operation FREEBORN.

As XIV Army prepared for Rangoon, another capability was added to the 1ˢᵗ Air Commando Group arsenal. Accompanying the group throughout the campaign, Mr. Burkhart, civilian technical representative of All American Aviation, Inc., provided continued assistance regarding snatch equipment and procedures. Exposed to the air commando spirit, Burkhart anticipated the time when a downed airman would require immediate extraction from enemy-held territory. He theorized existing glider snatch equipment could also be used to recover personnel. Equipping a UC-64 with a spe-

Invaluable Moonlight Savant
Field mechanics toiled long into the night with few parts and under miserable conditions. *Courtesy of 1ˢᵗ Air Commando Association*

L-5B Sentinel
Technical Sergeant Russ N. Krelle stands beside an L-5B Sentinel. The aircraft was modified for stretcher patients. The modification was unlike Gallagher and Snyder's version. *Courtesy of Russ Kreele, 1ˢᵗ Air Commando Association*

Fighter Wallas
(L-R) Captain William J. Hemphill; Captain Leon Reese; Second Lieutenant James W. Tate; Second Lieutenant Thomas A. Hight, Jr. *Courtesy of 1ˢᵗ Air Commando Association*

cially designed snatch reel, he submitted himself to an in-flight trial. At altitude, he slipped out of the Norseman—trailing behind the aircraft by a nylon tether. Despite difficulties reeling him back into the aircraft, the test was successful. After improving the design, Mr. Burkhart proposed a demonstration. A goat was selected as the live participant. Poles were positioned and the animal was secured in a harness. Swooping low, the UC-64 caught the looped cord and lifted the goat skyward. As the crew reeled the animal into the airplane, the critter was wide-eyed but alive.

Operation FIRST GUMPTION began favorably as the British 17ᵗʰ Division and 244ᵗʰ Tank Brigade encircled and soundly defeated the Japanese at Pyawbwe. By a twist of fate, Japan's 33ʳᵈ Army Headquarters was allowed to slip through the British web. The speed of the thrust canceled General Kimura's hope of establishing a stand in South Central Burma. Leapfrogging Pyawbwe, the 5ᵗʰ Indian Division passed through the 17ᵗʰ Division intent on capturing Pyinmana. Moving quickly, the en route airfield at Lewe was cleared of major Japanese resistance on 19 April. Airborne en-

Fighter Pilot Rescuer
First Lieutenant Frank N. Davis, Operations Officer of 166ᵗʰ Liaison Squadron, and Corporal Silas H. Rhodes, Crew Chief. Davis was recommended for a Silver Star after rescuing Captain William R. Hemphill. It was declined. *Courtesy of Frank Davis, 1ˢᵗ Air Commando Association*

Radio Communication Section
Staff Sergeant Michael P. Presti, Private First Class Marvin C. Morgan, Private First Class William Morison, and Sergeant Henry A. Galbraith manned air commando radio stations as the unit moved into Burma. *Courtesy of 1ˢᵗ Air Commando Association*

C-47 Nose Art *Big Snatch*
In later operations, Dakota crews decorated their airplanes with nose art. This C-47 Dakota reported having the most glider pickups. *Courtesy of 1ˢᵗ Air Commando Association*

gineers wasted no time repairing the airdrome. By the afternoon of 20 April, British and American engineers had leveled a glider strip 150 yards wide by 800 yards long and prepared a smaller 30 by 350 yard liaison runway on an adjoining taxiway. The parallel landing zones were outlined by corner markers and side panels; ground personnel positioned wind tees for each. When British Airborne Engineers signaled the two strips would be ready in the morning, operations swung into motion.

Crews from the 4ᵗʰ Combat Cargo Squadron departed Meiktila before sunrise on 21 April for the new glider strip at Lewe with 22.74 tons of rations. After airdropping the supplies, transport crews returned to fly glider tows. Eight gliders of the 2ⁿᵈ Air Commando Group flew in single ship sorties to Lewe and arrived between 0955 and 1015. Their cargo was 13.5 tons of equipment to widen and lengthen the runway for transports and fighters. A scraper, tractor, jeep, trailer, gasoline saw, 2 bulldozers, water, rations, gasoline, and 19 men were included. As the Waco pilots arrived, ground personnel set off smoke pots and fired green flares at the north end of the glider strip. Failing to see the signals, five of the gliders landed on the L-5 runway. The equipment was serviceable and there were no injuries although one glider ran off the taxiway and was damaged beyond repair.

Skirmishes occurred all day and on 22 April, the field was raided by eight Oscars. Strafing the area from the north, the Japanese pilots left five gliders burning from the gasoline that was on board. The gliders had acted as a decoy leaving the engineering area and equipment unharmed. Construction continued unabated and by noon the strip was 4,500 feet long. Before sundown, Dakotas from the 62ⁿᵈ Squadron, RAF, delivered the first precious shipments of aviation fuel. As FIRST GUMPTION came to a close, airborne engineers were lengthening the runway to meet specification for Brit-

ish Spitfires. In time, Lewe would become the primary enplaning point for the British march on Rangoon.

As engineers completed work at Lewe, 5ᵗʰ Indian Division was already entering Toungoo—Japanese opposition was light and confused. The airfield at Tennant required little work and was selected for another glider assault. Airborne engineers were flown to Toungoo from Lewe to fill craters, lay out an L-5 runway, position marker panels, and begin improvements at the adjacent Kalaywa runway for anticipated transport and fighter operations. The following day, thunderstorms and pre-monsoon rains made the airfields unserviceable until late in the day, so aircrews conducted supply drops to Tennant personnel. With weather in their favor on 23 April, six Wacos of the 1ˢᵗ and 2ⁿᵈ Air Commando Groups departed Meiktila at 4-minute intervals for Tennant. Duplicating operations at Lewe, the gliders landed about midmorning with 11.0 tons of equipment, supplies, and 13 personnel—10 engineers and 3 glider mechanics. After grading the craters again and extending the Kalaywa strip to 6,000 feet, engineers cleared transports to land. The first shipment of communication equipment arrived 3 hours and 30 minutes after the last glider touched down on the makeshift dirt airfield at Tennant. Between dawn and dusk the following day, 56 Commando and Dakota sorties reached the restored runway at Kalaywa.

Early in April, advanced liaison squadron teams arrived in Meiktila to bury the Japanese dead, cover their campsites, and prepare the base for liaison plane operations. Again the men and Sentinels of the 1ˢᵗ Air Commando Group accompanied IV Corps. Only the names changed. Captain Goodman welcomed new pilots into the 166ᵗʰ Liaison Squadron but was given little time to prepare them for Burma. With only 2 weeks to reorganize, the flying program for replacements necessarily was rudimentary, intended to develop aircraft familiarization. Operational mission training was done in-country. As the men flew deep into Burma, apprehension and bloodshed quickly tempered the new pilots with the reality of their task. The tone of Sergeant William F. Wellington's first mis-

C-47 Nose Art *Do It*
Courtesy of 1ˢᵗ Air Commando Association

Captain Hemphill bought help with 50 rupees and Captain Davis directed natives to free the Sentinel. He, Hemphill, and the Burmese pushed the plane to a section of the field; Davis lined up as best he could along a level stretch. It was clear there was not enough room to takeoff. Notified that Japanese troops were returning to the site, Captain Davis had to make a quick decision—face capture or risk certain damage to his airship and invite personal injury. Trusting his piloting skills, Captain Davis did not hesitate. While he revved up the engine, dropped the flaps, and held the brakes, a native knocked down a final section of dike to improve takeoff clearance. Once rolling, the Sentinel bounced four times over rice paddies before Captain Davis jerked the plane into the air and headed west. On landing at Meiktila, the aircraft had to be sent to maintenance for extensive repairs. After the rescue, Captain Hemphill gratefully wrote, "Needless to say, I have great respect and admiration for Captain Davis and the L-5 airplanes." (115:5 June 1945)

To ensure Rangoon before the normal 15 May start of the monsoons, Admiral Lord Mountbatten earlier ordered a paratroop assault on Rangoon as part of the combined attack called Operation DRACULA. General Leese described the objective, "The airborne operation was to consist of a parachute battalion dropped on the 1ˢᵗ May, west of Elephant Point, with the task of destroying the defenses in that area. This would permit the entrance of minesweepers which would sweep a channel up the river as far as its junction with the Bassein Creek." (109:1926)

Colonel A. L. McCullough, deputy chief of staff, Combat Cargo Task Force, and Major Holm were selected to command the airborne operation. Originally assigned to the mission were 14 Dakotas from the 319ᵗʰ Troop Carrier Squadron, 16 Dakotas of the 317ᵗʰ Troop Carrier Squadron, and the 2ⁿᵈ Gurkha Parachute Battalion. On 14 April, air commando aircraft arrived at Kalaikunda to prepare for training activities. Maintenance personnel immediately made modifications to the Dakotas. They moved static cables from the top of the cabin to the right side, laid paratrooper carpet, and installed external parapack racks on loan from 31ˢᵗ and 117ᵗʰ Transport Squadrons RAF. Parapacks contained signal equipment, grenades, explosives, ammunition, and supplies needed by paratroopers. The packs resembled bombs attached externally along the centerline of the Dakota's fuselage. To identify the contents, connected parachutes typically were distinctively colored. Table 9 shows the parapack chute colors for Operation DRACULA.

On 16 April training began. Indian Army paratroop methods were used. Initially Dakota pilots practiced 3-plane elements; as proficiency increased, the training was enlarged to 9-ship formations. On 22 April, 10 aircraft from the 2ⁿᵈ and 4ᵗʰ Combat Cargo Squadrons were added to complete the group complement. In all, Operation DRACULA included 40 aircraft. The following morning, Major Holm led a group formation on an actual day airdrop followed by a night formation simulated drop. Colonel McCullough directed a combined rehearsal, called Exercise MUFFIN, on 26 April to simulate conditions approximating those of the actual mission. The profile included a night takeoff, 2-hour flight, daylight jump, and employment of dummy parapacks loaded with 150 pounds of sand. The commander selected a practice drop zone near Kalaikunda. Two Pathfinder aircraft arrived 45 minutes before the main body. Pathfinder paratroopers quickly positioned drop zone equipment, marked the site (22-19-15N 87-24-30E) with panels in the form of a "T," and lit various flares to decide the best color for visual recognition. When the main body arrived over the drop zone, pilots reported white smoke was the most easily seen; blue was second.

After crews drew and checked equipment, the operation moved to Akyab for final preparations. Navigators were briefed on the route of the mission. A variety of navigational aids were available for the operation—LORAN, Rebecca, SCR-717-C search radar, and APN-1 radio altimeters. The drop zone was to be marked electronically with British Eureka Mark II transmitters. To assure success, navi-

C-47 Nose Art *Peaches*
Courtesy of 1ˢᵗ Air Commando Association

C-47 Nose Art *Umbriago*
Courtesy of 1ˢᵗ Air Commando Association

gators were instructed to use all aids to navigation. No method was to be used to the exclusion of others. SEAC assigned two Catalinas to provide air-sea rescue capability—one for the main route and the other near the drop zone. Six air commando aircraft were tasked to protect the formation. Additionally, a B-25D from the 2nd Weather Reconnaissance Squadron was included. It was to depart 3 hours prior to the takeoff of the Pathfinder aircraft and transmit continuous coded weather reports of the route and objective area.

TABLE 9
Operation DRACULA
Parapack Parachute Markings

Quantity	Container/Parapacks	Color
2	Medical Supplies and Equipment	White
9	Explosives	Black
10	Mortars	Red
18	Signal Equipment	Khaki or Orange
25	Machine Guns and Ammunition	Blue
43	Bombs	Red
49	Small Arms Ammunition`	Yellow*
65	Grenades	Green

* load of 6 mortar bombs on aircraft 29 was marked with yellow parachutes

On 30 April, squadron briefings provided operations, intelligence, medical, ditching, escape and evasion, and air-sea rescue procedures. The same day, an aircraft flying over the city reported English words were painted on the roof of the spoke-shaped Rangoon jail—the Japanese Prisoner of War Camp. In large white markings, someone had scrawled two messages:

JAPS GONE
EXTRACT DIGIT

Wary of a trick, SEAC did not take the information at face value. Admiral Lord Mountbatten decided to go through with Operation DRACULA.

The weather aircraft lifted off at 2330 that night. Colonel McCullough, in a Dakota named *Gravel Gertie*, followed at 0230. He was leading two Pathfinder aircraft carrying a small security force and a Visual Control Post. At 0300 on 1 May, Major Holm launched the main formation of 38 aircraft. The air armada flew to Myingyi Kyun Island at 140 miles per hour and 500-feet altitude before turning directly to Payagyi while climbing to 2,000 feet. Inbound to the initial point at Thandi, Maj Holm descended to 1,000 feet and then slowed to 110 miles per hour, set one-quarter flaps, and established 1,200 foot-spacing between 3-ship elements. The formation continued down to 800 feet drop altitude over the objective—a 1,000 by 2,200 yard rice paddy that marked the drop zone southeast of Elephant Point (16-27N 96-18E). The egress was a reciprocal route at 150 miles per hour.

The time spent rehearsing the operation was worth the effort. The mission was picture perfect. There were no mechanical or maintenance difficulties. Although the monsoons arrived 3 weeks early, weather even cooperated. Light rain and thicker weather was encountered over the mountains, but by the time the formation reached the objective area, visibility was unlimited and cloud decks were above the aircraft at 3,000 feet. Pilots reported the drop zone was exactly as briefed—recognizable by white smoke and panels in the familiar "T" silhouette. Colonel McCullough's Pathfinders arrived over Elephant Point at 0548 and the main formation called "green light" at 0633. Each was behind schedule by 3 minutes.

Over the objective area, the Pathfinder crew dropped a radar transmitter. It would be used by the main body to locate the drop zone. In case of radar failure, smudge pots were used as a backup. Private Byrne hunched over his radar scope as Major Holm adjusted azimuth to find the blip. Identifying a faint return, Byrne began timing as the blip reached 10 miles out. He recalled years later, "By the time we reached target, a semblance of light appeared in the sky and we could see smoke pots ahead...We no sooner made our pass and dropped the troops than the pilot yelled over the intercom, 'Byrne, you screwed up—we missed target by 50 feet.' Then he laughed like hell and dove for the treetops."(120:—)

The mission was one of the most successful paratroop operations of the war. The combat load of the initial insertion included 110 tons, 818 paratroopers, 221 parapacks, and 18 door bundles—8 bicycles, 6 flame throwers, and 4 signal equipment packets. Less than 5 hours later, Major Holm was in the air again leading 8 aircraft back to Elephant Point with 160 paratroop reinforcements. Bringing critical equipment behind the reinforcements were Dakotas loaded with 29.3 tons of weapons, ammunition, explosives, medical supplies, and signal equipment.

C-47 Nose Art *R. O. N.*
Courtesy of 1st Air Commando Association

C-47 Nose Art *Blue Bonnet City*
Courtesy of 1ˢᵗ Air Commando Association

C-47 Nose Art *Tail Wind*
Courtesy of 1ˢᵗ Air Commando Association

Synchronized with the vertical envelopment was a bomber attack on the main guns atop Elephant Point. The bomb run was the most ill-fated aspect of the entire Rangoon operation. While the paratroopers marched toward the objective, B-24 Liberator crews misidentified the aim point and dropped bombs short of the target. Gurkha soldiers suffered 30 casualties in a tragic case of fratricide. In the aftermath of the accident, Visual Control Post personnel canceled the bombing. The mission was turned over to the remaining Gurkhas. By late afternoon, the elite paratroop unit expelled 37 Imperial troops from Elephant Point and silenced the Japanese guns.

Meanwhile, XXXIII Corps and IV Corps marched toward Rangoon expecting to join the airborne assault in a final showdown with Japanese Imperial troops. In its path, XXXIII Corps swept through and captured the Burmese oil fields and towns. Lieutenant Colonel F. T. Wood wrote, "The result is that as May opened in Burma, British-controlled territory from Meiktila south is in two long fingers with confused Japanese on both sides and in the middle." Despite the rapid advance and heroics of the two corps, by the beginning of May, the British were still a considerable distance from the vital seaport needed to maintain XIV Army. It was not because of British shortcomings. One of General Messervy's ablest commanders, Major General P. T. "Punch" Cowan, reported he was bogged down in Pegu. In addition to the spirited and tenacious Japanese defense, XIV Army faced an old nemesis. Louis Allen described the circumstances in late April:

... Cowan was now bedevilled by another enemy. The monsoon arrived, a fortnight before it was expected. On 29 April, Pegu was deluged in torrential rain, like the rest of Lower Burma. At once, the airfields so recently captured began to be affected...The heavy rains kept the tanks and trucks confined to the main road. And any possibility of fording the Pegu River

and so ignoring the bridge demolitions disappeared as the waters rose in flood. (1:478)

Hours became critical because Admiral Lord Mountabatten's time table was tight. If Japanese resistance delayed or denied Rangoon to General Slim and the monsoons set in, the battle for Burma faced postponement until weather cleared. General Messervy's slow progress caused the airborne operation and General Slim's planned land attack of Rangoon to become uncoordinated by early May. These things preyed on the mind of Allied strategists as they raced against nature and her fury. With suddenness, just when the operation became acute, again the Japanese acted out of character. Prior to the pivotal confrontation with General Slim's army and air armada, General Kimura ordered the Japanese to abandon the port. The Emperor's field-tested army tucked tail and left the city uncontested suspecting General Slim was about to batter in the door. In their hasty retreat, the Japanese did not judge the capriciousness of nature. Nearly 2 weeks before normal, the monsoons fell upon Southern Burma in force.

Just before the storm broke, Wing Commander Saunders made a reconnaissance flight over Rangoon in a British Mosquito on the afternoon of 2 May. From the air, he stated the port city appeared deserted. Seeing signals from the ground and a Union Jack flying over the jail, the RAF pilot landed at the airfield north of town. Due to the condition of the airfield, he damaged his undercarriage during rollout. General Leese described the event that followed:

He was greeted by the local inhabitants, and made his way into the city and, after contacting our prisoners in the jail, went down river in a country boat and gave 26 Indian Division the news. By 2200 hours on the 3ʳᵈ May, 36 Brigade had occupied Dala Village, opposite the Rangoon docks, against minor opposition…. The liberation of Rangoon had cost us under one hundred casualties. Only one landing craft, unfortunately containing key engineer and medical personnel, [was] lost on a mine…. By the successful re-entry into Rangoon through the sea-gate, the port was re-opened at least 14 days earlier than if it had been left to XIV Army… With the capture of Rangoon a major phase of the war against Japan had been completed, a phase important in itself and decisive as far as Burma was concerned. It will be to the eternal credit of the sea, land, and air force of South-East Asia that this phase was completed before the 1945 monsoon. (109:1927)

The liberation of Rangoon was celebrated by a victory parade in the city, but the celebration was short lived. Winds and rain interrupted British efforts to establish port operations in Rangoon. As thunderstorms grew in strength and intensity, SEAC realized controlling the port meant the war was almost over. Accolades poured in regarding the extraordinary efforts of all involved in the reconquest of Burma. Admiral Lord Mountbatten and General Slim openly recognized the skill, sacrifice, and leadership of U.S. and British airmen. Air Marshall Sir Keith Park observed in Europe the army advanced *under* the wings of the air force, but in Burma the army advanced *on* the wings of the air force. General Leese recorded the contribution of the air campaign as follows:

Air power was a vital element and dominating factor in our strategy. The resources were never able to meet the demands without exacting the utmost from both man and machine…. I cannot speak too highly of the work done by the squadrons which swept the Japanese from the skies, disrupted their land communications, and provided our troops with close fire support which was all the more valuable owing to the restricted amount of artillery available… Air transport was used on a scale hitherto unprecedented in modern war….the tonnages handled daily are recorded, but to get the true measure of the effort, it should be remembered that the air-crews who delivered the goods often made three or four journeys a day over hazardous jungle country, often flying in appalling conditions of weather; many casualties were caused by these fearful conditions, but the risks were unflinchingly faced. The ground crews worked unceasingly by day and night in the open, sometimes in torrential rain, to keep the aircraft in commission and to enable the very high rates of service to be maintained. (109:1958)

General Stratemeyer was more specific in his praise of Colonel Hall's unit. He extended his "personal congratulations and commendations to every member of [the 1st Air Commando Group and 2nd Air Commando Group] without whose efforts the victory in Burma could not have been achieved…" (113:7 May 1945 Letter) Combat Cargo Task Force Intelligence Reports summarized with the following: "The whole campaign has been a striking illustration of a fact new in warfare that air power can be used to transport, supply, and support ground troops entirely independently of ground channels. This has been South East Asia's contribution to the art of war." (93:8)

In the glory of victory, the men who fashioned this new means of conducting war did not dwell on their contribution. Instead, they receded to their home base of Asansol. They were tired from nearly 8 months of front-line fighting. During the early days of May, the 1st Air Commando Group welcomed the unaccustomed leisure that followed the opening of Rangoon. While in Asansol, the air commandos did not know the fortunes of war had changed the focus of U.S. activities in Southeast Asia. After General Slim's successful campaign, the air commandos would no longer be a part of the Allied excursion in Burma. During the summer monsoons, American efforts were redirected to China. After a short rest and the announcement of victory in Europe, the men of the 1st Air Commando Group grew restless and looked forward to new operational assignments. For many, the wait would prove to be in vain.

Airdrop Ground Markings
Ground panels in the shape of a "T" and a triangle indicate the point of release. During Operation DRACULA, aircrews reported white smoke and panels in the shape of a "T" were easiest to spot. *Courtesy of 1st Air Commando Association*

13

Exit

When Rangoon fell, British and American interests diverged and SEAC became an Allied command in name only. Once Burma was retaken, Admiral Lord Mountbatten's plan for the next operation targeted Malaya. The United States had no strategic interest in the peninsula and wished to avoid the appearance of supporting European re-colonialism. This ideological separation also took place symbolically between air commando squadrons and their longtime counterparts, IV Corps and XXXIII Corps. As British, Indian, and African troops labored to establish Rangoon as a major supply center, the annual monsoons brought warm summer rains to blur the Burmese countryside. In the soaking curtain, sustained flight operations ceased; therefore, in early May 1945, Colonel Hall ordered the 1st Air Commando Group to retract its tentacles from the washed out, fair weather airstrips of Burma. The group reconstituted in Asansol for a much anticipated rest. Left behind was XIV Army.

Awaiting the 5th and 6th Fighter Squadrons in India were P-51D and P-51K Mustangs. Between 18 and 20 May, air commando fighter pilots delivered their P-47 Thunderbolts to Air Service Command in exchange for new Mustangs. The pilots accepted the trade with mixed feelings. Some stressed the increased speed and maneuverability of the Mustangs while others regretted the loss of the rugged Thunderbolts. Upon accepting the new aircraft into the inventory, the fighter squadrons flew to Kalaikunda for transition training. In mock combat, the air commandos adopted a "thatch weave" formation as a basic defensive configuration, and with time, developed more confidence in the sleek Mustang. While the fighter units waited for operational orders, Captain Wilkins transferred to 1st Air Commando Group Headquarters and then returned to the United States. Command of the 5th Fighter Squadron transferred to Captain Manuel S. Martinez.

Air Commandos receive P-51D Mustangs
First Lieutenant Anthony H. Dubois, Jr., checks out newly delivered P-51D Mustang at Dum Dum Field, Calcutta, India. *Courtesy of Allen W. Abrahams, 1st Air Commando Association*

Replacement Fighter Pilot
Arriving along with the new P-51D and P-51K model aircraft were replacement pilots. Flight Officer Adolph E. Giza stands in front of the Air Commando's third fighter. Staff Sergeant James Herrell maintained *Miss Joyce. Courtesy of 1st Air Commando Association*

6th Fighter Squadron
After delivery of the P-51D Mustangs to Asansol in August 1945, the 6th Fighter Squadron painted the tail with a showy checkerboard design. *Courtesy of Elwood Jamison, 1st Air Commando Association*

Doubts about the durability of Mustangs returned when Second Lieutenant Bruce V. Johnson was killed 10 miles west northwest of Kalaikunda. On 7 June during a dive bombing run, the 5th Fighter Squadron pilot attempted a routine pull out at 2,500 feet when the left wing separated. The aircraft snap rolled out of control and augered in. Adding to the gloom were the losses of 6th Fighter Squadron members Lieutenant Hainey, one of the 7 Volunteers, and Flight Officer William E. Mantel. Due to the accidents, the group adopted skip bombing techniques instead of the steeper dive procedure because of the Mustang's apparent wing weakness. Anxious to field-test the new planes before the war ended, the fighter pilots futilely waited for operational orders to take the Mustangs into combat. Only a Theater Air Show in Agra to commemorate Air Force Day disrupted the boredom. When the hot, humid summer wore on, the fighter squadrons concentrated on ways to boost morale. One of the results was the development of three innovative ways of cooling beer.

> … we used to put our beer cans in the wings of the fighters and the pilots would go up on a check flight at high altitude. When they got back the beer was real cold. Before that we used up practically all the CO_2 fire extinguishers cooling the beer until the word came down from the brass to stop. We also dug holes in the dirt, put a couple cans of beer in the hole, covered it with dirt, poured aviation gas over it, lighted it and when the flames went out, the beer was cool. (131:May/June 1993:3)

When the Flying Sergeants arrived in Asansol, they also suffered from inactivity. Captain Beasley's 164th Liaison Squadron had replaced Captain Davis' men at Sinthe in April. While XXXIII Corps moved southward toward Rangoon, the light planes followed and set up headquarters at Magwe, Burma. Operating from a rice paddy strip, Beasley's light plane pilots averaged more than 25 air evacuations per day while they continued to deliver cargo, supplies, and replacements; fly aerial reconnaissance; and transfer Japanese prisoners of war. As April became May, pelting rain turned Magwe's rice paddies into mire making flying impossible. By 10 May, the squadron pulled up stakes for their rear area base at Asansol.

At the same time, the 166th Liaison Squadron was forced to terminate operations at Toungoo as worsening conditions gradually turned the unit's camp into a lake. During breaks in the storm, the liaison pilots supported IV Corps as British soldiers and desperate Japanese units savagely clashed near Rangoon. Captain Goodman's men evacuated 182 casualties, flew in 49 replacements, and transported over 16 tons of supplies during the first 8 days of May. Then the tropical storm season shut down Toungoo. Unrelenting rain fell four more days before weather cleared enough for light plane pilots to chart a course to Eastern India. On 13 May, Major Austin's Dakotas completed the redeployment by extracting the remaining equipment and ground personnel from Burma. As the last fragments of the 1st Air Commando Group arrived in Asansol, the three liaison squadrons were reunited after 8 months of intense frontline activity.

During the early summer at Asansol, the light plane squadrons were concerned mainly with reorganization and training. With President Truman's Potsdam Ultimatum, the officers and enlisted sensed the end of the war was near and began counting points to decide who would return to "Uncle Sugar Able." Command of each squad-

Air Force Day Air Show
In the summer heat, the 1st Air Commando Group participated in a Theater Air Show in Agra, India. *Courtesy of 1st Air Commando Association*

ron changed hands during the summer of 1945. In June, Captain Beasley turned over the 164ᵗʰ Liaison Squadron to Captain Thomas H. Brown; Captain Elbert E. Davis rotated out of theater leaving the 165ᵗʰ Squadron to First Lieutenant Limburg; and Captain Goodman transferred the flag of the 166ᵗʰ Squadron to Captain Saxon. Only an occasional search and rescue assignment, courier mission, or flight over the Hump into China broke the monotony of training in the blistering India heat.

While air commando fighter and light plane pilots stewed in Asansol, a desperate shortage of airlift in China prompted a request for C-47 and C-46 aircraft. Fighters and bombers stationed in China were assigned the job of isolating Japanese troops in the south from their supply sources in North and Central China. For this, General Wedemeyer originally proposed moving all 10ᵗʰ Air Force assets across the Himalayas. Prematurely, China Theater issued a General Order on 1 May naming newly promoted Lieutenant General Stratemeyer as Commanding General, Army Air Forces, China Theater. Under the new arrangement, both 10ᵗʰ and 14ᵗʰ Air Forces were to be component commands.

To ease the reorganization of his theater, General Wedemeyer recommended sending both Major General Chennault, 14ᵗʰ Air Force, and Major General Howard C. Davidson, 10ᵗʰ Air Force, back to the United States. In this way the China Theater commander hoped to snuff out potential personality clashes. After coordinating the personnel transactions, the China Theater staff realized the logistics requirement for such a large force was not possible—Hump tonnage and supplies carried over the Burma Road could not support the massive commitment. Therefore, General Wedemeyer ordered a downsizing of assault forces being sent to China. At the same time, he snatched up all available transport units.

Coincidentally, on 17 May, SEAC dissolved Combat Cargo Task Force. As a result, the 319ᵗʰ Troop Carrier Squadron's new commander, Major Lester L. Bear, resettled his Dakotas in Asansol to await orders. An unassigned C-47 squadron was just what General Wedemeyer was looking for; he immediately directed the transport unit and the 72ⁿᵈ Airdrome Squadron to Warazup, Burma. Soon after setting up a base camp in the remains of the 490ᵗʰ Bombing Squadron buildings, a story that a Bengal tiger roamed the grounds kept personnel sleeping with one eye open. Some claimed to have seen the big cat, others swore they observed paw prints, but no one conclusively proved the tiger's existence.

Although tasked to fly Chinese troops over the Hump to Kunming, Major Bear was soon without a mission. Within a week of arrival, higher headquarters stopped all C-47 Hump flights—the mission was better suited to the larger C-46 Commando. In short order, the Dakota pilots were instructed to resupply isolated hill stations of the Air Warning System. Located atop the highest mountain crest in specified areas of Burma, these stations were totally dependent on airdrop for all rations and supplies. Corporal Charlie Brown, Dakota radio operator, later wrote, "I remember flying with [Major] Al Kaufman a few times on airdrops to radio and radar

outposts. Trying to push out food, mail, or gasoline and have them land on top of a mountain ridge is not easy. The poor guy who had to climb down in a canyon to recover it probably wasn't too happy about it either." (131:March/April:5)

The missions were very demanding and for the first time a 319ᵗʰ Troop Carrier Squadron aircraft was lost between Myitkyina, Burma, and Ledo, India. Among those who died were Second Lieutenant Robert L. Karnes, pilot; Second Lieutenant Clyde S. Slick, copilot; Corporal Donald L. Merrill, radio operator; and Corporal Joseph G. Speroni, crew chief. Despite this tragedy, whether delivering life saving serum to a man bitten by a rabid dog or accurately airdropping critically needed food and gasoline blindly through an undercast, air commando Dakota pilots established a reputation for skill, inventiveness, and steel nerves.

Just as the war neared an end, the 1ˢᵗ Air Commando Group officially ceased operating as a lone wolf. On 10 July, China Theater approved orders assigning Colonel Hall's organization to 10ᵗʰ Air Force. As a result, Major Bear's men were ordered immediately to join other Army Air Force transport units operating on the north side of the Himalayas in the China Theater. Once under 10ᵗʰ Air Force command and control, air commando Dakota pilots received missions that moved them deeper and deeper into China. Between May and August, members of the 319ᵗʰ Troop Carrier Squadron operated from the Chinese airfields of Loping, Nanking, Luliang, Liuchow, Chihkiang, Peishiyi, Hankow, and Kunming as well as Hanoi in French Indochina. At each stage base, news of Allied attacks on islands leading to the Japanese mainland gave aircrews the strength to continue.

Finally the news of Hiroshima and Nagasaki brought a swift end to the conflict. With Japan's acknowledgment of formal surrender aboard the battleship *Missouri* on 2 September 1945, the men of the 1ˢᵗ Air Commando Group were anxious to go home. Established for a 6-month mission, the organization had remained in Burma almost 2 years. Sergeant Jack Curtis described the reaction at Asansol:

> When the war ended, we had a bash at the mess hall. What a night. Free beer, all you wanted. In old style as we emptied the bottles, we threw them against the far wall. When the party was over, I bet there was a pile of glass 2 feet high. At that time, rationing in the PX was over and you could buy candy bars by the box and all the beer you wanted. Can you imagine sitting on the porch of the barracks eating *Baby Ruth*, *O'Henry*, and *Zag Nut* bars and drinking beer? (131:May/June 1993:3)

Within 3 weeks of the armistice, Colonel Hall's men transferred all the group's aircraft except those belonging to the 319ᵗʰ Troop Carrier Squadron to various depots: 44ᵗʰ Air Service Group, 61ˢᵗ Air Service Group, 305ᵗʰ Air Service Group, Bengal Air Depot, and South India Air Depot. Their inventory was a mixed bag of aircraft and models. Table 10 shows the diversity of the group.

TABLE 10
Aircraft Inventory
23 September 1945

Manufacturer	Type Aircraft	Count	Organization
North American	AT-16F Harvard II*	2	5th and 6th Fighter Squadrons
North American	B-25J Mitchell	1	1st Air Commando Group Headquarters
North American	B-25H Mitchell	1	1st Air Commando Group Headquarters
Consolidated Vultee	BT-13A Valiant	21	65th and 166th Liaison Squadrons
Douglas	C-47A Dakotas	2	1st Air Commando Group Headquarters
Vultee	L-1C Vigilant	1	1st Air Commando Group Headquarters
Stinson	L-5A Sentinels	66	164th, 165th, and 166th Liaison Squadrons
Stinson	L-5B Sentinels	33	164th, 165th, and 166th Liaison Squadrons
North American	P-51K Mustangs	40	5th and 6th Fighter Squadrons
North American	P-51D Mustangs	8	5th and 6th Fighter Squadrons
Beechcraft	UC-45F Expeditor	1	1st Air Commando Group Headquarters
Noorduyn	UC-64A Norseman	7	164th, 165th, and 166th Liaison Squadrons

*Some members of the 5th and 6th Fighter Squadrons stated the aircraft was an AT-6 Texan

Even though the war had ended, there was much work to be done. Soldiers and airmen were eager to return to their homes in the United States. Preparations had begun earlier in anticipation of Japan's surrender. To overcome inequities, a point system was designed to favor men over 35 years old and those with enough service to earn 75 points. In exchange for personnel with high points and lengthy service, 29 enlisted men were transferred from air commando fighter units to the 80th Fighter Group on 11 August. Because transport crews were needed to move personnel to ports, they wondered if they would be the last to leave. However, with the point system in place, airlift crew members competed alongside all others for a ticket home. Eligible aircrews and ground personnel reported to debarkation sites according to the number of points earned. When voids were created in transport units, crosstraining was used to fill authorizations. Second Lieutenant Bill J. Ravey recalled those days after the war ended:

> The old warriors had a lot of points and were sent home on the first available transportation. We new fighter pilots were left to the mercy of the gods, and suffered a fate worse than death. We were assigned to the 319th Troop Carrier Squadron as co-pilots on Goonie Birds (C-47 Dakotas).... We were to fly gasoline in barrels to Shanghai. I think we used more gas flying than we delivered.... On my first flight ... I automatically pushed in rudder for torque as you had to do [on takeoff] in fighter aircraft. There being none on twin engine aircraft, I was all over [the] runway, and parts of the shoulders too.... My "old first pilot" [also a Second Lieutenant] just sat back during the whole affair, with a big grin on his face. (131:April/May/June 1994:10)

This infusion of Mustang blood into Major Bear's squadron led to some wild rides all over China and an education for the former fighter pilots. On a trip to Shanghai, a C-47 crew reportedly hedge-hopped more than 200 miles knocking over sampans in the canals and rivers en route. During another trip while hauling gasoline drums from Siam, Dakota pilots buzzed the Hankow airstrip at 240 MPH. But Dakota missions also taught the fighter pilots something new as well. Lieutenant Ravey remarked, "I had been briefed that the time to Shanghai was [8 hours and 30 minutes] and that we had only 8 hours of fuel. To stretch our fuel we weaned out the fuel mixture until the cylinder head temperature rose to the maximum allowable limit." He added, "Thank God for the autopilot." (131:April/May/June 1994:10)

Asansol Inactivity
An L-5 Sentinel parked next to the Asansol tower. By mid-May all three liaison squadrons had pulled back to their rear base. For most of the summer, the light plane squadrons were concerned mainly with reorganization and training. *Courtesy of Bill Chapple, 1st Air Commando Association*

Chinese Air Commando
In late summer 1945, a Chinese P-47D Thunderbolt was seen with 1ˢᵗ Air Commando markings. *Courtesy of 1ˢᵗ Air Commando Association*

En route to Loping, Huhsien, Hankow, Shanghai or other former Japanese bases, the scenes were jarring or filled the men with awe. In Hanoi, Dakota pilots were met at the ramp by Japanese troops and transported downtown. The 319th Troop Carrier Squadron was unable to air evacuate the number of Allied prisoners of war held at the city in a timely manner. The unit's Operations Officer, Major Albert Kaufman, arranged the movement of a U.S. Army field hospital to the French Indochina capital so medics could minister to the needs of those who were liberated. Major Kaufman spoke about other scenes of postwar China:

My most vivid memory of Loping was the endless lines of Chinese troops that passed our base on their way to the east. The columns stretched out for miles... They were foot soldiers with an occasional pack mule, and most officers were mounted. The soldiers first came into sight as they descended from the mountains in the west, the unbroken column extended across the valley floor, and then disappeared into the foothills to the east...Another adventure is indelibly etched in my memory. One cloudless day with unlimited visibility, we took off and headed northwest just for a "look-see." We flew at a 14,000-feet flight

altitude up a valley with steep mountains on both sides. The valley was wide enough so that there was no danger of getting squeezed in. But as we peered out of the cockpit, the mountains on either side loomed up another 14,000 feet above. (131:May/June 1989:4)

Shanghai signaled the end of American efforts. Dakota pilots looked forward to the modern Chinese Provincial capital and always counted on hospitality at the end of the line. Major Moist had been reassigned from the 1st Air Commando Group to Shanghai and he often assisted his former mates in finding overnight accommodations, ground transportation, and aircraft maintenance. While serving as the Operations Officer in USAAF Headquarters China and with MAGIC—Military Advisory Group in China, the ever-thinking Major Moist gathered the 1st Air Commando Group's monthly reports before they were destroyed. Thus, he saved much of the organization's history.

For Lieutenant Colonel Bear and the men of the 319th Troop Carrier Squadron the end was near. In China, the last operational fabric of the 1st Air Commando Group finally was told it was time to go home. They would follow air commando fighter and light plane squadron personnel who had begun outprocessing in September. Captain John Knop captured the transport squadron's response:

> The officers threw their shindig on the 26 October and the enlisted men had theirs on 27 October. Everyone had a shot of "stateside" whiskey and Lieutenant Colonel Bear made a speech explaining the situation as it stood. He also said that he might be leaving the organization in a few days and wanted to express his gratitude for the support the men of the 319th had given him since he became its Commanding Officer in May 1945. (116:October Report:2)

Indeed, Lieutenant Colonel Bear was among the first to be processed for return to the United States; before leaving, he passed command to Major Kaufman on 29 October. The new squadron commander described the last actions taken before deactivating the 319th Troop Carrier Squadron:

Our orders were to burn, crush, and bury our surplus supplies. So we had a big bonfire of all sorts of flying clothes, aircraft instruments, and everything else that our capable supply officer had accumulated for us. We flew our airplanes to Kunming, pickled the engines, and left them to the elements. It was a sad ending for the birds we had relied on for so long. C-54s then brought us to a camp at Calcutta where we waited our turns to board home bound ships. Somewhere along the line the 319th was deactivated. We departed India for home as individuals, priority being on the number of points each of us had earned. (131:May/June 1989:5)

Many air commandos were transported from Eastern India and China airfields to Calcutta. At the port, most of the group's personnel boarded the *USS General Hodges*, a Coast Guard transport anchored in the Hooghly River. Their route would take them down the river to the Bay of Bengal and on through the Indian Ocean, Arabian Sea, Red Sea, Suez Canal, Mediterranean Sea, Straits of Gibraltar, and across the Atlantic. As the ship made its way, they had time to reflect on their commanders, their accomplishments, and the events in Burma.

Heading Home, Asansol, India, August 1945
Front Row (L-R) **First Lieutenant Allen W. Abrahams; First Lieutenant Anthony H. Dubois, Jr.; First Lieutenant Franklin J. Misfeldt; First Lieutenant Lloyd B. Coleman**
Second Row (L-R) **First Lieutenant Rudolph "Rudy" Melichar, Jr.; First Lieutenant George A. Patton; First Lieutenant Benton R. "Benny" Hall; First Lieutenant Robert R. Ferguson, Jr.; First Lieutenant James A. Knight, Jr.; First Lieutenant Ernest P. Dornbush; Captain Lee F. "Moon" Mullins**
Courtesy of Allen W. Abrahams, 1ˢᵗ Air Commando Association

14

Legacy

The 1st Air Commando Group had made a difference in the outcome of the war against Japan, but the events of Burma were largely unknown in America. Aside from episodic accounts of Hump operations, the *Flying Tigers*, or General Stilwell's combustible temperament, South-east Asia was ignored as much by the American press as military logisticians. Pentagon historians recorded Eisenhower's D-day invasion and MacArthur's island hopping strategy in great detail but left the documentation of the conflict in China, Burma, and India to our staunch ally, Great Britain. As a result, the

impact of the 1st Air Commando Group's extraordinary accomplishments are scarcely understood today.

At the close of the war, much had changed in the 2 years since the self-styled organization departed Miami. Operationally assembled to sustain General Wingate's unorthodox long range penetration operations, the 1st Air Commando Group also influenced events in the CBI as an instrument of U.S. national strategy. Its formation was intended to further United States interests in China by reopening the Burma Road. This was apparent after the Chindit mission was realized but the Burma Road remained sealed. Washington was unable or unwilling to disengage the unit. Left in the theater to finish its task, the 1st Air Commando Group effectively transitioned from special operations to conventional warfare during General Slim's march to Rangoon.

The 1st Air Commando Group was the product of General Arnold's intellect, but his foresight was equally important to the organization's success. By ensuring the unit was isolated from the existing military structure of the CBI, he sanctioned a "rock-the-boat" approach to warfare. This allowed the group's leaders to define a modular organization with various disciplines under a single banner guided by one mission. The freedoms provided by Arnold and the adaptable design encouraged men of character and vision to challenge a tradition-bound military. In a culture that allowed them to generate new ideas, experiment freely, and "road-test" new concepts, the 1st Air Commando Group were the exception to B. H. Liddle-Hart's axiom, "The only thing harder than getting a new idea into the military mind is to get an old one out." (22:190) Operating in the "forgotten" CBI without fanfare or recognition, the group's leaders shaped and developed future warfare, just as General Arnold had intended.

Colonel Philip G. Cochran, Commander
Project 9, 5318th Provisional Unit (Air), and 1st Air Commando Group. *Courtesy of 1st Air Commando Association*

(OPPOSITE): Little Natural
Captain Archie L. McKay's B-25H Mitchell. *Courtesy of 1st Air Commando Association*

Dangero...
Mainten...
Courtesy...

Assault Force Leaders
Colonel John R. Alison, Major Robert L. Petit, and Lieutenant Colonel Grattan "Grant" Mahony at Hailakandi, India *Courtesy of James Lansdale, 1ˢᵗ Air Commando Association*

merely r
ing out
flicted w
    Gen
and airp
results.
directly
keep the
Burma R
range pe
land line
hands by

TABLE 11
1ˢᵗ Air Commando Group
Group, Section, and Squadron Commanders

1ˢᵗ Air Commando Group   Colonel Philip G. Cochran
        Colonel Clinton B. Gaty
        Colonel Robert W. Hall

Fighter Section   Lieutenant Colonel Grattan "Grant"
                               Mahony

Transport Section   Major William T. Cherry, Jr.
Glider Section   Captain William H. Taylor, Jr.
Light Transport Section   Lieutenant Colonel Clinton B. Gaty
Liaison Section   Major Andrew P. Rebori
                           Lieutenant Colonel Clinton B. Gaty
Helicopter Section   Lieutenant Colonel Clinton B. Gaty
Bomber Section   Lieutenant Colonel Robert T. "Tadpole"
                           Smith

5ᵗʰ Fighter Squadron (Commando)   Major Roland R. Lynn
        Captain Malcolm J. Wilkins
        Captain Manuel S. Martinez

6ᵗʰ Fighter Squadron (Commando)   Major Olin B. Carter
        Captain Younger A. Pitts, Jr.
        Captain William J. Hemphill

164ᵗʰ Liaison Squadron (Commando)   Captain David C. Beasley,
                                    Jr.
        Captain Thomas H. Brown

165ᵗʰ Liaison Squadron (Commando)   Major Vincent L. Ulery
        Captain Elbert E. Davis
        Captain Donald C. Limburg

166ᵗʰ Liaison Squadron (Commando)   Captain Fred H. Van Wagner
        Captain Julius Goodman
        Captain Neil B. Saxon

319ᵗʰ Troop Carrier Squadron (Commando)   Major Neil I. Holm
        Major Orlo L. Austin
        Lieutenant Colonel Lester L. Bear
        Major Alfred Kaufman

Norseman
Maintenar
flightwortl

SSgt Jasper C. Thomason
Sgt Ngon T. Tom[D]
MSgt Kermit G. Torkelson
Cpl Robert E. True
Sgt Clifford J. Tucker
Capt Donald C. Tulloch[M]
SSgt Alfred E. Turkingham
FO Charles B. Turner
1Lt Frank M. Turney
1Lt Leo S. Tyszecki*
1Lt Vincent L. Ulery
1Lt Steve T. Uminski
Cpl Milan J. Urbancic
Sgt Charles J. Usey
2Lt Charles J. Vagim*
2Lt Aurele R. Van De Weghe*

1Lt Edward G. Van Hofe[D]
1Lt Fred H. Van Wagner*
SSgt Arthur H. Van Wye
TSgt Geoffrey S. Vore
TSgt Norman W. Wach
Capt Edward (Sam) Wagner
FO Robert Wagner
1Lt Howell T. Walker
FO Earl C. Waller
SSgt Preston W. Walling
SSgt William T. Walters
1Lt Stephen A. Wanderer*[D]
1Lt Albert T. Ward
TSgt Owen C. Warren
SSgt John Watson
Sgt Roy Watson
Cpl Warren G. Watts

SSgt Walter R. Waugh, Jr.
FO Mainord M. Weaver
Cpl Max V. Weaver
TSgt Jack H. Webb
1Lt Wesley D. Weber*
SSgt Jesse C. Webster
Cpl Robert J. Weeks
SSgt Selig Weinstein
Pfc Morris Weiss
1Lt Kenneth L. Wells[D]
TSgt Leslie E. Werner
FO Russell J. West[T]
TSgt James R. Westmoreland
Maj Edwin S. White
Sgt Warren G. Wilcox
2Lt Malcolm J. Wilkins*
SSgt Chet A. Willets, Jr.

FO Bruce Williams
1Lt Grant H. Wilson, Jr.
2Lt Elmer L. (Jack) Wingo*
1Lt Robert A. Wink*
Pfc William J. Winn[D]
Capt James R. Woods
Cpl Julius F. Yackie[M]
Cpl Gerald L. Yound
Sgt Walter E. Young
F/Sgt Arnold Z. Zahorsky
Sgt Stanley G. Zajac
Sgt Alexander Zalman
Pfc Morris H. Zalmonovich
Sgt Michael R. Zamenski
Pfc Carl J. Zarcone
Capt Carl E. Ziegler, Jr.
FO Leo Zuk

Gr
for
opp
ger
rea
ise,
the
case
Adr
re-c
seer

oper
war
the
weal
Brita
ing a
trade

Unkn
Seco
Must
tesy o

1ˢᵗ Air Commando Group Personnel Roster

1 September 1944

Unit designations are as of 1 September 1944. Officially, only the 5ᵗʰ Fighter Squadron (Commando), 319ᵗʰ Troop Carrier Squadron (Commando), 164ᵗʰ Liaison Squadron (Commando), 165ᵗʰ Liaison Squadron (Commando), and 166ᵗʰ Liaison Squadron (Commando) were constituted with the publication of orders. Night Intruder Section air and ground crews were assigned to Group Headquarters. Nonetheless, Special Order Number 151 clearly earmarked fighter pilots and personnel for duty with "Q" Squadron, the forerunner of the 1ˢᵗ Air Commando's 6ᵗʰ Fighter Squadron (Commando). It officially was formed on 22 September 1944.

1ˢᵗ Air Commando Group
APO 690 c/o Postmaster NY
1 September 1944

164	TSgt	Glenn Abell	HQ	Sgt	John M. Barth	5	Pfc	Daniel E. Brennan
165	TSgt	Paul H. Abernathy	HQ	Pvt	Leonard F. Bartosiewicz	285	TSgt	Ewald Brenner
6	2Lt	Allen W. Abrahams	HQ	Pvt	William C. Bates	HQ	Cpl	Chester L. Brown
319	TSgt	Muncy E. Adams	HQ	Pvt	Gerald A. Bauer	HQ	Pvt	George W. Brown
319	FO	Eugene L. Adoue	6	SSgt	George U. Baylies	319	Pfc	Burton F. Browning
319	TSgt	Lester C. Ahlbrecht	6	2Lt	Edward D. Bayne	HQ	Pvt	Foch A. Browning
319	TSgt	Kenneth J. Alexander	5	Sgt	Walter L. Beares	HQ	Pvt	David H. Bruce
165	TSgt	Alfred T. Almen	164	1Lt	David C. Beasley, Jr.	HQ	Pfc	Donald E. Bruce
319	2Lt	Samuel L. Altman	166	Sgt	Robert H. Beatson	HQ	Pvt	Harold J. Bryan
HQ	Pvt	Wayne F. Angel	5	TSgt	William R. Beaty, Jr.	5	Pvt	Thomas W. Buck
HQ	Pfc	Frank P. Aquino	HQ	TSgt	Charles F. Becker	HQ	Pvt	Samuel J. Bullock
319	1Lt	Gerald L. Arkfeld	HQ	Sgt	James F. Bedell	164	TSgt	Daniel W. Bunch
164	Pfc	Thomas J. Armacost	5	SSgt	George W. Beers	HQ	Pvt	John J. Burgess
HQ	Pfc	Chester Armstrong	HQ	Cpl	Edward A. Beether	5	2Lt	William S. Burghardt
HQ	WOJG	Donald M. Armstrong	6	Sgt	Thomas P. Behan	5	Pfc	Michael A. Burgiel
319	SSgt	Richard H. Armstrong	319	TSgt	Richard M. Belcher	HQ	Pfc	John D. Burkett
319	Sgt	Willie J. Arnold	HQ	2Lt	William W. Bendernagel	166	SSgt	Arthur E. Burrell
HQ	Pvt	Kenneth D. Ashcraft	6	2Lt	Harold L. Bennett	164	SSgt	William E. Bussells, Jr.
HQ	Pvt	William D. Aston	HQ	MSgt	Irving Berkowitz	6	Cpl	Claude H. Butler
319	Capt	Orlo L. Austin	HQ	Pvt	Roger Biagiotti, Jr.	319	FO	Ernest S. Butler, Jr.
HQ	Pfc	Frank Bailey	5	Pfc	Seymour Blatt	5	2Lt	Frank S. Byrne, Jr.
319	FO	Leslie D. Bailey	HQ	Pvt	Saul Blitzer	319	Pvt	Robert J. Byrne
HQ	2Lt	Theodore A. Baird	319	1Lt	Neal J. Blush	HQ	Pfc	William L. Caflisch
5	SSgt	Leroy H. Baker	HQ	Lt Col	Richard W. Boebel	HQ	Pvt	John W. Caldwell
5	Sgt	William W. Baker	HQ	Pvt	Frank J. Bonelli	HQ	Cpl	Harry H. Camp, Jr.
HQ	Pfc	Russell L. Bakke	319	1Lt	Ralph C. Bordley	319	Cpl	Charles J. Campbell
5	2Lt	Marion C. Ball	319	Sgt	Robert S. Bovey	HQ	Cpl	Donald J. Campbell
HQ	Pvt	Vance E. Banks	164	MSgt	Charles E. Bowden	HQ	Pfc	Edward A. Campbell
HQ	Pfc	William H. Barber	319	SSgt	Velmar L. Bowls	HQ	SSgt	Jeter Campbell
6	Pfc	William T. Bardsley	166	Sgt	Arthur M. Bowman	HQ	Pvt	Thomas H. Campbell
5	SSgt	Joseph E. Bardzinas	HQ	Pvt	David Bowman	319	Cpl	Salvatore Canale
HQ	Pvt	Burrell S. Bare	HQ	1Lt	Frank M. Bowman	319	SSgt	George H. Cancienne, Jr.
HQ	2Lt	Morris M. Baren	319	FO	George E. Boyle	164	Cpl	Allen H. Canter
319	Capt	Edgar L. Barham	5	SSgt	Wayne E. Bozarth	164	SSgt	Leo J. Carroll
6	2Lt	Edison D. Barker	319	2Lt	Anthony J. Bracaliello	6	Capt	Olin B. Carter
6	SSgt	Ralph E. Barker	HQ	Cpl	Eugene E. Brady	HQ	TSgt	William O. Casebolt
319	Pfc	James D. Barnet	HQ	Pfc	Robert D. Bratcher	165	SSgt	Benjamin G. Casey

HQ	2Lt	Benjamin C. Cavender	HQ	Pvt	Bernard T. Dahms	6	Sgt	James F. Eubank
HQ	Pvt	Joseph Cerrado, Jr.	6	Pvt	Joseph F. Damiano	164	SSgt	Rupert S. Eudy
285	SSgt	Jerry Chalupa, Jr.	5	Capt	Hamer R. Davidson	319	CWO	Bruce H. Evens
319	FO	Amos B. Chambers	6	Pfc	John W. Davidson	319	2Lt	Robert E. Everett
165	MSgt	Robert E. Chambers	HQ	Cpl	Ancil O. Davis	6	Pfc	Frank W. Fahrer
HQ	2Lt	Robert S. Chambers	164	1Lt	Elbert E. Davis	5	Pfc	Leo M. Farmer
164	2Lt	William R. Chappelle	166	2Lt	Frank N. Davis	319	Cpl	Ralph A. Fasano
HQ	Sgt	John T. Chasse	HQ	Pfc	Jack W. Davis	6	2Lt	Glen R. Feickert
166	SSgt	Woodrow W. Cheek	165	TSgt	Lemuel A. Davis	5	Pvt	Otto F. Feiler, Jr.
165	SSgt	Arthur M. Cherry	285	Pvt	Finley E. Dawsey	HQ	Pvt	John Felice
166	TSgt	Jack W. Chesrown	HQ	Pvt	David A. Deaderick	HQ	SSgt	Harry D. Fenwick
164	SSgt	Julian Chmil	319	MSgt	John L. Dean	6	2Lt	John M. Ferron
			HQ	Pfc	William S. Deardeuff	165	MSgt	James C. Ferry
165	Cpl	Carlous L. Christian	HQ	1Lt	Herbert J. Delaney	164	SSgt	Charles S. Fessler
HQ	Cpl	Junior L. Christie	HQ	MSgt	Benjamin J. Delaware, Jr.	164	SSgt	Robert J. Fiske
5	SSgt	Eugene J. Chrystler	6	SSgt	Robert D. DeMarko	6	Sgt	John D. Fitzgerald
319	FO	Paul E. Chumbley	164	SSgt	Thomas H. Denlea	HQ	Pvt	Lowell E. Fletcher
HQ	Pvt	Edward A. Clark	319	Pfc	John V. DePalma	285	Pfc	Clinton E. Fleury
HQ	Pvt	Ernest Clark	HQ	Cpl	Ernest H. Dixon	285	Pvt	Leo Flores
319	Pvt	Robert W. Claunch	166	SSgt	Bernard P. Dole	HQ	Pfc	John W. Fontaine
165	TSgt	Daniel G. Claus	5	2Lt	Daniel A. Donovan III	5	Capt	Irving W. Forde
HQ	Cpl	Charles H. Clay	319	Cpl	Edward J. Donovan	HQ	Cpl	Gerald Foster
319	SSgt	Marion L. Clay	5	2Lt	Ernest P. Dornbush	HQ	Maj	John W. Fox
164	Pvt	Peter A. Clementi	285	Pvt	Leo R. Dorrell	5	TSgt	Oswald C. Francisco
165	SSgt	Robert L. Clements	319	2Lt	Gene R. Douthit	6	2Lt	Jean E. Freiwald
166	MSgt	Charles J. Clephas	HQ	Pvt	William J. Driscoll	285	Cpl	Eldon W. Fricks
165	SSgt	Frank M. Clifford	164	SSgt	Stanley Drobysh	HQ	Sgt	Marion L. Friday
164	Sgt	Joseph L. Cochran	HQ	Pvt	Fernad A. Drozdowski	166	SSgt	Duane K. Fudge
6	2Lt	Lloyd B. Coleman	6	2Lt	Anthony H. Dubois, Jr.	HQ	Pfc	John R. Fulkerson
164	SSgt	Hugh A. Coll	HQ	Pvt	James Dudas	164	SSgt	Walter D. Fulton
HQ	Pfc	Joe Collins	319	TSgt	Ralph E. Duddeck	HQ	Pvt	William G. Gaither, Jr.
HQ	Pvt	John S. Collins	165	SSgt	Leonard C. Duke	HQ	Sgt	Henry A. Galbraith
285	Cpl	Marvin L. Collins	6	Sgt	Jack K. Dunifon	166	TSgt	John C. Gallagher
HQ	Pvt	Olie L. Combee	HQ	SSgt	Charles D. Durden	HQ	Cpl	John Gallo
165	Pfc	Jose Compean	HQ	SSgt	Joseph A. D'Urso	165	SSgt	Joseph F. Gambill
319	FO	John W. Conner	HQ	Pvt	James F. Dwyer, Jr.	5	2Lt	Eldon W. Gandrud
5	Cpl	John E. Cook	HQ	Pvt	Norman L. Earnest	285	Pvt	Fred Garcia
6	SSgt	Carl L. Corbin	HQ	SSgt	William L. Easley	HQ	Pvt	Curtis A. Garner
HQ	Pvt	James H. Corbin	5	Cpl	Robert J. Easom	HQ	Pvt	Hubert Garrett
5	Pvt	Leonard Cornwell	319	Capt	Nelson E. Eddy, Jr.	165	SSgt	Loyd W. A. Garrett
HQ	Pvt	Frank C. Corsillo	319	1Lt	Robert H. Edwards	319	FO	Bertel B. Garrison
HQ	Pfc	Aubrey Cosper	164	SSgt	Joseph P. Eagan	164	Sgt	John F. Garrity
HQ	Pfc	John W. Courtney, Jr.	164	TSgt	Robert L. East	319	TSgt	Perry L. Garten
HQ	Pvt	Russell S. Courtney	HQ	TSgt	James D. Edenbo	HQ	Col	Clinton B. Gaty
319	TSgt	Thomas T. Crabtree	6	Cpl	Abraham Effress	HQ	Pfc	Robert L. Gaus
164	TSgt	John B. Craighead	5	Sgt	Wade M. Egelston	HQ	Pvt	Gilbert E. Geeting
165	SSgt	Thomas J. Crosby, Jr.	166	Cpl	Elvy W. Ellis	HQ	Pfc	Hedley J. George
HQ	Pvt	George P. Cruikshank	319	FO	Harry H. Ellis	HQ	FO	Kenneth Georgeson
164	MSgt	Joe L. Cunningham	164	2Lt	Winfield C. S. Eng, Jr.	HQ	Pfc	Louis J. Gerace
166	Cpl	John J. Curtin	HQ	Pvt	Donald A. Engelhardt	HQ	Pfc	Herbert E. Gerrish
6	Sgt	Jack Curtis	319	1Lt	Donald I. Erikson	HQ	TSgt	Leslie F. Ghastin

164	SSgt	Lawrence A. Giargiari	HQ	2Lt	William M. Healy	319	TSgt	Edwin L. Karns
HQ	MSgt	Thomas H. Gibbons	285	Cpl	Phillip J. Hein	HQ	Sgt	Gene O. Kaschel
HQ	Pvt	Walter B. Gillespey	319	Sgt	Robert E. Henderson	319	2Lt	Jack W. Keiser
319	Sgt	Earl F. Gillett	319	2Lt	Ronald A. Hennig	HQ	Cpl	Samuel B. Keller
HQ	TSgt	William Gilliam, Jr.	319	FO	James W. Henry	165	MSgt	Stanley C. Kelley
5	1Lt	Richard T. Gilmore	HQ	Pvt	John K. Henry	6	1Lt	Everett L. Kelly
165	MSgt	William D. Gleaves, Jr.	319	1Lt	Jesse B. Hepler	319	2Lt	Gene A. Kelly
165	SSgt	George H. Goodfellow	5	2Lt	Charles H. Hess, Jr.	164	SSgt	Miles E. Kempf
166	1Lt	Julius Goodman	319	2Lt	George D. Hess	285	SSgt	Robert J. Kendrigan
HQ	Pfc	Clifford H. Goodson	319	FO	Paul B. Higgins	166	SSgt	Irwin J. Kersey
319	2Lt	John E. Gotham	319	2Lt	Thomas A. Hight, Jr.	HQ	Capt	Marlin F. Kerstetter
165	SSgt	John M. Gourley	285	Cpl	Stanley W. Hilderbrandt	HQ	Pvt	John E. Kimar
HQ	Pvt	Francis J. Grace	166	SSgt	James O. Hill	HQ	Pfc	Charles A. King
HQ	SSgt	Winfield S. Graham	166	SSgt	William E. Hitt	319	Sgt	John A. Kinner
HQ	Maj	Don K. Greelis	165	SSgt	Edward F. Hladovcak	HQ	Pfc	Frank Kinsella
HQ	Sgt	Roy F. Greene	HQ	MSgt	John J. Hoffman	6	2Lt	James M. Kirby
6	TSgt	Robert L. Greenlund	319	TSgt	Wayne Hoffman	6	1Lt	Jack U. Klarr
164	Pvt	Robert E. Greer	319	Maj	Neil I. Holm	6	2Lt	Guernsey P. Knapp
166	SSgt	George C. Gregson	319	2Lt	Charles R. Hon	5	2Lt	James A. Knight, Jr.
HQ	Capt	Lyle R. Grey	165	SSgt	Ralph E. Horton	5	Pfc	Stanley J. Knox, Jr.
HQ	Pvt	Kenneth B. Grier	HQ	Pfc	Oscar O. House	HQ	Pfc	Steve Kolas
165	Cpl	George W. Griggs	6	SSgt	Charles I. Hovermale	HQ	Pfc	Melvin O. Kolterman
319	2Lt	Woodrow W. Grimsley	5	SSgt	Anton Hrna	5	TSgt	John Koniar, Jr.
6	Sgt	John H. Gross	HQ	Pvt	John Huff, Jr.	6	Cpl	John L. Koranda
5	Pvt	Robert J. Groya	319	MSgt	Paul R. Hughes	6	TSgt	John P. Kropp
HQ	Pvt	Daniel J. Gruchy	285	Cpl	Edwin H. Hurd	6	Sgt	Jack Kubler
6	SSgt	Robert P. Grutsch	HQ	TSgt	Edward M. Hurley, Jr.	319	1Lt	Richard E. Kuenstler
HQ	Pvt	Haig A. Gulezian	5	2Lt	James C. Hutchinson	319	Cpl	Floyd B. Kyea
HQ	Pvt	Carl W. Gustke	319	1Lt	Frank M. Huxley	166	Sgt	Claude Lacy
319	1Lt	Patrick H. Hadsell	165	TSgt	John J. Hyland	HQ	Pvt	Charley L. Laffoon
319	Pvt	Allen R. Haggard	6	2Lt	Dean Illingworth	6	Pvt	Gordon C. Landon
164	FO	Albert E. Hainey	5	SSgt	Austin L. Jameson	HQ	Pvt	James E. Lare
319	FO	Allen Hall, Jr.	6	SSgt	Ellwood H. Jamison, Jr.	166	2Lt	Erwin H. LaVarre
164	SSgt	Mathew B. Hall	285	Cpl	James R. Jaynes	HQ	Cpl	June R. Lay
319	2Lt	Robert D. Ham	HQ	Maj	John H. Jennette	164	MSgt	Charles M. Lee
319	Pvt	Rolland B. Hamilton	5	TSgt	Lynn E. Jennings	HQ	1Lt	William C. Lehecka
319	FO	Nimrod F. Hankins	HQ	Pvt	Vivian A. Jessup	HQ	Pvt	Ernest A. Leogrande
164	1Lt	Carter Harman	319	Sgt	Donald L. Johnson	319	Cpl	Martin Levitz
166	SSgt	Ben T. Harris, Jr.	319	FO	Harlie D. Johnson	HQ	Pvt	Jack W. Lewis
HQ	Cpl	Felix E. Harrison	319	FO	James M. Johnson	319	1Lt	John E. Lewis
319	Cpl	Glenn R. Harsdorff	319	2Lt	Kenneth Johnson	319	Capt	John K. Lewis, Jr.
HQ	Sgt	John M. Hart	166	Pvt	William A. Johnson, Jr.	319	FO	David H. Lieberman
319	FO	Edwin F. Harter	319	1Lt	William W. Johnson, Jr.	165	SSgt	Alfred J. Lieto
HQ	Pfc	Jimmie B. Hathcock	319	MSgt	John H. Johnston	164	2Lt	Donald C. Limburg
5	MSgt	Melvin Haug	6	2Lt	Voyo Jovanovich	319	Cpl	Charles Lindgren
166	MSgt	Thomas J. Hawes, Jr.	319	2Lt	Burton B. Jones	166	TSgt	Clarence A. Lingle, Jr.
HQ	Pvt	H. B. Hawkins	HQ	Cpl	Marvin C. Jones	HQ	Pfc	John L. Linn
HQ	Pvt	Edmund F. Haycock	165	SSgt	Willie P. Jones	HQ	Cpl	Lyman M. Linson
319	FO	William F. Hayden	5	MSgt	Elmer L. Jumper	6	SSgt	Robert P. Little
319	Sgt	Billie H. Hayes	319	TSgt	Francis M. Kaman	319	Sgt	Robert A. Livermore
6	FO	John M. Haynes	HQ	Cpl	John T. Kane	164	SSgt	Felix C. Lockman, Jr.

HQ	Cpl	Melvin E. Lohsen	319	2Lt	Sam S. Medford	165	TSgt	James Oliveto
HQ	Pvt	Samuel C. Long, Jr.	HQ	Cpl	Melkon Melkonian	HQ	MSgt	Arthur R. Olson
HQ	Pvt	James P. Loughlin	166	TSgt	Harold C. Mendelson	HQ	Pvt	Wilmer W. Olson
HQ	TSgt	Joseph C. Lucke	5	Sgt	William C. Mercer	HQ	Pvt	Frank B. O'Neal
HQ	Cpl	Dallas H. Lynch	319	Capt	Frank B. Merchant	319	Pvt	Leonard J. Oney
HQ	Sgt	Howard W. Lynch	5	Capt	John E. Meyer	5	1Lt	Paul A. Oram
5	Capt	Roland R. Lynn	165	FO	Donald K. Miller	165	Pvt	Dale Overlease
165	Pfc	James A. Lyon	5	Sgt	Donald W. Miller	5	Capt	Randolph K. Owen
166	MSgt	Joseph Lysowski	5	SSgt	Ernest O. Miller, Jr.	HQ	Pfc	George E. Padula
165	SSgt	Warren C. MacArtney	5	Sgt	George R. Miller	HQ	Cpl	Edwin P. Padykula
HQ	Sgt	Lewis R. Mackenzie	HQ	Pvt	Harry R. Miller	5	SSgt	Everette L. Page
HQ	Pvt	Wilfred V. Madruga	319	Pfc	John J. Miller	319	Pvt	John Palesano
165	TSgt	Fintan F. Maegerle	HQ	SSgt	James Millholland	HQ	Sgt	Everett H. Palm
HQ	Pvt	Carl S. Magnuson	6	SSgt	Clyde E. Millstead	HQ	Pvt	Joseph T. Panessiti
319	Sgt	Linn E. Magoffin	HQ	Pvt	James J. Misto	319	1Lt	Fred P. Paris
164	SSgt	Robert J. Magruder	HQ	Pvt	Christopher C. Mitchell	164	TSgt	Russell L. Parrott, Jr.
HQ	Cpl	James C. Mansbarger, Jr.	5	1Lt	Daniel B. Mitchell	HQ	2Lt	Jim Patterson
165	SSgt	John A. Manter	6	2Lt	Ernest W. Mitchell	165	SSgt	Robert J. Patterson
166	TSgt	Christopher J. Marion, Jr.	HQ	MSgt	John A. Mitchell	5	Pvt	Edward N. Patton
HQ	Pfc	Warren R. Marquardt	HQ	Pfc	Doyt L. Mohler	HQ	Pvt	Mike Pavlovich
166	SSgt	Francis H. Marshall	319	2Lt	Billy Mohr	319	TSgt	Winston G. Pearson
285	Cpl	John W. Martin	HQ	Maj	Robert E. Moist	HQ	Pvt	Walter R. Peevy
HQ	Pvt	Leo S. Martin	319	2Lt	George L. Molitor	319	1Lt	Stanley Pelcak
319	2Lt	Nesbit L. Martin	6	2Lt	Michal E. Mongan	164	1Lt	Paul L. Pennekamp
5	TSgt	Paul W. Mason	6	Capt	Charles F. Moore	HQ	Pvt	Leslie F. Peper
164	MSgt	Charles E. Mathews	6	TSgt	James W. Moore	6	Sgt	Chester Petrowsky
165	Pvt	Frederick E. Mattson	HQ	Capt	Temple C. Moore	164	SSgt	Rodney E. Petty, Jr.
319	MSgt	Samuel L. May	HQ	Pfc	Marvin C. Morgan	166	1Lt	Allen O. Pfander
6	Pfc	John E. McArdle	HQ	Pfc	William H. Morison	166	Sgt	James D. Phelan
5	SSgt	Clifton F. McCabe	HQ	Pvt	Ralph R. Mros	HQ	Cpl	Ben Phillips, Jr.
HQ	Sgt	Joseph P. McCartney	HQ	Pvt	Joseph R. Mullen	HQ	Maj	Duke Phillips, Jr.
165	SSgt	Bruce H. McCormick	5	Cpl	Harold E. Mueller	6	Pvt	Melvin T. Phippin
6	1Lt	Roy J. McDonald	5	2Lt	Lee F. Mullins	HQ	1Lt	Wesley C. Pierson
319	FO	ChChester R. McDowell	166	SSgt	Bernard H. Mulvihill, Jr.	6	SSgt	Albert E. Piester
319	Sgt	Edgar W. McDowell	HQ	Pfc	Donald W. Munroe	319	Cpl	William A. Pinta
5	Cpl	James F. McDowell	319	TSgt	Irvin L. Murphy	285	Capt	William S. Piper
6	TSgt	Elbrige B. McDuff	5	SSgt	James B. Murphy	6	Capt	Younger A. Pitts, Jr.
319	2Lt	Robert F. McFarland	166	TSgt	Herbert H. Myers	HQ	1Lt	Alvin J. Plouff
319	2Lt	Bernard P. McGaulley	319	Cpl	Howard G. Myers, Jr.	164	SSgt	Alexander Podlecki
HQ	TSgt	Alexander McGregor	319	2Lt	Melvin L. Nadell	165	SSgt	Lawrence N. Poepping
319	2Lt	Harry L. McKaig	HQ	SSgt	Bennie Nance	6	TSgt	Walter J. Polak
319	Capt	Archie L. McKay	165	2Lt	Roy S. Nelsen	285	Pfc	Ray H. Pollington
6	2Lt	James F. McKeighen	285	Pvt	Fred C. Newell	166	SSgt	Harrell M. Pope
166	SSgt	George E. McLain	319	2Lt	John F. Newland	319	Pvt	Frank Popp
285	Pvt	Francis P. McLaughlin	6	2Lt	Thomas H. Newman, Jr.	HQ	Pfc	Clarence Porter
319	Cpl	Harry D. McLean	164	SSgt	John A. Nicholson	HQ	Sgt	Eli Porter
319	SSgt	William J. McMahon	319	2Lt	Vernon Noland	HQ	MSgt	John H. Porter
165	TSgt	Morris D. McManama	319	SSgt	Bernard Nowakowski	HQ	Capt	Andrew B. Postlewait
5	Sgt	Thomas J. McNally	6	Pfc	Harry L. O'Bannon, Jr.	165	Sgt	Kenneth J. Powell
165	TSgt	John D. McNamee	319	Pfc	Carlon H. Ober	6	2Lt	Walter F. Pratt
HQ	TSgt	John Meck	HQ	Pvt	Leo M. Ogul	HQ	SSgt	Michael P. Presti

Unit	Rank	Name	Unit	Rank	Name	Unit	Rank	Name
165	TSgt	William H. Protz	HQ	Pfc	J. E. Salyer	HQ	Lt Col	Samson Smith
HQ	Pvt	Lee R. Purcell	166	TSgt	Lloyd I. Samp	319	TSgt	Zane L. Smith
165	TSgt	Grant B. Putnam	6	Pvt	Theodore P. Sanders	HQ	Pfc	Edward L. Snead
HQ	Sgt	Donald Pyne	319	Capt	John C. Sanichas	HQ	SSgt	Elmer R. Snyder
6	SSgt	Lewis J. Qualkenbush	319	Sgt	Joe F. Satarino	166	MSgt	Glen W. Snyder
HQ	Pvt	Richard L. Qualters	319	2Lt	Marlyn O. Satrom	166	TSgt	Richard D. Snyder
HQ	Cpl	William H. Quinn	166	2Lt	Neal B. Saxon	285	1Lt	Ben Solomon
HQ	Pfc	Glenvil L. Rackley	6	SSgt	William J. Schatz	HQ	CWO	Burton E. Sommers
5	Cpl	Jennings B. Rader	HQ	Pvt	Raymond S. Scheirer	HQ	Pvt	Frank F. Sowa
319	2Lt	Francis L. Randall	319	Cpl	Robert J. Schieferstein	285	Pvt	Howard R. Sowden
5	SSgt	George F. Randall	HQ	TSgt	Karl K. Schmidt	165	1Lt	John O. Spangler
HQ	Pvt	Hugh L. Randall	164	MSgt	Edward W. Schnatzmeyer	165	SSgt	Joseph H. Sparrow
HQ	Pfc	John W. Randall	HQ	1Lt	Soloman Schnitzer	HQ	Sgt	John E. Sprague
HQ	Pfc	Joseph S. Randazzo	HQ	Pvt	Freeman P. Schofield	HQ	1Lt	Ralph J. Stafford
319	MSgt	Texas J. Rankin	166	SSgt	Harry J. Schroeder	6	MSgt	Gerald W. Stake
6	MSgt	Fred J. Rannalli	319	SSgt	Marshall C. Schuler	HQ	Pvt	Thornwell B. Staley
HQ	MSgt	Harry A. Raymond	6	SSgt	Robert C. Schurr	319	Sgt	John L. Stalker, Jr.
HQ	SSgt	John J. Raynak	166	2Lt	Jack A. Schweier	HQ	Cpl	William R. Stawiski
HQ	Pfc	Robert E. Reed	319	FO	John L. Sciez	165	2Lt	James R. Steel
HQ	Sgt	William G. Reed	HQ	1Lt	Virgil E. Scobey	166	SSgt	George Steele, Jr.
319	2Lt	Earl E. Reeves	319	2Lt	Edward G. Scott	319	WOJG	Peter E. Stefonich
HQ	Pvt	James L. Reeves	319	Cpl	John W. Seagren	HQ	FO	Walter M. Steinke
5	2Lt	Edward L. Reimel	HQ	Pvt	Joseph F. Selbitschka	319	Pvt	James W. Stephen
HQ	1Lt	Joseph Rettinger	6	2Lt	Ralph A. Selkirk	5	2Lt	Fred H. Stevens
165	SSgt	Woodrow W. Reynolds	HQ	SSgt	Peter C. Serio	HQ	Pvt	Wendell W. Stoker
HQ	Pvt	Victor L. Rhine	5	Pfc	James S. Sessions	319	Cpl	Warren J. Stotz
HQ	Sgt	Silas H. Rhodes	6	2Lt	Joe Setnor	164	SSgt	John A. Stroebeck
HQ	Cpl	John W. Rice	319	Sgt	Derald K. Settles	HQ	Pfc	John E. Strubol
5	FO	Raymond S. Richard	319	1Lt	James E. Sever	6	Pvt	Howard C. J. Sturek
319	1Lt	James E. Richmond	HQ	Pvt	Walter H. Shamblin	164	SSgt	Franklin O. Suckow
166	Sgt	William B. Ringwood	319	2Lt	Troy C. Shaw	6	Pfc	L. D. Sutherland
HQ	TSgt	Clarence F. Rippl	HQ	Pvt	James L. Sheldon	165	MSgt	Harley V. Sutton
319	Cpl	Maurice R. Roberts	319	1Lt	Jackson J. Shinkle	319	Cpl	Joseph S. Sweeney
6	Pfc	Robert L. Roberts	319	FO	Jack M. Shipman	319	TSgt	Walter R. Sweeney
164	SSgt	Stamford N. Robertson	164	SSgt	Hal H. Shurley	HQ	SSgt	Shyojiro T. Taketa
166	SSgt	Lee R. Rodawalt	HQ	Pvt	Robert M. Simmonette	285	Pfc	Fred L. Tando
HQ	Cpl	Grady D. Roddy	165	FO	Henry Simon	6	Cpl	Charles S. Tanner
HQ	Cpl	Walter L. Rodgers	6	Pfc	Louis Simon	HQ	2Lt	James W. Tate
HQ	Pvt	William F. Roldan	HQ	Pvt	Robert M. Sims	164	2Lt	Dexter J. Taylor
HQ	Cpl	George D. Rosenblatt	HQ	Capt	Daniel A. Sinskie	5	Pfc	Wycliffe D. Temples
166	2Lt	Rodger L. Rosenwald	HQ	Pvt	Robert A. Sipila	HQ	TSgt	Andrew M. Ternosky
6	Pfc	Mitchell Rosolowski	5	Cpl	Charles E. Sisson	6	2Lt	William S. Terranova
HQ	Sgt	William J. Rossman	319	2Lt	Dean D. Skelton	HQ	CWO	John M. Teten
166	SSgt	Willard L. Roy	HQ	Pvt	Charles D. Smith	5	1Lt	Nelson C. Tewksbury
319	Cpl	Alfred I. Royce	6	SSgt	Frank H. Smith	HQ	Cpl	Donald E. Thomas
166	SSgt	Robert N. Ruehlen	HQ	MSgt	George Smith, Jr.	HQ	Pvt	George C. Thomas
319	2Lt	Eugene L. Ruiz	319	SSgt	Harlan P. C. Smith	166	TSgt	Jasper C. Thompson
164	TSgt	Raymond J. Ruksas	HQ	Sgt	Harry W. Smith	285	Pvt	Lester B. Thompson
319	MSgt	Ray R. Rumfelt	164	TSgt	Howard L. Smith	165	SSgt	Walden J. Thompson
5	Sgt	Forrest J. Russell	5	Pfc	John P. Smith	6	Pvt	Noal G. Tillman
319	FO	Victor Sakryd	HQ	Capt	Lewis S. Smith	HQ	Pvt	Fred S. Toal

285	Cpl	Albert H. Tortorello	319	1Lt	Howell T. Walker	166	SSgt	John E. Whitaker
5	2Lt	Carl H. Townson	HQ	Pfc	Russell S. Walker	HQ	Pvt	Howard C. White
319	Pfc	Ralph W. Trent	165	SSgt	Preston W. Walling	HQ	Capt	Frank R. Whitelam
HQ	Cpl	Robert E. True	HQ	Pvt	Harry L. Walters, Jr.	6	Sgt	Warren G. Wilcox
164	Sgt	Clifford J. Tucker	319	1Lt	Albert T. Ward	5	1Lt	Malcolm J. Wilkins
HQ	Capt	Donald C. Tulloch	HQ	Pfc	Kenneth P. Warneke	HQ	1Lt	William F. Wilkinson, Jr.
319	2Lt	Charles B. Turner	5	SSgt	John Watson	319	2Lt	Bruce Williams
5	Pfc	Norval G. Turner	319	SSgt	Warren G. Watts	HQ	Cpl	Walter E. Williams
164	SSgt	Delbert J. Tyler	166	SSgt	Walter R. Waugh	HQ	Capt	Grant H. Wilson, Jr.
319	1Lt	Leo S. Tyszecki	319	2Lt	Mainord M. Weaver	6	2Lt	Elmer L. Wingo
164	Capt	Vincent L. Ulery	5	Sgt	Max V. Weaver	HQ	Pfc	Ezell D. Wise
6	Sgt	Milan J. Urbancic	HQ	Pvt	Willie O. Weaver	HQ	Pvt	Delmar Witt
319	Sgt	Charles J. Usey	319	TSgt	Jack H. Webb	HQ	Maj	James R. Woods
5	2Lt	Charles J. Vagim	166	SSgt	Jesse G. Webster	HQ	Pfc	Ben Worsham
HQ	Pfc	Nolan A. Vail	5	Cpl	Robert G. Weeks	HQ	Pvt	Douglas Yoon
319	Pfc	Arthur J. Van Bremer	5	2Lt	Hilton D. Weesner	6	Cpl	Gerald L. Young
6	2Lt	Aurele R. Van De Weghe	HQ	Pfc	Henry Weiner	HQ	Pvt	Phillip R. Young
6	2Lt	Allen H. Vanderyerk	5	SSgt	Selig Weinstein	5	SSgt	Walter E. Young
319	FO	Lloyd L. Van Nest	285	Capt	Carl Y. Werelius	5	Pfc	Zane G. Young
166	1Lt	Fred H. Van Wagner	319	MSgt	Leslie E. Werner	166	MSgt	Arnold C. Zahorsky
5	Cpl	Earl H. Varner, Jr	319	FO	Russell J. West	164	Sgt	Alexander Zalman
HQ	Sgt	Sam Virgone.	5	MSgt	James R. Westmoreland	319	Pfc	Morris H. Zalmanovich
319	Capt	Edward Wagner	319	Pfc	Warren J. Wetzel	319	Cpl	Carl J. Zarcone
319	2Lt	Robert Wagner	165	SSgt	George R. Wharen, Jr.	HQ	Capt	Carl E. Zeigler, Jr.
285	Pfc	Virgil L. Wagner	5	2Lt	Francis W. Wheeler	319	2Lt	Leo Zuk

Bibliography

Books

1. Allen, Louis. *Burma: The Longest War 1941-45.* New York: St. Martin's Press, 1984.
2. Bateson, Charles. *The War With Japan: A Concise History.* Hong Kong: Michigan State University Press, 1968.
3. Bidwell, Shelford. *The Chindit War: Stilwell, Wingate, and the Campaign in Burma: 1944.* New York: Macmillian Publishing Co., Inc., 1979.
4. Bond, Brian (ed). *Fallen Stars, Eleven Studies of Twentiest Century Military Disasters.* London: Brassey's, 1991.
5. Burchette, W. C. *Wingate Adventure.* Melbourne: F. W. Cheshire Pty. Ltd., 1944.
6. Callaghan, Raymond. *Burma: 1942-1945.* Newark: University of Delaware Press, 1979.
7. Calvert, Michael. *Prisoners of Hope.* London: Jonathan Cape, 1952.
8. Cannon, Hardy D. *Box Seats Over Hell: The True Story of America's Liaison Pilots and the Light Planes in World War II.* 1985.
9. Cate, James L. and Wesley F. Cravens. (Eds). *The Army Air Forces in World War II, Vol IV.* Chicago: University of Chicago Press, 1948.
10. _____. (Eds). *The Army Air Forces in World War II, Vol V.* Chicago: University of Chicago Press, 1953.
11. Christian, John L. *Burma.* London: Wm. Collins & Sons & Co., Ltd., 1945.
12. Churchill, Winston S. *The Second World War: Closing the Ring.* New York: Houghton Mifflin Company, 1951.
13. _____. *The Second World War: Triumph and Tragedy.* Boston: Houghton Mifflin Company, 1953.
14. Costello, John. *The Pacific War.* New York: Rawson, Wade Publishers, Inc., 1981.
15. Dank, Milton. *An Eyewitness History of World War II Glider Combat.* Philadelphia: J. B. Lippincott Company, 1977.
16. Drew, Dennis M., Lieutenant Colonel, USAF and Dr. Donald M. Snow. *Introduction to Strategy.* Maxwell AFB, AL: Air University, 1985.
17. Edmonds, Walter D. *They Fought With What They Had: The Story of the Army Air Forces in the Southwest Pacific, 1941-42.* Boston: Little, Brown and Company, 1951.
18. Esposito, Col Vincent J. (ed). *The West Point Atlas of American Wars, Volume II: 1900-1953.* New York: Frederick A. Praeger, 1959.
19. Greenfield, Kent Roberts (ed). *Command Decisions.* Washington DC: Office of the Chief of Military History, 1960.
20. Griess, Thomas E. (ed). John H. Bradley and Jack W. Dice, Contributing Author. *The Second World War: Asia and the Pacific.* West Point, New York: Department of History, United States Military Academy. Wayne, New Jersey: Avery Publishing Group, Inc., 1984.
21. Haughland, Vern. *The AAF Against Japan.* New York: Harper & Brothers Publishers, 1948.
22. Heinl, Robert D., Jr. *Dictionary of Military and Naval Quotations.* Annapolis MD: United States Naval Institute, 1984.
23. Hogan, David W. *India-Burma.* Washington DC: U.S. Army Center of Military History, 1992.
24. Kirby, S. Woodburn, et al (ed). *The War Against Japan; Volume II: India's Most Dangerous Hour.* London: Her Majesty's Stationery Office, 1958.
25. _____. *The War Against Japan; Volume III: The Decisive Battles.* London: Her Majesty's Stationery Office, 1961.
26. _____. *The War Against Japan; Volume IV: The Reconquest of Burma.* London: Her Majesty's Stationery Office, 1965.
27. Klein, Wilhelm. *Burma.* Singapore: APA Publications (Hong Kong), Ltd., 1988.
28. Livesey, Anthony. *Great Commanders and Their Battles.* New York: Macmillan Publishing Company, 1987.
29. Lowden, John L. *Silent Wings at War: Combat Gliders in World War II.* Washington DC: Smithsonian Institution Press, 1992.
30. Masters, John. *The Road Past Mandalay.* New York: Harper & Row, Publishers, Inc., 1961.
31. Matthews, Geoffrey. *The Re-conquest of Burma 1943-1945.* Aldershot, UK: Gale & Polden Limited, 1966.
32. Maurer, Maurer (ed). *World War II Combat Squadrons of the United States Air Force: The Official Military Record of Every Active Squadron.* New York: Smithmark Publishers, Inc., 1992.

33. Mende, Tibor. *South-east Asia between Two Worlds.* London: Turnstile Press, 1955.

34. Moraes, R. R. and Robert Stimson. *Introduction to India.* Longdon: Oxford University Press, 1946.

35. Moser, Don (ed). *China-Burma-India.* Alexandria, VA: Time-Life Books, 1978.

36. Mrazek, James E. *The Glider War.* New York: St. Martin's Press, Inc., 1975.

37. Peters, Thomas J. and Robert H. Waterman. *In Search of Excellence.* New York: Harper & Row, Publishers, Inc., 1982.

38. Ravenstein, Charles A. *Air Force Combat Wings: Lineage and Honors Histories 1947-1977.* Washington DC: Office of Air Force History, 1984.

39. Rolo, Charles J. *Wingate's Raiders.* London: George G. Harrap & Co. Ltd., 1944.

40. Romanus, Charles F. and Sunderland, Riley (ed). *United States Army in World War II: China-Burma-India Theater; Stilwell's Mission to China.* Washington DC: Office of the Chief of Military History, 1953.

41. _____. *United States Army in World War II: China-Burma-India Theater; Stilwell's Command Problems.* Washington DC: Office of the Chief of Military History, 1956.

42. _____. *United States Army in World War II: China-Burma-India Theater; Time Runs Out in CBI.* Washington DC: Office of the Chief of Military History, 1959.

43. Saunders, Hillary St. George. *Royal Air Force 1939-1945, Volume III: The Fight Is Won.* London: Her Majesty's Stationery Office, 1954.

44. Slim, Field Marshall, the Viscount. *Defeat into Victory.* New York: 1961.

45. Smith, E. D. *Battle for Burma.* New York: Holmes & Meier Publishers, Inc., 1979.

46. Spector, Ronald H. *Eagle Against the Sun: The American War With Japan.* 1985.

47. Stilwell, Joseph W. *The Stilwell Papers.* New York: W. Sloane, 1948.

48. Swimson, Arthur. *The Battle of Kohima.* New York: Stein and Day, 1967.

49. Sykes, Christopher. *Orde Wingate: A Biography.* Cleveland: World Publishing Co., 1959.

50. Thomas, Lowell. *Back to Mandalay.* New York: The Greystone Press, 1951.

51. Toland, John. *The Rising Sun.* New York: Random House, Inc., 1970

52. Tuchman, Barbara W. *Stilwell and the American Experience in China, 1911-45.* New York: Macmillan Publishing Co., Inc., 1970.

53. Tulloch, Derek (ed). *Wingate In Peace and War.* London: Macdonald and Co., Ltd., 1972.

54. Wedemeyer, Albert C. *Wedemeyer Reports!* New York: Henry Holt & Company, 1958.

55. Williams, Douglas. *194 Squadron: Royal Air Force "The Friendly Firm."* 1987.

Articles and Periodicals

56. "10ᵗʰ Combat Camera Took Meiktila Scenes." **Roundup** (Newspaper), May 3, 1945, pp. 8.

57. Arnold, H. H. "The Aerial Invasion of Burma." **National Geographic Magazine**, Vol. LXXXVI, No. 2 (August 1944), pp. 129-148.

58. Bainbridge, John. "'Flip Corkin,'" **Life**, Vol. 15, No. 6 (9 August 1943), pp. 42-48.

59. Bellah, James Warner, Lieutenant Colonel, USAF. "The Password Was Mandalay." **Reader's Digest**, September 1944, pp. 33-36.

60. "British Raid Burma." **Life**, (28 June 1943), pp. 19-24.

61. Caufield, D. C. "The Bright Flame." **Marine Corps Gazette**, Vol. 48, No. 10 (October 1964), pp. 41-46.

62. Cunningham, Ed. "Cochran's Commandos." **Yank**, Vol. 1, No. 38 (22 April 1944), pp. 41-46.

63. Gelder, Stuart. "Transport Planes Ensure Victory in S.E. Asia Incalculable Moral Effect of Continuous Air Supply." **The Statesman** (Newspaper), circa 1945.

64. "Gliders Carry Air Engineers For Toungoo." **Roundup** (Newspaper), May 3, 1945, pp. 4.

65. Goodman, Thomas L. "American Gliders Evacuate Wounded From Jungle Front." **Sidney Morning Herald**, November 3, 1944.

66. Mead, P. W. "The Chindit Operations of 1944," **Royal United Service Institution Journal**, Vol. 100, No. 597 (February 1955), pp. 250-262.

67. McCann, John A., Col, USAF. "Air Power and 'The Man'." **Air Power Historian**, Vol. 6, No. 2 (April 1959), pp. 108-124.

68. Miller, Moscrip (ed). "'Snatching' Wounded in Burma: American Air Commandos run an ambulance service with gliders to evacuate jungle battle casualties." **Look**, February 6, 1945, pp. 38-39.

69. Prather, Russel E. "Broadway Burma." **Ex-CBI Roundup**, Vol. 22, No. 10, (December 1967), pp. 6-10.

70. _____. "Easy Into Burma, Part I." *Ex-CBI Roundup*, Vol. 21, No. 2, (February 1966), pp. 8-25.

71. _____. "Easy Into Burma, Part II." *Ex-CBI Roundup*, Vol. 21, No. 3, (March 1966), pp. 8-25.

72. Sciutti, W. J., Captain, USAF. "The First Air Commando Group August 1943-May 1944." *American Aviation Historial Society Journal*, Vol. 13, No. 2 (Fall 1968), pp. 178-185.

73. Stratton, Bill (ed). "L-Pilot, aircraft historian shares stories, wartime experiences." Stamford Robertson, *Liaison Spoken Here, International Liaison Pilot and Aircraft Association*, pp. 10-11.

74. "Two Divisions Flown To China." *Roundup* (Newspaper). May 31, 1945, pp. 10.

Official Documents

75. AAFSAT, Intelligence. Glider Operations on Two Fronts; Special Intelligence Report No. 54, September 1944. 248.532-63, in USAF Collection, USAFHRC.

76. AC/AS, Intelligence. Air Room interview with Lt Col John R. Alison, 3 July 1943. 142.052 in USAF Collection, USAFHRC.

77. AC/AS, Intelligence. Special Informational Intelligence Report No. 43-11; Interview with Lt Col Philip G. Cochran, 28 June 1943. 142.034-2, in USAF Collection, USAFHRC.

78. AC/AS, Intelligence. Chronological History of Project 9 (Cochran), 17 August 1943-28 January 1944. 142-0411-9, in USAF Collection, USAFHRC.

79. AC/AS, Plans. 1st Air Commando Force and Combat Cargo Groups organization and redeployment correspondence and memoranda, 1943-45. 145.81-170, in USAF Collection, USAFHRC.

80. AC/AS, Plans. Interview with Col John R. Alison, 25 April 1944. 145.95, in USAF Collection, USAFHRC.

81. Allied Forces, Southeast Asia Command. Report to the Combined Chiefs of Staff by the Supreme Allied Commander, Southeast Asia, 1943-1945, Vice-Admiral the Earl Mountbatten of Burma. London: HMSO, 1951.

82. British Air Ministry. *Operations in Burma*. 15 Dec 1941-20 May 1942. 512.952, in SAF Collection, USAFHRC.

83. British Air Ministry. Wings of the Phoenix: The Official Story of the Air War in Burma. London: HMSO, 1949.

84. British Information Service. Victory in Burma. New York: British Government, 1945. 168.7097-13, in Ronald F. Kennedy Collection, USAFHRC.

85. Burma Research Society. Burma Facts and Figures. London: Longmans, Green & Co. Ltd., 1946.

86. Central Office of Information. The Campaign in Burma. London: His Majesty's Stationery Office, 1946.

87. Eastern Air Command. Collected narrative reports of operations in CBI Theater from December 1943-May 1945. 820.306, in USAF Collection, USAFHRC.

88. Eastern Air Command. Weekly Operational Reports, 1943-45. 820.607, in USAF Collection, USAFHRC.

89. HQ 3TAF. Photographic report of 1st Air Commando Force, September 1944. 822.08, in USAF Collection, USAFHRC.

90. HQ Army Air Forces India Burma Theater. Miscellaneous correspondence concerning "Employment of 1st and 2nd Air Commando Groups," 1944-1945. 820.452-1, in USAF Collection, USAFHRC.

91. HQ Combat Cargo Task Force. Operation Multivite, Intelligence Extract No. 10, 22 March 1945. 824.609-1, in USAF Collection, USAFHRC.

92. HQ Combat Cargo Task Force. The GUMPTION and FREEBORN Operations, Intelligence Extract No. 16, 20 May 1945. 824.609-1, in USAF Collection, USAHRC.

93. HQ Combat Cargo Task Force. Operation DRACILA—Airborne Phase, Intelligence Extract No. 19, 1 June 1945. 824.609-1, in USAF Collection, USAFHRC.

94. HQ Combat Cargo Task Force. Unit History, 12 October 1944-4 June 1945. 824.01, in USAF Collection, USAFHRC.

95. JICA/CBI. First Air Commando Force Invasion of Burma; Report No. 1448, 29 March 1944. 810.6091A, in USAF Collection, USAFHRC.

96. JICA/CBI. Glider Operations in Burma; Report No. 1449, 1 April 1944. 810.6091A, in USAF Collection, USAFHRC.

97. JICA/CBI. Wingate Report on Airborne Invasion of Burma; Report No. 1833, 12 April 1944. 810.6091A, in USAF Collection, USAFHRC.

98. JICA/CBI. Final Operations of First Air Commando Group in Burma; Report No. 3137, 30 May 1944. 810.6091A, in USAF Collection, USAFHRC.

Also from the publisher

WITH CHENNAULT IN CHINA
A Flying Tiger's Diary
Robert M. Smith

It's all here – the whole story of how the AVG shot down over 650 Japanese planes using obsolete P-40s and a communications network that covered China with a protective "umbrella." This ground based radio network (in which the author operated) kept the pilots so well-informed of enemy air activity that they were seldom surprised by Japanese attacks. Enjoyable to read, this memoir will give you a taste of the "local flavor" of life in China while under Japanese attack. You'll find amusing anecdotes and accurate descriptions of the author's duty as a radio operator as well as the wartime activities of other AVG members. Robert M. Smith was a sergeant-air mechanic first class for the U.S. Air Force when the recruiters arrived on base looking for volunteers for the Chinese Air Force. He was discharged from the Air Force and went to China to join the American Volunteer Group, "The Flying Tigers."

Size: 6" x 9", over 110 b/w photographs
176 pages, hard cover
ISBN: 0-7643-0287-6 $29.95

**FLYING TIGER: A CREW CHIEF'S STORY
- THE WAR DIARY OF AN AVG CREW CHIEF**

Frank S. Losonsky & Terry M. Losonsky.

This book is the war diary of a Flying Tiger American Volunteer Group crew chief
from the 3rd Pursuit Squadron. A thorough account of the activities that occurred in
and around the AVG during their time fighting along the Burma Road, this war diary
also describes the trip over to China and gives insight into the days and thoughts of a
crew chief working in the AVG. *Flying Tiger* will also give aviation historians new
insights into the days shortly before the Flying Tiger successes in late 1941.

Size: 8 1/2" x 11"
200 photographs
112 pages, hard cover
ISBN: 0-7643-0045-8 $35.00